TWO WOMEN

TWO WOMEN

STORIES

Gemini Wahhaj

Luka Press

Cover art by Maha Rahman. Designed by Md Siddiqur Rahman.

Gemini Wahhaj has a PhD in creative writing from the University of Houston. Her fiction has appeared in *Granta, Cimarron Review, The Carolina Quarterly, Crab Orchard Review, Chattahoochee Review, Apogee, Silk Road, Night Train*, and *Northwest Review*, among others. At the U. of Houston, she won the Inprint/Michener Fellowship in Honor of Donald Barthelme for 2004-5. She received an honorable mention in Atlantic Monthly's student fiction contest in 2005 and in Glimmer Train's fiction open contest in 2009 and was a finalist in Glimmer Train's short-story award for new writers in Spring 2005. She won the Phi Kappa Sigma Award for Best Fiction by an Undergraduate at the University of Pennsylvania in 1993. She attended the University of Pennsylvania for her undergraduate degree and Princeton University for a master's degree. An excerpt of her Young Adult manuscript The Girl Next Door was published in Exotic Gothic Volume 5. In Bangladesh, she was a regular writer for the Daily Star newspaper and weekend magazine. She teaches English at the Lone Star College in Houston.

Acknowledgments

Wheels of Progress was published in *Granta*. Voices was published in *Crab Orchard Review*. First Snow was published in *Apogee*. Rental Car was published in *The Carolina Quarterly*. Marker was published in *Chattahoochee Review*. How to Break an Iraqi was published in *Night Train*. Funny-Looking People was published in *Cimarron Review*. Mita was published in *Silk Road*. Exit was published in *Northwest Review*.

CONTENTS

The Wheels of Progress

Bakher Khan bought a shell key chain on Cox's Bazar beach from one of those bare-chested girls who sell trinkets in the dark. He had had the name "Mohua" carved on the shell. He showed it to Mr. Vincent when Mr. Vincent climbed in the Jeep the next morning. "Very nice," said Mr. Vincent said. "Your wife?"

"No, my daughter," replied Bakher Khan. The Bangladeshi engineer Siddiqi, who had also climbed into Mr. Vincent's car, said, "You have a daughter? In that case there is no question of writing your wife's name."

Mr. Vincent's car was full today. Bakher Khan was pleased that he was driving more people Robiul, the driver of the other car. Mrs. Ann was coming with them, too; she had left her daughter behind in Dhaka. They had flown in the night before to Chittagong Airport, Mr. Vincent, Mrs. Ann, Mr. John, and Mr. Frans. Bakher Khan and Robiul had driven down from Dhaka ahead of time to wait for their arrival. Bakher Khan thought they could have made the trip to Sitakunda on the way from the airport to the hotel in Cox's Bazar–Sitakunda was only 37 kilometers away from Chittagong–but the foreigners had been tired.

Geological tour by the exploration department! Bakher Khan had memorized the words. He was good at memorizing, learning, improving himself.

He drove in a trance-like state, thinking about his three-year-old daughter: how she ran about the small flat in Mohammedpur in circles, her bangles tinkling all the time, even when she slept in the dark between Bakher Khan and his wife. He thought specially about her feet, so tiny and fat that they always made him think this moment with her would pass, she would grow, the feet would get bigger, and she would no longer run about his little home.

Mrs. Ann and Mr. Vincent also had babies, Mrs. Ann's was just four months. After some moments of eavesdropping, Bakher Khan gathered that they were discussing what Mr. Vincent and his wife, and Mrs. Ann and her husband did when their babies cried at night. He felt an immense satisfaction in gleaning this from their softs; his English had improved vastly since he had become Mr. Vincent's driver.

"So Mary says you get up, and I say, it's your baby," Mr. Vincent was saying, "and we both lie there groaning. Then it's always me . . . Mary just can't do it at night."

Mrs. Ann chuckled, said her Bill was quite good at handling little Cara, but she just couldn't let them be. There was more laughter in the back seat, a warmth in the car. Bakher Khan was especially happy to be in Chittagong, his hometown. Siddiqi, sitting in the front passenger seat, was also laughing.
Then Mr. Vincent asked Siddiqi, "Do Bangladeshi fathers ever take care of their children?"

Siddiqi stopped laughing and said he didn't know, he was not a father yet. Something about Siddiqi's

2

manner and his long face soured the atmosphere in the car. Bakher Khan did not know what was wrong. Siddiqi had seemed cheerful enough when they had driven down together. Siddiqi had traveled ahead with the drivers to settle on the hotel, buy the supplies, choose locations for the tour. Bakher Khan had driven him in Mr. Vincent's car. They had laughed a lot then and sat in circles singing popular film songs, but now Siddiqi had ruined the sense of camaraderie. His scowls, his silences, and his short replies to the foreigner experts disturbed Bakher Khan greatly.

They were stuck in traffic. Mr. Vincent gave Bakher Khan smart directions from the back. Then he cried out, "Can you believe that? Look at those trucks blocking the shoulders and coming the opposite way. Sure, go ahead, make it worse. I've never seen more idiotic behavior in my life!"

Bakher Khan watched with a sinking heart as the trucks took up the road space that would have allowed the cars to pass by. After a year of driving Mr. Vincent, Bakher Khan had become increasingly aware of Bangladesh's shortcomings: drivers who did not follow rules and blocked the roads, police sergeants who did not know their own duties, not to mention the corruption, the greed, the lack of law and order, the dirt everywhere. He now looked at his country, which he had always regarded with a lazy warmth, through new eyes. When he drove Mr. Vincent home at night—Mr. Vincent worked late every day at the office, after everyone else at the gas company had left—they would have philosophical conversations about Bangladesh.

"I don't know, Ba-ker," Mr. Vincent would say, "I get depressed every night. This place is so corrupt, I wonder if we can make any progress at all. This country

3

could have been so much. You have so much gas, Ba-
ker, if only the officials weren't so pig-headed and
corrupt. If you could develop this gas, there would not
be one hungry man in your country."

Bakher Khan honked his horn and Mr. Vincent
said not to; it wouldn't do any good. Bakher Khan
immediately recognized the wisdom of his advice. He
was very proud to be working for the gas company.
When his old gas company sold out to this one, he had
become an employee instead of a mere contractor. These
people were so intelligent, they had so much to teach.
Bakher Khan often dreamt, when he was waiting in the
car for Mr. Vincent while he attended a meeting, that his
country would change; there would be super highways,
electricity in every village, and high-rises for everyone to
live in.

At last, the traffic cleared and they began to
move. Mr. Vincent asked Siddiqi if he had remembered
to load all the food for their trip to Sitakunda, and
Siddiqi sullenly said yes. Mrs. Ann coughed in the
sudden gust of exhaust and roadside tar work (which had
probably been the cause of the traffic jam). She told Mr.
Vincent that her little Cara had been ill with breathing
problems at least three times since she had been born–
the doctors thought it was the pollution of Dhaka. Mr.
Vincent had the same problem with his boy, who had
developed asthma. Bakher Khan felt disappointed that
his country was so backward, and that Mr. Vincent and
Mrs. Sarah were having to making such grave sacrifices
to help it progress.

The road was clear now and he sped on, the wind
flying against the outside glass, the air inside cool from
the AC. He had to brake only occasionally, when he
passed a slow rickshaw or van, or a fool of a man

4

walking his cow by the road. Bakher Khan thought that perhaps one day his daughter would attend the local university and become an engineer, too, become what Mrs. Ann was: a…reservoir engineer. He loved Mohua so much: her long cotton dresses that reached her ankles, the bell that tinkled around her waist, the drop of *kajal* on her forehead that protected her against evil.

Mr. Vincent"s firm was so advanced that when the managers met to decide the company's mission and the vision, even the drivers had been invited. It was a long-drawn-out process, with every department making several proposals, and in the end there was a big meeting with lunch–sandwiches from Coopers. In the meeting, the most popular slogan was 'Circles of Progress'. But the exploration manager, who was Mr. Vincent's boss, pointed out that progress was linear. Someone joked that circular was a good slogan for their partner company in Bangladesh because all the Bangladeshi officials talked only in circles. Everyone thought hard, and so did Bakher Khan, and finally, when they chose a phrase–something that would appear underneath the company's title–it was 'Wheels of Progress'. Bakher Khan really liked this slogan because wheels had something to do with driving and his own role in the company.
At last they were approaching Sitakunda. They were beginning to climb uphill. The other car, with Mr. John and Mr. Frans, followed behind.

"Go slow," said Mr. Vincent. "Ease up on the brake." Mr. Vincent always gave him tips on driving, how to handle the Jeep on dunes and uphill, in mud and through water. There were signs announcing that Sitakunda would soon become an eco-tourism park. For now, it was green and quiet: terraced agricultural fields along the steps of hills. Little boys walked with the harvest or with goats up the hill. Bared walls of hills had been cut for quarries. A quarry was a good place for a geological exploration, Mr. Vincent explained. Mr. Vincent was too good, always explaining things and educating him.

"Vincent, I think we should park here," said Siddiqi.

"No, let's go further up," said Mr. Vincent.

They continued on until the stalks of the paddy pushed up against the windows. The boys who walked along the narrow path had to jump into the ditches.

"All right, let's get out," said Vincent. "Siddiqi, bring the equipment. Leave the lunch in the car."

Mr. John and Mr. Frans stepped out of the other car, laughing and making jokes. Mr. John was the leader of the tour.

"Siddiqi, come here," he would say, showing him something. The group would stop, measure, look, discuss. The drivers followed behind, and Robiul said to Bakher Khan wasn't it nice to see their Bangladeshi engineer walking alongside the foreigner experts? But Siddiqi looked so dark and shriveled that it was impossible to be proud of him. Bakher Khan hovered close to the group, and from time to time Mr. Vincent drew his attention to interesting features in the landscape, pointing with his slender white finger with the gold band. He wore a stylish white hat to keep off the sun and he carried a camera in the pocket of his slim white pants. Bakher Khan repeated the words to himself: shale, sandstone, dislocation, faults, formations. He had once worked for an NGO, and he had learned some terms that he still remembered: sustainable, participatory, development. These expressions continued to serve him well. As they climbed, Mrs. Ann and Mr. Vincent discussed that the development of gas was the means of sustainable development for Bangladesh.

"Think," Mr. Vincent was saying to Mrs. Sarah. "Now Bangladesh only survives on aid, on other people feeding its people. It's eternal, this giving. But with gas, Bangladesh could feed its own people."

Bakher Khan was hopeful. He imagined his country making linear progress, his Mohua in a slim skirt like Mrs. Ann's, long boots, pushing up her glasses to study a quarry.

The local people were now crowding round the group and the drivers had to shoo them away: "Go, go. There is nothing to see here." Sometimes a man would ask what the foreigners were doing and they would explain that these were great technical experts come to get gas out.

"Is there any gas here?" the boys asked. But mostly they stared at Mrs. Ann or at Mr. Vincent's camera. Mrs. Ann smiled sweetly at them, although Bakher Khan could see that the staring made her uncomfortable. They stood right behind her when she stopped, followed her when she walked, breathed the shampoo in her hair. When one group chewing on sugar cane disappeared, another soon appeared.

"Are they bothering you?" Mr. Vincent asked, and Mrs. Sarah smiled: *no.*

Mr. Vincent explained to him that the sandstone held the gas—he pointed with his finger at the lines of sand—and the shale acted like a cap to hold in the gas. He pointed at lines of shale. Bakher Khan memorized the phrase 'trapped gas'. At last, when he thought there was no end to the information that he should swallow and keep within—as if by being able to keep it all in he could apply his knowledge and help his country move forward on the path of progress in the energy sector—they reached the top of the hill. The temple of Sitakunda appeared suddenly as they rounded the corner. They stood at the edge of a cliff that fell to the valleys of cultivated fields below. Steps led up to the temple where pilgrims had climbed to pay their respects for hundreds of years. For hundreds of years it had stood unchanged and unchanging. Bakher wondered what would happen once the eco-park opened. Mr. Vincent and Mrs. Ann were discussing the options if they discovered gas or oil under the temple. They joked that they could put a rig there and make it resemble a temple.

The survey was over for now. Mr. John lowered his bulky body to the sandstone and sat by the edge of the cliff. Mr. Vincent sent Siddiqi back to the car with the other driver to gather the lunch supplies. Perhaps Siddiqi was sullen because he was an engineer, but he was having to do all this menial work. Although Bakher Khan found Siddiqi's twin roles slightly confusing as well; he disapproved of his attitude; he thought Siddiqi shouldn't look down upon any work as menial; he was their guide on the tour. Without him how would the foreign experts know which hotel to stay at, how to negotiate with boats and ferries for tomorrow's trip to Maheshkhali? This was the trouble with Bangladeshis: they thought work was beneath them.

Mrs. Ann and Mr. Vincent stood by the cliff's edge looking down below and admiring the scenery. They compared it to Scotland. Bakher Khan felt proud. Mr. Vincent had once said Dhaka was all concrete, it was bewilderingly depressing, and Bakher Khan had always been depressed by Dhaka ever since then: the alleys that got clogged up with plastic bags, the children who got wet in the rain, the dirty buses with their black exhaust which choked the lungs of infants. Mr. Vincent had once visited Bakher Khan's home when Mohua was very sick. She had pneumonia but Bakher Khan hadn't realized. She would have died if Mr. Vincent and his wife had not admitted her to PG Hospital. Bakher Khan felt indebted to the kindness of Mr. Vincent. He felt sure that the company would bring progress at last to his country, which he had begun to feel was a very sad place to live in. But here, at Sitakunda, he felt happy. Here was something he could be proud of, the open air, the story of Ram and Sita, the temple overhead, the children who walked with their goats. This was the Bangladesh Bakher Khan had grown up in, the essence of his soul, and he was happy that Mr. Vincent and Mrs. Ann also appreciated these surroundings.

The night before, Mr. Vincent had asked the two drivers to join them for dinner at a local restaurant in Cox's Bazar, to which Siddiqi had directed the party. Mr. Vincent said he had been happy in his job, until he arrived in Bangladesh. He had such high hopes at first, but now he had begun to despair. If only he could change things, if only all his efforts resulted even in the infinitesimal change. But this country was unchanging and unchangeable, solid in its decrepitude.

"Can you even hear birds in the morning in this place?" he had asked. The party had been silent for a long time, considering this. Also, Mr. Vincent had not been pleased with Siddiqi's choice of a restaurant. Even though it was a five-star restaurant, they saw a mouse run over the carpet.

There was a cry. Bakher Khan turned to look, his heart trembling a little. Mr. Vincent had a protective arm about Mrs. Ann's shoulder and was leading her away.

Bakher moved closer to Mr. Vincent and Mrs. Sarah to ask, what happened, what happened?

A group of boys who had been standing by them, teenagers wearing Sando shirts and lungis. The boys had been staring at Mrs. Ann, then they had formed a circle around her and someone had touched her golden hair. Mr. John had stood up and moved swiftly to her side; she was very shaken. Mr. Frans had been studying the sand and the shale a little distance away, and even he answered her call of distress. They all surrounded Mrs. Ann to comfort her.

Bakher Khan said to the boys, "Go, go! Don't you have anything better to do? Go!" He wanted to explain to Mrs. Sarah that they had meant no harm. They simply wanted to touch her golden hair, which seemed just as unreal to them as dreams of gas and wealth would seem to any Bangladeshi now. But he knew he could not explain this to Mrs. Sarah, that he did not possess the English to do so. And it was more than just the lack of language—it was something he couldn't put into words. So he hovered, feeling sorry for everything.

Then Mr. Vincent said to Bakher Khan, "Just ask them what they're doing for their country, standing around with nothing to do, the silly fools."

Bakher Khan stood like a statue, unable to move. His chest throbbed with pain. Siddiqi and Robiul were back with the food in ice boxes. From where Bakher Khan stood, he could see the Sitakunda, the mossy steps that led to the derelict temple, and out of the corner of his eye, under the cover of his lashes, he could also see the boys; their checked collars, the faces and eyes that reminded him of his own youth, and he felt very downcast about them. He felt that he was a silly fool himself. What had he done with his life after all, what good was he, what good was anybody in his country? Even the professors of the engineering university where Bakher Khan wanted to send Mohua were never trusted to do work on the exploration team collected; they had to send everything for analysis abroad. He felt disgusted with the boys, with all the worthless youth of Bangladesh, and with himself, for he saw how they all seemed to Mr. Vincent–absolutely useless.

"Let's eat," said Mr. Vincent. "Siddiqi, fetch the food."

Siddiqi had forgotten to bring a bottle opener. He stood awkwardly with two Coca Cola bottles in each hand, apologizing. But even when he apologized, he did it resentfully, as if he were about to explode. Bakher Khan looked away. Robiul tried to help by fumbling inside the bags.

"Not to worry," said Mr. Vincent. "We shall make do. We can eat our sandwiches dry and swallow our saliva."

"I can do something, Sir," said Siddiqi. "I can open."

Bakher Khan didn't look to see how he would manage this, but he heard a smash. Siddiqi had broken a bottle trying to open it against a rock.

"Good job, Siddiqi," said Mr. Vincent. But Bakher Khan could feel his anger and he sank further within himself. He wanted to sit down. Mr. John held out a sandwich to him and his fingers closed around it weakly. He didn't trust his grip.

Then Siddiqi, dark and sulky in a dirty white shirt, threw the bottle to the ground, and Bakher Khan was astonished to see him standing with his hands at his waists, shaking like a stalk of paddy in the wind.

"Mr. Vincent," he cried in a shrill voice. "Mr. Vincent, I want to quit. I . . .I have been very unhappy in this company. I am get no respect."

Bakher Khan folded his arms around his chest and watched Siddiqi.

"What kind of respect do you want?" Mr. Vincent asked quietly.

"I get ordered, I don't get a promotion, and you talk to me in that tone."

"What tone?" asked Mr. Vincent. Then enunciating his words slowly, carefully: "Really, Siddiqi, I have been very patient with you. Your performance in the company has been dismal, but I have waited. The trouble with you people is that you want to climb fast to the top by means other than hard work and competence. So cut your bullshit about tone and respect."

Siddiqi began to cry like a woman, the way Bakher Khan's wife cried when he scolded her for burning the rice or making the daal too thin. He shook and he cried. Bakher Khan half expected someone to walk over to Siddiqi and put an arm around him, but no one moved. Then Siddiqi turned and walked away down the hill.

The rest of them stood silently finishing their sandwiches in silence.

Then Mr. Vincent said, "Well, I guess we had better pack up. Ba-ker and Ray-bial, can you manage?"

"Yes, Mr. Vincent," Bakher Khan assured him. He busied himself packing up the trash and lifting the ice boxes. He waited for Mr. Frans and Mr. John, Mrs. Ann, and Mr. Vincent to lead the way. As he did so, he stared again fondly at the temple, which was now radiant in the sunlight. The pounding in his chest had stopped. The boys began to go on their way, waving their sticks gaily, returning to their work in the fields that would be harvested the same way year after year. Mr. John had been explaining last night over dinner the cyclical nature of tides and its importance for geologists, but Bakher Khan could no longer remember that lecture. He watched the children and hoped that their lives wouldn't change too soon.

Siddiqi refused to return with them; he would find his own transport and he was going to hand in his resignation at the office in Dhaka.

"You simply cannot do that, my good fellow," said Mr. Vincent kindly. "There are procedures. You need to give notice."

But Siddiqi walked away, childishly. Robiul and Bakher Khan assured the foreigner experts that they knew the way back to the hotel. Bakher Khan climbed into the driver's seat and let Mr. Vincent advise him down the hill. He drove back on the highway to Cox's Bazar, taking his time, no longer in a hurry, no longer even listening to the hushed conversation, about Siddiqi no doubt, in the back seat. Instead he admired the scenery around him. Mohua would be home now, playing by the drains, dropping beads down them, or perhaps she would have gone down to the river in Mohammedpur with her mother to watch the fishermen and the boats. He thought of Chittagong's great harbors, and its container ships, the hundreds of years of naval history, and the ocean. He thought of Ram and Sita and the beautiful stories that he had heard in his childhood, stories that never led anywhere but started where they had stopped the night before.

When they had reached Cox's Bazar, it was getting dark. Mrs. Ann and Mr. Vincent sat in the shadows. The two cars pulled up side by side in front of the hotel and Mr. John rolled down this window to confer with Mr. Vincent. They decided to shower and go on to dinner. The foreign experts went to their rooms, telling the drivers when to meet them again in the parking lot. Robiul and Bakher Khan did not shower or wash. They sat together in silence thinking of Siddiqi, whose duty it would have been to act as guide for the evening, and to organize the next day's trip. Presently, the four experts came out and Mr. Vincent and Mrs. Ann, both in clean starched shirts and cotton pants, climbed into Bakher Khan's car.

Mr. Vincent said, "Bakher Khan, you have the great honor of choosing where we should eat tonight. Lead us. Onward!"

Bakher Khan was from Chittagong. He had grown up in Chittagong. He had visited Cox's Bazar many times. Although he had never eaten in the best restaurants himself, he could have led them to any number of good ones, efficiently and expertly, in a straight line. But to his own surprise, he took no initiative. When he had reached the busy town center, where all the restaurants were, he just drove around aimlessly.

Mr. Vincent tapped him on the shoulder. "Ba-ker, you're on the same street we just passed," he said. "We're hungry, my man."

Bakher Khan nodded at Mr. Vincent's clean-shaven reflection in the mirror. He thought again of Siddiqi, who would be hungry now, walking still or on some dusty bus, and he thought that he cared nothing for the hunger of these foreign experts. Let them tell him where they wanted to eat, when they wanted him to stop. He just kept driving. His shell keyring jangled, reminding him of his musical Mohua, and he forgot everything else.

14

Marker

Four weeks after their father had been buried, Salma and Asif finally drove up to the cemetery office to choose a tombstone. The woman at the desk, with close-cropped hair and wearing a neat green suit, asked them if they could wait, please. Mr. Munoz was meeting with another family. Panic gripped Salma. She had called ahead to make sure that they would be served on time, that it wouldn't be a wasted trip. All official business seemed to her a looming task, a rabbit hole down which anything could happen.

Both brother and sister smiled politely, and Salma sat down on the wooden church bench in the front office while Asif excused himself to use the restroom. Salma could see the family inside with Mr. Munoz and hear them speaking in muted tones. Soon, when it was her turn, she would have to make decisions. She wanted a stone headstone, something old, like a grave in an English churchyard, natural and close to the earth, the way her father would have liked it. The kind of grave that would reflect his personality best. But she already knew there would be disappointments. Compromises would have to be made. The question of money would enter into it. Already, looking around, the decorations hanging in the front office, large plastic sculptures of cherubic angels and vases with plastic flowers, did not give her high hopes about what options would be available.

The time passed quickly enough. While Asif was in the bathroom, the woman at the reception was on the phone, and Mr. Munoz kept on talking with the other family. But suddenly everything happened at once. As soon as Asif returned, Mr. Munoz walked the other family out, and the woman in the front office said something, smiled, and led them inside to the small sales room at the back.

"Please have a seat. He'll be with you shortly."

Salma and Asif kept standing. The room was small and cold, crammed with samples of gravestones on the walls and on tables shoved in corners. Four upholstered chairs were drawn up around a large center table. Various blocks, bricks, and tiles were laid out on this table, as well as on a side table pushed against one of the walls. All kinds of plaques hung on the walls, large rectangular plaques and small ones, with wreath-like boundaries, pictures of angels, and different letterings.

"I think Abba would have liked something plain," Salma said, turning away from a plastic-looking brownish rectangle. "These are really ugly."
She had majored in Art History and English in college. Now she was an English teacher who wore long, flowing skirts. She felt particularly burdened by their task. She felt there had to be aesthetics and meaning in the choice of a gravestone.

"I was looking for stone. You know?"

"This is interesting!" Asif said, reading a tomb marker on the wall. "This plaque says Linda Grissell. 1974. That's younger than you."

Salma turned to look. For several minutes, they read the names and dates on the plaques, and commented on the different designs (flowers and petals and leaves), precious details that family members had eked out of the unnatural materials they had to work with.

Mr. Munoz entered, smiling, his face round and cherubic, wearing a pale summer suit, and warmly shook their hands. Salma was slight and thin. She often felt cold in rooms. Now she felt the warmth return to her skin with Mr. Munoz's handshake, as if she had been abandoned in this room and Mr. Munoz had come to take care of everything.

"Do you have stone gravestones? Is that what they're called, gravestones?"

"Unfortunately, we don't have stone in our cemetery. What we have is a granite base. Like this."

Salma frowned at the sample Mr. Munoz held up. She had to be rational about the choices offered to her. Mortality itself was a reality she had come to acknowledge in the last days of her father's life. She had seen this man who had once seemed so powerful and full of life unable to stand, or feed himself, or go to the bathroom.

"Touch it. So smooth and supple." Mr. Munoz handed the tile to Asif when Salma looked away.

"Ah. So this is granite," Asif said amiably. Salma was glad of her brother's presence. Through the funeral and afterward, he had been friendly and calm. Everything about him was pleasing: his average height, thick hair, dark, flashing eyes, and even the way he dressed, laid-back khaki pants and polo shirt.

"I'm sorry for your loss," Mr. Munoz said, putting his hands together and smiling sincerely. He had a nice mouth and even white teeth.

Salma and Asif nodded quickly, yes. They didn't want to talk about it. They had avoided everything having to do with their father's death so far. Salma's husband, Kamal, had taken care of all the official business, checking out the gravesite ahead of the funeral and paying for the plot.

Since the funeral, the cemetery office had been calling Kamal; to make arrangements for a permanent marker. They had sent a bunch of letters along the same lines: *sorry for your loss—your loved one's courtesy temporary marker will be kept for one month—please make arrangements to pay for a permanent marker.* But this was one decision that Kamal couldn't make. He had been insisting for several days that Salma visit her father's grave and choose a permanent marker.

"Please. Have a seat." Mr. Munoz was a salesman, yes, clean shaven, with slicked back hair, in a blue-grey suit, but not quite so pushy. He was easy to get along with, in spite of his gaudy granite wall plaques.

Salma slid into an overly soft, yellow chair. "So it's all granite. We just have one choice."

"Yes, let me show you." Mr. Munoz took blocks and piled them on top of each other. "The base is granite and on top of it you have a bronze marker. All our graves are bronze on granite."

"Oh! My father had never liked gaudy things."

He had been a deeply philosophical man. He would not have liked a grave at all, perhaps. Or perhaps he would have cared very much. He had been a sentimental man as well.

After he had died in Salma's home in Houston, there had been a lot of confusion about where he ought to be buried. Salma had always assumed that when her father died, he would be buried in his village home in Bangladesh. It seemed wrong, pointless, all of these decisions involved in burying him in a foreign land as an unknown man.

When their mother had died a year ago in Bangladesh, she had been buried in a hurry in her family graveyard in Dhaka. Salma and Asif had both flown there immediately, taking advantage of summer vacations from their respective schools. They had known even then that there was no space for their father's body in that same graveyard. Their parents could never be buried next to each other.

A few days after their mother was buried, Mukul Bhai, a cousin on their father's side, invited Salma and Asif to his house for dinner. Mukul Bhai told Salma and Asif that he had had a nightmare the night before. In the middle of the night, he had been awakened by a deep restlessness. Salma's dead mother's spirit had come to him, distraught. She had walked around his room in a lost and sad way, begging him for something. In his dream, Mukul Bhai realized what she was trying to say: that it had been wrong to bury her in Dhaka. She should have been buried in her husband's family graveyard in the village.

This story had alarmed Salma. She had just wanted to think of her mother as being in peace. But after hearing her cousin's story, it felt as if the burial itself had been a wrong that could never be righted, a choice that would lead to other difficult choices in the future.

After her mother's death, Salma had brought her father to America to live with her. He had declined rapidly. Salma couldn't remember a single happy day since he had arrived in her home in Houston. He had been quite a famous scientist in Bangladesh. He had published a few important papers on the topic of fluid mechanics in international journals and received a few awards from the government. He had always seemed larger than life to her in his baggy slacks and ink-stained shirts, gliding above the dust and noise and quarrels of everyday life in Dhaka in his own intellectual plane. But after arriving in Houston, he had rapidly lost control of his brain and his body. His last days had been tainted with all the baseness he had seemed to escape all his life. The night he died, Salma's husband Kamal called the Islamic society in Houston because he and Salma had no idea about the traditions of burial. What did someone do with a dead body? Salma's cousin—the same cousin who had claimed to have seen her mother's ghost—called from Bangladesh saying that his uncle's body should be flown home to his village to be buried in his family graveyard.

"Please, I beg you," Mukul Bhai cried over the crackling phone line. "At his death, his body belongs alongside his parents. Both his parents were buried in the graveyard in his village. It is so beautiful. It is in the middle of the family orchard of mango trees and guava trees, many of which had been planted by your father himself! As a child, he played among these trees, climbed them, and ate their fruits. Think about it. It's the right thing to do."

"But how will I move the body?" Salma asked.

"You don't have to do anything. I'll do it all. I'll get the permission from the embassy. I'll fly there myself right away."

While they spoke, the four men from the Islamic Society in Houston, who had arrived at their house within an hour after the firefighters had pronounced Salma's father dead, sat in Kamal's office. When she put down the phone and went to see them, they told her sternly that the custom according to their religion was that 'a body should be buried immediately, wherever a person died'. A person's burial should be where he had come to die, not where he had been born, they said. Salma's father's body lay on the cold hardwood floor in his room where Kamal had lowered it from his bed to practice CPR with instructions from the 911 operator. A police officer had arrived after the firefighters left and cleared the death as being from natural causes. While the police officer waited outside for the Islamic funeral home to take away the body, Salma and Kamal negotiated with the men from the Islamic society argued inside about what to do with the body. They didn't even want to wait for Asif to fly in from California—he was frantically calling for flights to Houston—and Kamal had to put up a fight. At last, the men said that they would wait until Thursday, two days, to bury the body in Houston.

Over the next two days, the battle over where to bury Salma's father continued. Her cousin called several times a day to plead to bring the body home where it belonged, so that Salma's father could be given his due respects and lie in peace. Other relatives and her father's friends called with counter arguments. Putting a body on a plane would mean that it would have to sit in a freezer for weeks while Salma would have to apply for a permit from the embassy in Washington, D.C. to fly the body. The body would have to be embalmed—an intrusion that seemed violent when described by various passionate voices on the phone.

In the end, Asif decided the matter by calling via Skype from the airport.

"Listen, sis," he said, "I want my father buried where his children can visit his grave, in Houston. Yeah?"

"I didn't have a strong opinion myself," Salma explained apologetically to her cousin later that night. "I see your point. I know you are hurt. But this is what Asif wants. He's arriving tomorrow. And we'll bury the body then."

"You are his children. So of course, you have first right over his body," her cousin said tightly.
"It's not that," Salma said. "I agree with you that he should be buried where he was born. I'm sorry. But it's what Asif wants."

Secretly, she was convinced that her father, who practiced no religion, would not have liked to the hassle of being embalmed and flown on a plane. She was sure he would have abhorred such a fuss being made of his body.

She, with whom he had lived, felt most strongly how futile it was to fight over his dead body when she had not been able to care for him while he had been alive. Only Salma knew the ugly truth about how his life had ended, in so much neglect. Often, he had called to her and woken her in the middle of the night. Salma had run down from her upstairs bedroom to his room, her heart stopped from being jerked awake suddenly. She was sleep deprived from his chronic nighttime calls and moaning.

"Please stay with me!" he begged. "I'm scared. I see something in the dark."

"I can't!" Salma shouted. "Do you know what time it is? Go to sleep. You'll make us all mad."

Everything had been exhausting for Salma and humiliating for her father. Feeding him, which involved sometimes forcing things down his throat because he could not swallow, and taking him to the bathroom, which involved him slipping and sliding.

Mr. Munoz slowly coaxed Salma and Asif into taking at least some pleasure in their decisions. He had a salesman's art of convincing. Or perhaps all three wanted to get it over with, one another toward their common goal, moving through the laborious steps of making choices. Mr. Munoz explained that there were several colors available in the granite base. They could choose black or brown granite. The bronze plates had various textures as well. On top of those combinations—he pulled a brochure in front of their eyes (they had been trying to choose from the samples on the walls and tables, but apparently the right way to go about it was to look at the brochure)—they could have different designs for the marker. They could even have a slab that covered the entire grave, like a mausoleum, or they could dedicate a bench to their father!

"How much is a bench?"

"Starts at two thousand."

"Ah."

They stopped moving in the direction of the mausoleum or the bench. Their father would not have liked to spend thousands of dollars on such a thing as a mausoleum. Still, every dollar withheld felt like a curtailment of their love.

Mr. Munoz left the room for a few minutes to consult the lady in the front office about the prices for the different sizes of bases (it turned out that she was his boss rather than his secretary), and Salma and Asif quickly made their decision in his absence. They chose the simplest design, the one that would best describe their father's personality, a man of high thought and a low regard for show and recognition.

When Mr. Munoz returned, Asif quickly pointed out the plain rectangular design to Mr. Munoz and also quickly decided on the size of the base and marker, spelling out his choices while Mr. Munoz wrote rapidly with a ballpoint pen on a yellow notepad. In a few minutes, it was over.

"There, all done," Asif said happily, leaning back in his chair with his feet planted on the ground.

"And now for the words you want on the marker," Mr. Munoz said.

Salma gasped. She had forgotten that a tombstone required words. Mr. Munoz smiled apologetically. There were more discussions about fonts and sizes, more back and forth with prices. Salma mechanically pushed through the decisions, always choosing the simplest and cheapest option.

"Now are we done?"

Mr. Munoz smiled. "We're done."

Suddenly Asif asked, "Can we have a poem? There is a poem that best describes my father, a poem that my father used to recite."

"Yes, of course!" Mr. Munoz said, his face lighting up.

More words meant more money, Salma thought.

"Actually," Asif said, "can we have the poem written in Bengali letters?"

"Yes, yes, definitely," Mr. Munoz said. "People have done different scripts. We had some people request writing in Arabic, for example."

Painstakingly, Salma wrote down the foreign words on a piece of paper, words that meant nothing in English. Someone could easily make a mistake with the characters. Mr. Munoz said he would send them the proofs first for their approval.

"What do the words mean?" he asked with childlike curiosity.

"They mean: When will there be born in our land a boy, who speaks little and is big in deed?" Asif chatted easily with Mr. Munoz, telling him what kind of man his father was.

Mr. Munoz seemed interested in hearing about their father. He had an open face and a sweet, kind smile. His manner was mild and his voice slow and gentle.

"All done now?" Salma smiled brightly, standing up.

A man in jeans walked in and spoke in Spanish with Mr. Munoz. He had been hired to cut the tree in the parking lot, and he needed Salma and Mr. Munoz to move their cars. When they came back in, Mr. Munoz finally finished calculating the price from the quotations list and writing down the design details on his notepad. At last, it was over, and they were joking, talking about the World Cup Football games taking place. Mr. Munoz was Colombian, and they discovered that they were all three supporters of the South American countries. Then Salma and Asif were free.

They shook hands with Mr. Munoz and walked out, spilling out into the beautiful sunny day at the end of summer. As they hurried down the steps, they passed a mother and daughter entering the cemetery office. The mother and her daughter, about twelve or thirteen, smiled weakly at Salma and Asif. Their eyes were red, and they looked uncertain whether to behave normally or to show their grief.

Back in her car, Salma said, "I'm glad we did it now. You know? Instead of just immediately afterward, like them. We would have been like them, just paralyzed.

It would have been painful. At least this way we were able to enjoy it. You know what I mean?"

"Yeah," said Asif, pulling his seatbelt on. "Can we visit the grave before we go?"

"Of course. I was thinking the same thing!"

The car followed the narrow road, crowded with parked cars along the side, to Garden nine, where the Muslims were buried. They walked on the lawn, stepping over other graves, trying to find their father's. Had Kamal been with them, he would surely have told her it was disrespectful to walk on graves.

Salma felt lighter, a world away from the day they had buried him four weeks ago. Everything had seemed still and foreign on that day. They had stood around watching, unbelieving, as a crane had lowered a slab of concrete and then piled dirt on the grave. A few people had come to pay their respects, but the words of condolences had seemed miles away. There were so few people, for a man who had had so many friends. Salma and Asif had just wanted to get away, into the comfort of their car, back home, where a warm meal awaited them, and television, and the World Cup games.

"Strange," Salma said now in the sunlit day, after they had walked for a few minutes. "His grave was at the end. Where is it now?"

They both realized at the same time what had happened. Their father's grave was no longer at the edge because other people had been buried since they had been there last. They walked on, still stepping over other graves, trying to find an unmarked grave with a temporary bronze vase filled with plastic flowers, a small paper marker with their father's name and date of birth pasted on.

In the distance, Salma could see a cantilever tent that had been set up by the roadside for the spectators of a new burial to take place on that day. A crane stood ready to dig. As they plodded on, Salma and Asif began to idly read the markers on the other graves. Then they became really interested.

"Look, Salma. This one says it expires a month from now," Asif said. "So this is a completely new grave, since a temporary marker is supposed to expire in a month."

"1954. You can tell their ages from the markers."

They passed an infant's grave, so tiny that it took up no space. "It's comforting, in a way, to see that so many people have died in the last two weeks. It's almost as if death is natural," Asif commented.

Salma let his words fall around her, comforting and natural. She walked nimbly now, her steps light in the warm day. They kept walking, reading the markers and letting themselves be surrounded by the commonness of death.

"Look!" Salma said, stopping at three graves with the same last name. "What could have happened?"

"Car accident?" Asif guessed.

"You're right."

By the dates of birth on the graves, they calculated, the three dead had been a twenty-year-old, an eighteen-year-old, and a fifteen-year-old of the same family, all buried at the same time. Salma and Asif tried to guess the relationships among the three dead people. Salma read their names: Miriam, Sara, and Haider—two girls and a boy. Their deaths could only have been tragic. Their last name was unusual, Muquddum. Salma memorized it, interested, determining to Google it once she returned home.

At last they found their father's grave, surrounded by fresh mounds of earth. They sat by it, touching the mound of earth, and wondered aloud what was happening to his body now.

When their mother had died, suddenly, from cancer, Salma had felt an acute urge to steal her back. She had wanted to raise her from the grave when no one was looking. She had felt that urge for a long time after her mother's death, every time they visited her grave during their month-long stay in Bangladesh. But now Salma felt no such longing to pull her father back from his grave. She felt removed from her father's body.

"He was so far gone," Asif said when she confided in him. "When I looked at his dead body, when I was washing him, he didn't feel like my father to me. His body was emaciated and changed."

"You know, he starved to death," Salma said. She was sitting with her knees on the earth, pulling grass at her feet. "He was thirsty, but he couldn't drink water. He couldn't swallow. I kept trying to push him to get better. If only I'd realized he was dying, I could have been kinder to him."

"Don't be hard on yourself," Asif said soothingly.

He was looking away, squinting into the sun. After they returned home, Salma Googled the name Muquddum on her iPad. At first, it didn't seem a particularly deliberate act, just an idle way of browsing the Web. She did so many things just to pass the time, to distract herself. For most of Asif's visit, they had been watching the World Cup games, cooking elaborate snacks together, eating, taking walks, and eating out at restaurants. And they discussed football, and read about football, and Googled various statistics on football. So, from researching the World Cup, it was an easy stretch to Google other things as well. Marvelously, with a few strokes of the key, the keywords Muquddum and Houston thrown in, the news came up.

It hadn't been a car accident, after all. Thrilled, Salma lay in bed that evening reading all the articles she could find on them on her iPad. She could hear Asif and Kamal downstairs, talking together in a soothing, distant drone. She kept searching the name in different browsers and different search engines, with different combinations of keywords, and the story emerged.

The Muquddums had been siblings. It was a murder suicide. Salma kept reading. For the first time in weeks, she was focused on something outside of herself. According to all the news articles, no one knew what exactly had happened to the three siblings. It was a mystery. All the children were polite and nice, according to friends and neighbors. There had been nothing out of the ordinary about them. The twenty-year-old sister had dropped out of school and was working as a nurse's assistant. The fifteen-year-old sister was a sophomore in high school. The police suspected that their teenaged brother had shot them both and then turned the gun on himself.

No one called Salma for hours. At last, when it got dark outside her window and she realized her room light wasn't on, she put away the iPad and came downstairs. Kamal and Asif were watching a detective show on TV.

"Do you remember that family of the three siblings who died?" Salma said, standing in front of the TV. "I just Googled them. It was a murder suicide."

"Wow. Really?" Asif sat up and slapped his knees, exclaiming.

"No one knows what happened exactly. But they think the brother probably killed his two sisters and then shot himself."

"That's really sad," Kamal said.

Asif and Kamal returned to watching the show. Salma sat on the sofa and patiently waited for them to finish. But after the show ended and she switched off the TV, they moved on to other topics. When Salma brought it up again at dinner, Kamal and Asif seemed suitably touched. They talked about it, but no one else bothered to Google the story. The three ate dinner, talked some more, went outside to stand on the front steps drinking coffee under the full moon, came inside, and went to sleep, never once mentioning the Muquddums again.

In the middle of the night, Salma crept out of bed, moved to the window seat, and turned on the iPad, hoping its light would not spread to the bed and wake up Kamal.

More of the story had built over time. People were referring to the victims' Twitter accounts and Facebook pages that hadn't been taken down. The boy, Haider, had a Facebook post looking forward to the World Cup games. Friends of the victims were now writing their own accounts on their blogs. Also, by going back to the original news stories, Salma discovered a growing thread of comments. A friend of Miriam, the younger girl, wrote about how Miriam had been "the sweetest person on earth, not just on the outside, but also on the inside." Several people speculated about how the parents must be feeling.

Now it seemed to her that her father had lived a normal life and died a quiet death. The more Salma read, the more comforted she felt. After Salma's father had died, friends had dropped by and said nice things, but none of those visits had offered Salma as much comfort as this story about the murder suicide of the three siblings. She stayed on the iPad until the first markings of daylight. Then she crawled back into bed beside Kamal, exhausted.

For the next several days, Salma Googled the name repeatedly on her iPad. Muquddum. It was an addiction. She regained an interest in talking on the phone with people who had wished to console her before, whose calls she had not received. What would she have said to them then? The only way to truly understand his death was to avoid it, to do anything but focus on it, so that understanding came in brief flashes, suddenly, after a good TV show or in the middle of tea with her brother and husband. But now Salma called those friends back to tell them about the tragedy of the Muquddum family. She wondered about every detail, what the mother must have felt on her first discovery of her babies lying dead in her home, or how the sisters must have been scared in the moment when their brother had attacked them. She could have gone on for hours thinking about them.

They had spent most of Asif's visit lounging around at home, just resting from the world. Being academics, they were both off for the summer. One day, toward the end of Asif's visit, Salma suggested to Kamal that they should all drive to the cemetery again to visit her father's grave.

"Yeah, let's go," Kamal agreed. "Let's go there today."

The cemetery was an hour away. The motion of the car was soothing. They played music. At Garden Nine, Salma looked around furtively for other visitors. On the way to her father's grave, Salma led Kamal and Asif back to the three siblings' graves. Someone had stuffed fresh flowers in the bronze vases, Salma noted, as Kamal and Asif started to walk away. They seemed strangely uninterested.

As on the previous occasion, they had trouble finding Salma's father's grave. At last when they reached it, it seemed even more buried by new dead bodies all around. Salma felt curiously detached from her father's grave. Her father's living self was still alive in her memory. She remembered his every discomfort and suffering. At home, she felt a shiver when she passed his empty room. But his grave had no effect on her. "Hey, someone left flowers," Asif cried happily.

Perhaps another visitor. Some of her father's friends and students lived in Houston. Salma studied the flowers, tall irises and lilies bent and spilling over the vase. She and Asif wondered aloud who it might have been, a welcome distraction. The day was beautiful, clear blue, with a light breeze that slanted the grass near the grave. There was a small apple tree nearby in the otherwise characterless land and an embankment with pine trees in the distance, possibly planted to cut off the view and sound of the highway. Asif said the tree could serve as a marker for their father's grave in the future.

Salma thought of her mother's grave in the Azimpur graveyard in Bangladesh, where she lay next to her parents and two of her sisters. That graveyard had character, planted with trees by the family members of those buried there, mango trees and guava trees and flowering plants that filled the air with a heavy scent. In the evenings, crows came to sit on the trees and a nearby mosque belted out its call for prayers, making the atmosphere gloomy and somber.

But here, in a foreign land, in a commercial cemetery, there was just a body under the earth, fast disappearing. Salma sat down near her father's grave. Asif sat down, too. The breeze lifted Salma's hair. There was a drone of cars on the highway. They sat together silently, searching for meaning.

Salma realized she had been hoping that she might run into the Muquddum siblings' mother come to visit their graves and discover more of their story. She had found out a lot more about the family. The father had moved out only a few days before the murder. The boy, Haider, had hated his father. The father and son had gotten into fist fights several times. The more Salma found out, the more she wanted to know. Why had the brother killed his sisters? Why did the father move out? And how did the father feel now?

For the next few days, Salma suggested to Asif and Kamal that they visit the cemetery again. But Asif had caught a cold and said he was too sick to go, and he was flying home in only four more days. Kamal had to work on a paper he was writing. So Salma drove to the cemetery herself. She stayed for a long time, sometimes sitting by her father's grave and sometimes walking around reading the markers on other graves. She still did not feel any connection to her father's grave. Her proximity to his body did not yield any special thoughts, except to make her wonder how much more his body had decomposed since she had last visited.

She had posed such questions to Asif, as well as questions about life after death. Her father had been an atheist, so the question about what had happened to his body after his death was interesting to them. He must have found out at last what happened after death.

Salma kept looking to see if other visitors would arrive. Other graves held more interest for her, distracting her. She kept wondering about a grave where the person had been born in 2000 and died in 2013. That would make the person a mere child. Then she would wonder how the child had died. She was also impressed by how many old people were buried in the cemetery. Her father was not the only one, after all, to be buried far away in another country. There was some romance in starting one's life in one place and ending it in another, as if life were an adventure and one could never know where it would end. Her parents could not have known how things would look for them in the end, the sudden death of one leading to the other's journey to another country and his humiliating, lonely death.

Squinting in the sunlight, staring ahead, Salma saw a middle-aged woman in a shapeless shalwar kameez with her head loosely encircled by a dupatta and an elderly man wearing a dirty, collared shirt, and baggy slacks climb out of an old Toyota Corolla. The elderly couple walked slowly to the three graves of the Muquddum siblings. Then they stood side by side offering prayer. Salma stared open-mouthed at the couple in the sun, shading her eyes and squinting, facing them nakedly. They did not look in her direction or pay her any heed, so she had an open view. Salma drank them in greedily. She could not be sure, but they could only be the father and mother of the three dead siblings. They appeared to her as abject, tragic figures. Their gaits were slow and their facial features were vague, washed out by their sorrow. They held their hands at their breasts, their heads bent low in prayer. Several times, they knelt, stood up, and knelt again. Then they rose and left.

Salma watched their departing backs as they walked slowly to the Toyota Corolla and climbed inside. She stared straight at them as the car reversed, made a K turn, and drove off. There had been no encounter, no contact; they had told her nothing of their story or their feelings. Salma was satisfied, nevertheless, with just seeing the Muquddum parents.

She wondered why. Perhaps they had just been entertainment for her. A distraction. Perhaps they wouldn't have been able to answer the questions she had after all. Why did the boy not wait to watch the World Cup games before taking his life? And what was he thinking at the moment he killed his sisters, one by one, or earlier in the morning when he probably had no intention of killing anyone? Or later, if he had had a later, what regrets would he have felt?

When she returned home that day, Salma didn't tell Kamal or Asif about her sighting. They seemed to have forgotten the Muquddum family. After four days, Asif left for California, still sniffling. Kamal drove him to the airport. It was too much for Salma to accompany them, to face another difficult parting.

After Asif left, Salma settled into bed, trying to get as much rest as possible before the end of summer and the start of classes and students and syllabi. The World Cup games ended a few days after the semester started. Then Salma started pulling novels from the shelves downstairs and carrying them up to her bed. She would read them lying down, skipping meals, depending on Kamal to take pity on her and bring her a jam and butter sandwich. She kept reading. For days, weeks. She was late on grading, distracted during office hours, slovenly about most things she did. By then, Palestine was being bombed and children were dying, but death was entirely natural to Salma. She had discovered an antidote to life's stubborn miseries: the distraction of fiction, the made-up world of what happened next.

In October, when the few maple trees on campus had begun to shed their leaves, Salma walked to her car parked in the faculty lot at the end of the day, checking her cellphone. There was a voicemail from the cemetery, leaving a courtesy message that the permanent marker 'for her loved one's grave' was ready.

Salma had fretted about it before, wondering why it wasn't ready yet, but now she felt only relief that the business had been completed. She felt no desire to actually see the cheap tombstone. However it looked, it was an inadequate marker to her father's life. Even if Salma had erected a marble mausoleum in her father's honor, it could not take away the disappointments and the guilt and the sadness. Those feelings could only be squashed under other things.

Salma walked across the parking lot in the setting sun, climbed in, tossing the phone in her bag, and started the engine. Then she turned on an audio recording of a new novel, a long one.

Two Mothers

The rain pooled outside the house in Katy as Simi poured the food into warmers for the party. This was the problem with Katy, she had discovered when they moved to Houston: If it rained, floods became an immediate concern. But all their Bengali friends had recommended buying a house Katy, the suburb to the west of the city which had become home to the never-ending flow of fossil fuel engineers to Houston. The subdivision had expanded to accommodate its workforce, past Cincho Ranch to new territories, over prairie lands and rice paddies where field mice had once roamed. Simi and Sumon had bought a modest house, with three bedrooms to accommodate an occasional guest, but Sumon thought they could have bought something grander. The houses in the new subdivisions were much larger, with six bedrooms, three garages, and two stairways, with Roman Columns and Mediterranean balconies reaching out to the sky. Whenever he drove by these new mansions, Sumon stared at them with awe. They seemed to him to be death defying, as if the massiveness of the houses and the sheer number of rooms, could secure one from the world outside.

Sumon poked his head in the kitchen. "Everything ready?"

Simi nodded. She was used to working quietly and steadily, like a squirrel. Everything was planned and neatly done. She had bought a dozen warmers for parties just like these when they had lived in Louisiana, and she had brought them with her to Houston when they had moved.

"Don't mention to anyone that it's Maria's birthday," she reminded him, setting candles under the warmers and lighting them with a stove lighter.

Maria, turning eight, would have protested and made a fuss had she been around, and Simi would have had to turn on her and scold her. But thankfully the child had settled down to play on the computer in her room. Usually, Maria refused to do anything quiet, like watch TV. She liked to prance about the house and make a mess, pulling flours out of the pantry for her chemistry experiments or cutting up paper and spilling them all over the floor. For now, her anticipation of the birthday party and her friends arriving had helped to buy her cooperation for a few hours.

As the sky darkened, the rain drummed more loudly, ominous now in the dark. The wind whistled, lashing the saplings in the yard violently. Even the crepe myrtle, the only mature tree in the yard, creaked dangerously. Just a few weeks ago, acting on advice from her neighbors, Simi had made Sumon call men to cut down the two oak trees, lest they fall on the house during a storm. She was glad of it now.

As it grew closer to seven, Simi began to worry that the rain would upset everything, that no one would be able to drive through it, and the party would be canceled. But the first guests began to arrive on time, right on cue, at eight, running from their cars with umbrellas, shaking off wet saris and squishy shoes, the men carrying the children, one in each arm. There were umbrellas everywhere, and Sumon hurried to get these off the wood floor and find a place for them, because Simi was particular about such things. He dragged a big plastic sheet for the wet shoes and dripping umbrellas. It was a mess, and most of the guests were flustered and out of temper.

"It was impossible to see on the road. So dangerous!"

"Almost got into an accident!"

Simi and Sumon stood at the door, receiving their guests, commiserating, and soothing.

"Maria, your friends are here!" Simi called. "Take them to your room."

It was the custom for the children to go away, to disappear upstairs to the den or into various rooms, separated by age and gender, where they would be no trouble.

Maria, a stout and pretty girl, came out of her room wearing a heavy brocade party dress and scratching her neck from the itchy fabric, her mouth downturned and her eyebrows raised, with her little brown hands poised on her hips, in an extreme expression of suffering. She was under orders not to reveal that this was her birthday party. Her bright black eyes pooled with intelligence, expressing–everything, if only someone would ask.

Simi's closest friend in Houston was Bithi. Bithi's two daughters, twins, were Maria's age and her best friends. Most of the other eight-year-olds had arrived with tablets and chargers and were already demanding the password, which Sumon had presciently taped onto the back of the front door so that he only had to point. But Bithi's two children liked to play without technology, like Maria. The three got along well.

Bithi entered complaining of a sore throat. "Sorry we're late. I had to take a Tylenol to lie down first." She wore a heavy blue sari and blouse, with a silver choker at her throat, her hair pulled back from her round face in a ponytail.

"You look very nice," Simi said, taking her by the hand to ease her inside.

Bithi paused near the shoes and umbrellas to talk more.

"Oof. It was so difficult getting the twins ready. One ran this way and the other said I have to play first. She said, I have to finish my dolls' birthday party! So then I had to lock them up in a room in the end and dress them by force, while they were screaming!"

Simi laughed. Bithi was always telling funny stories about the travails with her children. But Bithi was blocking the door to other guests, so Simi gently nudged her toward the kitchen.

Soon, the kitchen pooled with women in silk saris and three-piece satin outfits, dangling fashion jewelry, crying out in mutual admiration, until no one could hear the rain anymore.

"Appetizers are served," Simi said, getting down plastic bowls and spoons.

"Need any help?" someone asked.

"No. Everything is ready. Being tall and thin, I'm able to reach up to both the high cupboards and bend down to the low cupboards," Simi joked. She was overly skinny, so she wasn't bragging.

"How is the gym going?" someone asked.

"Good. I go every day to build muscles, so I can carry you all in case of a flood," she said, working as she talked. She was dressed efficiently, in a no-nonsense kameez and shalwar and house slippers that would allow her to work fast without obstruction.

"Ooh, it's warm, let's sit down a little." Bithi withdrew from the heat of the kitchen, where other women were still serving themselves fried spicy things and tomato chutney, and walked to the adjacent dining area, sinking into one of the tall chairs arranged around the high round table. "No one knows how difficult it is to raise two kids. It's very hard on me." Bithi poured herself a glass of lemonade into a blue plastic cup from the jug placed on the table. Her hands shook. "Sit, sit." She waved some women to her, who hesitated before sitting down.

"Are you alright?" a young woman asked as Bithi raised her trembling hand with the cup to beaded lips. "Your hands are trembling."

"Yes, I have had hypertension since the twins were born. It was so difficult when they were newborns. I had tremendous heartburn, so I could not lie down at night. I would walk around all night with one of them in my arms. Oh, those days…what shall I say? They were terrible. I cannot describe them to you."

"Are those real glass bangles, Bithi?" the young woman interrupted her.

Someone snickered and moved away. Bithi was fond of talking about her difficult pregnancy and childbirth. It was a constant refrain with her. Her face was swollen, and her body heavy and round. She had difficulty breathing in the silk sari and blouse and often panted to get her breath back. Simi's other friends often gossiped about her, that she should just exercise instead of reveling in her bad health. Others joked and said, "Seems like she's the only one raising kids. Haven't we raised kids ourselves?"

Dinner was served. Simi asked Sumon to call the men first. His mother had just passed away two months ago after suffering for years from kidney failure, so Simi checked his face to see if he was holding up okay. He had flown back to Bangladesh in June and turned right back after the funeral. He had never spoken a word about it afterward. She hadn't seen him shed a tear. They were throwing Maria's birthday party now, two weeks belated, as soon as they could managed after he returned. The women had served the children the pizza from boxes laid out on the kitchen counter. Now they took plates of rice and meat for themselves, slipping into the living room next to the open plan kitchen with foaming Coca Cola in red plastic cups. As they ate, they watched a Bengali serial on satellite TV and talked idly. But the conversation in the men's drawing room near the front door was loud and heated. It often happened this way at the parties, with the women exchanging pleasantries, trying their hardest to talk about nothing, while the men exploded into conflict immediately.

"No! A coal plant *cannot* be clean. A coal plant in the Sundarbans forest would destroy the habitat!" Someone was shouting, arguing about a project plan in Bangladesh to build a clean coal plant to export power to India.

The women recognized the voice as belonging to Mr. Haidar Khan, an elderly graduate of their engineering university in Bangladesh. They were all engineers and had all graduated from the same university in Bangladesh, then they had all come to America to get their master's degrees before getting jobs in oil and gas.

Mr. Haidar, a thin man in his fifties with glasses held together with scotch tape, was always creating conflict. He would get agitated debating some point that went over everyone else's heads, causing unpleasantness.

Whenever he expressed one of these explosive opinions, the other men looked away and started talking about something else. Once, Sumon had explained to Simi that Mr. Haidar's frustrations sprung from the fact that he was an unsuccessful scientist at the university, earning very little money, compared to the younger men, who worked at various oil and gas companies. Even in appearance, Mr. Haidar stood apart from the others. While the younger men had assimilated into American society, eating chips and drinking Coca Cola, rounding out, with receding hairlines, their rice bellies announcing their newly acquired American wealth and prosperity, Mr. Haidar had held onto his indecent famine-like figure from Bangladesh, with sunken eyes, stretched taut skin over his forehead and cheeks, and skeletal, stick like arms and legs.

"Why is it bad? It's called clean coal, after all." someone laughed.

"So you think technology can solve everything?" Mr. Haidar shouted, getting more excited.

This objection was so laughable that the other men could only guffaw in response. Everyone who lived in Katy had a deep faith that technology could solve everything. Sumon had often explained to Simi that to ignore the man was the best thing. Any response got him only more excited.

"Is the food okay? Is it edible?" Simi asked, to drown out the men's voices.

"First class."

The women considered it unseemly to let politics invade their drawing rooms, or to even consider what was going on in the world outside. If someone surfing through channels accidentally crossed a news channel, with scenes of war and mayhem, people looked away quickly. Someone might remark, I don't understand politics. Others would nod.

"It's raining much harder than before!" Bithi exclaimed. She stood up suddenly from the round table where she had been sitting and walked to the window by the table looking out into the dark yard. "Oh, my God. I can't see anything!"

Mr. Haidar Khan's wife Pansy joined Bithi at the window, looking out through the glass, burying her face in the darkness. "That crepe myrtle tree is rolling around dangerously. Its branch could break," she said. Pansy's cool bare arm under the sleeveless blouse brushed Bithi's hot arms. To the other women, Pansy was an embarrassment, like her husband. She wore long, dangling earrings and green nail polish, frosted lipstick, at her age! She pulled her hair up high on her head and drew down tendrils at either side of her face. And when she talked, she spoke of smoking and drinking and wild parties in her youth, old boyfriends. Of her two sons, both grown, one had married an older woman with a child and another was living together with a woman, according to rumors. When Pansy spoke, the younger women at the parties, clad in more modest blouses with sleeves covering their upper arms and their saris covering their navels, and with higher aims for their own children, would stand up, their ears burning, and walk away before they heard too much. It seemed that Pansy wanted to talk, that she had a lot to say, and that she didn't mind spilling her scandalous secrets, that in fact, she might have no idea that these were scandalous things to say. The crepe myrtle swayed dangerously toward the house, as if lending evidence to their constant fears about trees and all things in nature. The two women stood together in companionable silence, staring into the darkness outside, witnessing the horrifying theater of nature outside. They feared snakes in gardens, the infestation of squirrels and mice.

"Once, I saw a bright, leaf-green lizard on the pine tree," Bithi said. As she had stared at it, through a glass window, from inside the house, the lizard had suddenly unfurled its disgusting red dewlap. Bithi had screamed and had her husband Ali cut down the tree within the week, she said.

"Oh, my God!" Pansy reacted with satisfying horror to the story of the lizard, putting her hands to her lips. "These things can be poisonous."

"Do you know what happened a few weeks ago?" Bithi continued, staying away from the subject of coal and her offensive husband (she was an engineer herself and excited about clean coal). "I came home with my two children and parked in the garage, and my twins said, something is moving, mother. So I scolded them and said, overactive imagination! But later I saw that there were right. There was a snake! Like a ribbon. It was caught in the trap I set out for the rats. Our house is built on what used to be rice fields with field mice."

"Oh, my god. What did you do?"

"I locked them up in the house and ran inside and called animal control. They took hours to come. And when they came, would you believe it, they scolded me, saying it was a rare snake, and I shouldn't have set the mousetraps in my garage."

"Good for you that you trapped it. Oh my, I don't like snakes at all."

Again, the men's voices were raised.

"What do you think all you young men are doing here? Do you think you are helping this society? Hmm? Do you know how many poor people sleep on the streets of Houston? Do you know how often we have a h…h…hurr…hurricane or floods?" The older man was stuttering, his words coming out in angry, guttural barks.

"Oh, Haidar Bhai, calm down," someone said in a honeyed voice like salve. There were some coughs, a clearing of throats.

"Noooo! You think you can stop the world outside, the c–c–climate change, by going on going to your f–f–fancy jobs in your suits and living in these massive houses?" Haidar Khan stood up and started gesticulating with his harms, loosening the top buttons of his shirt.

"Calm down. You don't have to insult people. We can be civil." Still the responses were polite. "Do you know a reservoir was supposed to be built here in Katy to hold the flood water? But the city abandoned those plans and sold the land to developers to accommodate you guys. This is prairie land. It's supposed to be barren to let the water flood it! Now where will that water go, huh? You're scientists, for God's sakes!"

The children ran out of a side room to see what the fight was about, their eyes wide and mouths open. "What's going on?" Maria clapped her hands and jumped up and down, the heavy party dress bobbing with her. The plastic band Simi had placed on her hair had come off, and her curls fell over her face in wild disarray.

"Nothing. Go and play," Sumon said.

Maria came up to him and put her plump arms about his neck, rubbing her soft cheeks against his rough skin. "Are you sure?" she said tenderly, remembering that his mother had died.

"Yes." He smiled and sent the children back.

Simi froze in the kitchen, where she had been serving the dessert quietly, and stood with her two hands clasped in front of her chest. It was her night to serve, to make that everyone had enough to eat and a good time. She stood until Sumon came into the kitchen smiling brightly at his wife. He had a round, fair face, handsome, with long eyelashes, pink lips, and even teeth. Everything about him aimed to please.

"Is the dessert ready?"

"Yes. I'll get it right out," Simi said. She started to move again, with purpose.

Pulling open the fridge doors, she lifted out an orange caramel custard she had made, yogurt and pink custard with little bits of colorful fruit. Sumon started the percolator, expertly getting out teabags, sugar, and condensed milk from the cabinet for the evening tea that would complement the dessert.

Slowly, the raised voices faded away into murmurs. When the men filed into the kitchen to serve themselves sweets and tea, with the waft of sugar and warm milk in the air, talking about salaries, work, and the share market in low voices, the rain could be heard again.

As usual, Bithi and Ali stayed behind long after the other guests had left. Their children liked to play together, and the fathers were classmates: The adults got along as well as the children. Besides, the other guests lived nearby in Katy, whereas Ali and Bithi would have to drive further off, an hour's drive down to Clear Lake, so it was worth their while to stay longer and make most of the trip.

"Sit, sit," Simi said, settling down herself on the sofa that had been occupied all evening. She had just said good-bye to Mr. Haidar and his wife Pansy, who had both shuffled away into the rain in an embarrassed and angry way, without any umbrellas. She felt easier now, having got rid of the trouble.

Bithi, who had been hot under her silk sari after eating and from the overcrowding of guests (she often became overheated and breathless after eating), wiped her forehead with the back of her hand and breathed more easily. "Oof, it feels much cooler now."

The children had been huddled together all night in one room watching TV and playing on their devices, but now Maria and the twins, freed from the party decorum, rushed upstairs and started to jump up and down noisily, banging the pool sticks on Sumon's pool table.

"Never mind, let them play," Simi said, suppressing a yawn with her hand and raising the same hand to stop Bithi, who was about to get up. "Do you want another cup of tea?"

"The other children don't play," Bithi agreed. "This is why yours house is the only place I feel comfortable. Here they can be normal and run around and be naughty."

"Yes, children need to play," Simi agreed, her eyes heavy with sleep.

"I have grown so fat. I need to exercise. Do you work out, Simi?"

"Yes. I go to the gym. You look very nice. The lipstick is very nice."

"You always look like you are going to work out," Bithi said. "That's what I like about you. You never dress to impress, as if looks don't matter. Don't take it the wrong way. I really admire it, that you're not overdressed like the other women."

Simi laughed. When she went to work, as a pharmacist, she dressed in efficient blouse and slacks. When at home, she adorned an apron and got down to cook in her always tidy, clean kitchen. Her only role in life was to raise her daughter, to work, to keep in good health and keep her family in good health.

"But of course, you look good because you are slim. I was skinny myself before my marriage," Bithi said. "I should say before having the twins. It's hard raising the children."

Simi nodded sympathetically. She spoke little, but she was a good listener. The rainwater guttered down the drainpipes. There was a drumming on the ventilator and on the glass of the narrow skylight upstairs. There was a large window upstairs, beside the pool table, that led out to the roof. Sumon had walked out on the ledge to rake the leaves on the roof before the guests arrived.

Bithi was telling a story...

"When I was a young girl, my parents lived in Iraq. My father was working there in oil. They were employing a lot of foreigners all over the world. And in Iraq, I remember going to the hospital with my mother when my little sister was born. It was during the Iraq war. These soldiers had gone off to fight, and their young brides were having babies. These poor girls. One of them had given birth to two premature babies. The hospital didn't know what to do with the babies. So the girl put them in cotton under the bed on the floor. They were like little mice, smaller than my palm." She held out her swollen, pink palm. "I don't know what happened to the babies. I was too scared of the whole thing. That pale little girl giving birth to those little creatures mewling under the bed."

Simi nodded wordlessly.

"Maybe they died…"

Sumon came inside with Ali. They had been standing outside having a smoke, checking out the weather. Just that morning, Sumon remarked to his friend, he had gotten out on the roof through the open window in the den upstairs and cleaned out the leaves on the roof. Now the roof was covered up with fallen leaves again!

"Turn on the news," Sumon said to Simi. "My phone just went off with a flashflood warning."

"I remember when the twins were born, that night it was raining like this. Do you remember, Ali?" Bithi said. Her voice rose, searching for sympathy. Ali, a tall, silent man, was as stoic as his wife was talkative, willing to bear the burden the world had given him on his wide shoulders. She shivered and closed her eyes recounting the horrors of that night. "I can never forget it. The long labor, the emergency C-section. My parent had both passed away and there was no one to help us. It was just the two of us. It is too cruel being so alone in a new country, with no family around to help."

Sumon rolled through the cable channels until he found a local channel with weather news. His pretty face crumpled into a frown. All the highways were under water. Bithi shrieked at an image: The water on I-10 in one place had reached the highway sign on the bridge.

"In this situation, we cannot go home!"

"You must stay," Simi insisted at once. "We'll have a party."

"An after-party party," Sumon joked. "More tea?"

"Yes, I'll put on a proper kettle on the stove now," Simi said, standing up. She was tired and needed some strong tea with milk to stay up for her guests.

The children could be heard jumping on the pool table. There were thumping and scratching sounds.

"Ei!" Sumon called halfheartedly. "No jumping on the pool table. Also, too much jumping will make you cough again, Maria."

Once, a kid had dropped a pool ball from upstairs in the middle of a party at Simi and Sumon's house. The ball had crashed into a glass table directly in its path, and the table had shattered, spewing glass among the women sitting with their handbags around the table. Luckily, no one had been hurt. But since then, Sumon confiscated the pool balls before a party.
"I didn't think they would think to jump on the table," he said, shaking his head.

"These children," Bithi said. "They are not human. Monkeys, I say." She said it proudly.

They heard Maria coughing again upstairs. Sumon said, "Her allergies are acting up again. We are worried about her. The doctor said to put her back on steroids."

"Steroids!" cried Bithi. "That's very bad. I was on steroids. Don't you see, my body is all swollen up? Steroids save you, only to kill you. Never put her on steroid."

"She's been on them on and off, her whole life. There were complications when she was born…"

Sumon began to tell the story, but Bithi, who had been feeling hot again, stood up to go to the kitchen, where Simi had put a silver kettle on the stove.

She whispered to Simi, "Do you have a cotton nightie or something? I have hypertension, so I can't wear these rich clothes for too long you see." She laughed.

"Wait, I'll give you a whole selection to choose from. A whole wardrobe. You can have your pick!" Simi joked and took Bithi into the bedroom.

"What kind of complications does Maria have?" Ali asked politely.

But Sumon had stopped talking. He was thinking of his parents. If he turned his head around to face the back windows of the living room, he would be looking at the crepe myrtle. After his mother's funeral, he had flown back immediately. He would sit in his den on the second floor, working at his desk. He would carry work home from the office, determined to bury himself in work. One day, he found himself staring at the crepe myrtle full of pink flower, bursting with life. The tree had not been in bloom the day before. He had felt that a startling reaffirmation of life had crawled back, after the violence of what had happened to his mother– the frightened hospital run, being stuck in traffic in the ambulance, the cold, sallow skin of his mother after death. He had stared at the crepe myrtle with wonder. When Simi had been pregnant, they had discovered that she was going to have twins. But she had pre-eclampsia. There were complications, so the doctors decided to get the babies out early. During the surgery, the doctor came out to Sumon and told him that they didn't know if they could save both babies and the mother. Both babies survived in the end, but the doctors said they were in poor health. They had to get them out two months early. They were tiny, two pounds each, in NICU.

Sumon was startled. It was this very day. Maria's birthday. And his mother had come to the rescue for him. In the old days, they used to speak of raising such babies in cotton balls. They stayed in the hospital for months, it seemed. Up to that experience, he had been a sheltered boy who had been raised by two loving parents. Like Bithi's father, his father had worked in oil in Iraq during the seventies and made his money. They were upper middle class, well to do. Sumon had never had a moment's sorrow in his life. The worst memory of his entire childhood was from before his parents made money in the middle east, when they lived in a tiny flat in Dhaka with a roof on top that had no guard railings. A child who was visiting had escaped to the roof and had been walking around the edge of the roof one day and had fallen off. It had been afternoon and he was sleeping. He woke to his mother screaming. She ran into their one bedroom, picked him up from the bed, and clutched him to her bosom. "Sumon, Sumon. You are alive."

Later his mother said death had been calling to that child that day. But his mother's relief that Sumon had escaped death, that it was not he who had died, was the only conception Sumon had had of death until his wife gave birth to two premature babies. It was too much for him. They lived in New Orleans then, where he was a graduate student. He would walk by the levee, smoking one cigarette after another. Simi was at home. Two creatures he could not fathom were waiting for him at NICU.

They went regularly to touch the babies. The nurses said contact was good for the babies.

"The baby needs to be touched, comforted, listened to, understood," the nurses said. "It's a human need."

But that human need of his babies took everything from him. Then, one baby died in NICU. Only Maria came home. The doctors said they didn't know if she would live.

At the time, his parents were comfortably ensconced in their retired home in Gulshan, where they took daily walks on a lane lined with krishnachura flowers, with other retired people, who had also made their money in the Middle East oil, whose children were also comfortably settled in America. Their proud greeting to each other were about their offspring settled abroad.

"How is your son?"

"My daughter bought a big second house in California!"

"My son just got his Phd."

When Sumon always chose the brief period when the krishnachura bloomed blood red to visit. His parents called him early in the morning to walk with him and their retired friends under the Krishnachura (Sumon was up anyway from jetlag), showing him off proudly to his friends–their American son.

Hearing news of Maria's illness, his parents decided to come out of retirement. They offered to fly to America to take care of their son's child for him. Simi, too sick to stand, got up in the morning and went to work, while his mother took care of the baby all day. His mother taught Simi how to feed Maria, how to hold her, how to give her a bath. She stayed up all night holding the vomiting baby, listening to its mouse like wails, forcing herself to stare back at those large eyes staring out of that horrifying bony face, with no flesh on it. These was no flesh anywhere on that body, so that they had to be careful not to break her bones. It was his mother who had saved Maria, had given her last strength to her granddaughter. No one asked anything of Simi. She had been dumb, mute.

Sumon started to think about his dead mother, whom he missed very much. The last time he went home, to her funeral, he had walked on that path under the krishnachura trees again, but they were not in bloom.

"I'm sorry for your loss," Ali said, understanding why Sumon was distracted. He did not have many words, so these words were meant sincerely.

Sumon nodded, wiping a tear from his face. They went on quickly to talk about his work, where Sumon had just been promoted. He was ambitious and was rising rapidly through the ranks.

"I have five engineers working for me now."

"Wow. That must take a lot of work on your part."

"I have to work till at least eight every night. Weekends. But Simi manages at home…"

As the men talked, with the women gone, and the TV turned up by Sumon, no one paid attention to the noises upstairs. There were loud noises of dragging, scratching, and jumping.

Sumon grabbed the remote control and raised the volume on the news louder, shouting, "Stop it! No naughtiness."

Then there was a thud. Even this invasion of their tranquility the adults would have ignored, had it not been followed by screams. The twins ran downstairs to them in a fright of limbs, scurrying across the carpet like squirrels. They burrowed their heads in their father's chest, crying. "She fell! She fell down!"

Bithi called Simi daily, but Simi did not answer the calls. So Bithi urged her husband Ali to call his friend Sumon, and the two men spoke quietly, practically, for two minutes.

"What? What did he say?"

"You know. It's tough. Why don't you cook something, and we'll drop it off?"

The twins, sitting between their parents on the sofa—the little rascals never gave them a moment's peace—, chimed in, "It was horrible, what happened. I get nightmares every night."

"Hush and go to bed," Bithi scolded.

The men had rushed upstairs that night. Simi and Bithi had not heard the screams because of the heavy insulation of the master bedroom. But upstairs was the wrong way to run. The child had fallen out the window that Sumon had unlocked to go out on the roof and clean it out for Maria's birthday party. The men ran downstairs again. Maria had fallen by slipping on the wet roof and cracked her head on the concrete road, broken her neck. She lay under the water that was a foot deep on their road, until they found her. Sumon called 911 and could barely answer the barrage of questions. Ali had to seize the phone from him and answer calmly, walking up and down, his pants soaked in dirty water up to his knee.

"Sir. Sir? We can't get there soon. There is high water on all the roads. A lot of people are stranded and looking for help. Meanwhile, what you do is…"

"Oh god, oh god!" Sumon kept crying, standing on the road in the rain and holding Maria in his arms. Her neck and limbs were twisted at an impossible angle to her torso. He tried to take her breath the way he used to when she was an infant and he had to check every night if she was alive. He couldn't hear anything.

Simi came out of the house, screaming, "What happened? What happened?"

They carried Maria inside and laid her wet body on the carpeted floor of the formal drawing room where the men had sat a few hours earlier arguing about the disaster of climate change and overbuilding in Katy. Since Simi had been trained as a pharmacist in lifesaving, she bent down to take the child's pulse, her heartbeat, taking her away.

"Give her mouth to mouth resuscitation!" Sumon shouted.

Simi nodded and worked hard, blowing into the child's blackened mouth again and again. She pounded on her chest and started again. And then again. But she was already dead.

The fire truck didn't come till the next day. Simi had been pounding Maria's chest and blowing into her all night. She had refused to give Maria cake and candles to blow out, so she thought it a little painful that now she was doing all this blowing of air. There was still water on the road the next day. Sumon and Ali had moved their cars into the garage earlier. Other cars were lying submerged in the water. Water had crept into neighbors' yards. The firefighter came to their house first. They said they had orders to do so. They checked with their instruments and confirmed that the child was dead.

Simi and Sumon didn't miss a day's work. They had a funeral at the mosque, a burial, all as should be done. After forty days passed, and people had stopped bringing food, they cooked as normal people do. They ate facing each other at the high kitchen table, looking out at the backyard and the crepe myrtle tree.

Once, Simi said, "The next time there is a storm or rain like that, that tree could fall on the house. You better cut it down."

Sumon nodded.

Simi had a sister in New York and another in New Jersey. But she never called them to cry or tell little anecdotes about Maria. She found the candles and balloons Maria had insisted on buying for her birthday, that had never gotten used, and threw them away without tears. Only sometimes, when she returned after work before Sumon, and she had worked herself to the bones washing the kitchen floors and all the bathrooms of the house, Simi sat down with a steam cup of milk tea and stared out the double-glass window at the backyard, where the rain had dried up, and the sun shone in the new and bright suburb of Katy, covering up all the things that had passed a month ago.

First Snow

The first time I saw snow was in Philadelphia when I
was a freshman in college, an international student from
Bangladesh. I was staying with my father's friend's family
for the Thanksgiving holiday, sharing a room with their
daughter Bina, who was my age.

"Look, snow!" she cried when we awoke on
Thanksgiving morning.

I walked to Bina's bedroom window on the
second floor and watched the white flakes falling softly.
Bina was beautiful. She had skin the color of milk and
honey, rose spots on her cheeks, and long reddish curls
that were possibly permed. She wore green glasses. I
imagine her room being pink, floral—feminine—with
masses of pillows on the bed, and a soft, white, sinking
mattress. I was obese, having already gained my
freshman twenty eating cafeteria food at Penn. Bina was
half White and half Bengali. I didn't know it, then, but
had she been born of two Bengali parents, she would
still have been as foreign to me as I was to her.

I had visited the family before. My father's friend
Anwar Uncle (all my father's friends were uncles to me)
and his wife Margaret had received me at the airport

when I first arrived in August and brought me to their house. They had driven me to campus during move-in, waited in the long line of cars on the tree-lined streets full of parents, grandparents, and students in shorts with boxes in their arms.

Margaret took an interest in me and explained things about America to me. She was a kind, generous woman, with pale brown hair, wisps of it escaping from her bun, and sharp blue eyes. Her skirts were long and flowing. Her books lay strewn on the tables and floors of every room in the house, and any chance remark from me on any of the titles would lead to long philosophical conversations on the topic.

On the first day I had visited them, Margaret cooked bland chickpeas and garden vegetables with no spices. Other Bengali guests had been invited to lunch, including some relatives of Anwar Uncle and a Bengali graduate student at Drexel. We ate in the kitchen overlooking the garden. I liked Margaret's food, but I remember her saying to one of the other Bengali guests at the table that 'Anwar complained that the food was tasteless'.

It was an old-fashioned house, a cottage, with small rooms crammed with interesting things. I must have stayed several days that first time because I remember long hours and masses of experiences. Anwar Uncle showed me his garden, full of bright vegetables and colorful flowers. The house was full of books. I remember picking up one or the other in my solitude and reading it through to the end. I remember Carl Sagan's *Cosmos*, and a book by a man who did children's comedy.

I observed everything with interest and delight: the football game that my uncle watched through the weekend, the long lines of guests to the house, the two younger boys, John and Tommy, who chatted with me and brought me their comic books and school journals as little offerings, and the older boy Alan, who hung around in the shadows watching the game, looking forlorn and depressed, seemingly neglected by his father. I also remember watching the movie *Addams Family Values*, in particular the scene of the Thanksgiving play, with its obscure American humor, which completely escaped me.

Bina and I, although close in age, were not friends. On that first visit, as on all others, we skirted around one another, never finding common ground. I had plenty of contact with her. I accompanied her and her mother to shopping trips to buy new clothes and school supplies for the fall. I remember standing in the stationary aisle with Margaret as Bina walked off to buy her brand of shampoo. Margaret complained to me that Bina only bought the most expensive shampoo for her highlighted hair.

I remember accompanying all the children to their dentist for their annual teeth cleaning. Bina came out complaining that the hygienist who had cleaned her teeth had hurt her badly, but 'she was sweet', so Bina hadn't given her a hard time about it. Had the hygienist been a *b--*, Bina said, she would have let her have it. I listened intently to Bina's summing up of the world. All of these things, dentists, fall shopping, and special shampoos for color-treated hair, were new to me.

One evening, a boy named Mark came to the house to take Bina on a date. He was tall and lanky, with pale skin and longish brown hair. Margaret and I sat cooped up in the drawing room to give them privacy. Bina took Mark around the house, standing in front of the paintings that Margaret had brought over from Bangladesh, commenting on each one. There was a painting on the stairs of a boat on water and several of rural scenes hung on the walls of the hallway. Margaret told me that all the paintings were originals. Anwar Uncle was a great lover of Bengali art, and they had bought several paintings while they had lived in Bangladesh in the first few years of their marriage. Bina's date was a secret between mother and daughter. Margaret said that Anwar Uncle didn't believe in dating. In his view, people fell in love only to get married. But Margaret wanted Bina to have a good time, be young, enjoy life. Later, I found out that Anwar Uncle liked the boy anyway, since he was an engineering student at Penn State, one of the few students from Bina's school who had made it to college. Bina and all her other friends from school studied at the nearby community college. Anwar Uncle was disappointed in Bina. He told me this on the train ride when he brought me home for Thanksgiving. He worked at a firm in downtown Philadelphia, so I met him near City Hall to catch the train to Devon. I spotted him from a distance against the grey columns of City Hall, a tall, forlorn figure in a grey trench coat with a long, gray face. On the train, he asked me about my engineering classes and nodded when I told him my grades. Then he sighed. "None of my children are smart like you," he said.

The day before Thanksgiving, a Pakistani family came to lunch. We sat in the family room while Margaret prepared food in the kitchen. The Pakistani parents were well dressed, emanating an aura of respectability and excellence. They had two high school children, who were lavishly praised by their proud parents. The Pakistani girl was tall, her hair styled in a boy cut like her mother. The boy dressed in a sweater and khakis like his father. The boy played in band and he was applying to Princeton as his school of first choice. His parents asked me questions about Penn, as they were just then researching all the Ivy League schools.

"Bina will never get into Princeton," Anwar Uncle said with a long face. "She doesn't stand a chance."

"He thinks I'm stupid. He says so all the time," Bina said. Her face was puffed up and she blew air through her mouth.

"Your grades are very bad. You don't try," Anwar Uncle said sternly.

"See?"

A piano on which Bina had played *Edel Weiss* on my first visit stood in the corner. On top of it, there was a photo of Bina, taken for her high school graduation, wearing a blue dress, laughing.

The others made sympathetic noises to assure Bina that in their eyes she was talented. Bina moved to a sofa to sit with the Pakistani siblings. In a few moments, they were laughing together. The Pakistani family had just visited Karachi in the summer and the brother and sister chatted about what it was like there, how there were loud parties, and how it was so modern, how, instead of covering themselves, the Pakistanis in Karachi wore the latest American clothes. I sat near them and heard every line, yet I was sitting with their parents, separated from the American born people of my age by a vast distance.

That night, Bina confided in me that her father hated her. Just a week ago, her car had skidded on fallen wet leaves and hit a tree. Anwar Uncle had to come home from work and call a tow truck. The whole time, he scolded her, but both the tow truck driver and the mechanic at the garage said it wasn't Bina's fault. Wet leaves were more treacherous than ice, they said. It could have happened to anyone.

"My dad thinks my boyfriend Mark is smart because he goes to Penn State. He thinks I'm stupid."

"You're not," I said.

"He hates me. He thinks I'm dumb because I'm not in engineering like you. But I don't want to study engineering. I want to be an artist. He doesn't respect that."

Large works of graphite on canvas hung on the walls of her room, framed by Margaret, who quietly shielded her children from their father's disappointment.

In the morning, after the night's easy confidences, we were strangers again. The snow falling outside the window made the room appear extra cozy. I sat on the carpet, rummaging in my bag for my toothbrush and something decent to wear for the dinner party that evening. I had gained so much weight that none of my clothes fit me.

Bina had to step around me to get to the bathroom. "Sorry!"

"It's alright." The glib American expression fell out of my lips automatically. I paused, self-conscious, waiting to be caught out like an imposter.

But Bina was already in the bathroom, brushing loudly.

By mid-day, Bina's school friend Jodie arrived. They sat together on her bed gossiping and painting their nails. I sat facing them. Every now and then they broke off their confidences to fill me in. Bina said she wished she were pale.

"But you are already so pale," I cried. "To me you look white."

"I'm lighter than you, but I'm still very tan."

"It's a beautiful color, Bina," Jodie said.

We both gazed at her in admiration.

"But listen, you guys. I have something juicy to tell you," Bina said. "There's a match being arranged at dinner tonight."

"That's crazy! Tell us more," cried Jodie.

Bina said that an Indian family with two marriageable daughters was coming to the party. The elder daughter was going to be introduced to an Indian bachelor. This was the secret purpose of the party, to bring the two young people together. The three of us were equally shocked, scandalized, and filled with romantic anticipation about the meeting of this young couple, whom we considered, in our innocence, to be practically married. At our age, the arranged meeting of two lovers was no less exotic and fascinating to me than it was to Bina and Jodie.

By evening, the house filled with a flow of guests, mostly middle-aged, successful South Asians living in the suburbs of Philadelphia. They appear now in my mind in greys and blacks and browns, women in saris and *shalwar kamiz* suits in muted colors with cardigans on top, and men in dress pants and jackets, grey faced, silver haired, hawkish, talking animatedly about their professional accomplishments. The veneer of respectability was everywhere, from the solid wood furniture, the piano in the corner, and the paintings on the walls to the drone of middle-class conversation.

The two Indian sisters were both slight, petite, demure, and dressed in embroidered Indian *shalwar kamiz*, with angular faces and large eyes. Margaret had said that their parents were eager to get the older sister Preeti married within the year, as she had already turned twenty-five, and Neeti was only two years younger. What I remember most is that they were very Indian, more like me than Bina. They were Penn graduates also, and I believe they were both engineers. They were very kind to me, and we chatted easily about books and classes and majors and professors, about the mechanics of things and the surfaces of things, taking pleasure as only young people can in simply naming things.

The sisters had been brought up according to the strictest ideals of both worlds—to excel academically in America, attend Ivy League schools, and go on to careers in medicine, engineering, and finance, but also to learn Sanskrit, play Indian musical instruments, and marry an Indian guy by arranged marriage.

We discovered that we had grown up watching the same Indian movies and admiring the same Indian heroes. This hero had a few unchangeable qualities. He was quiet, thoughtful, often a lawyer or a doctor, a poor boy from a village who had gone on to earn the highest degree, whose principles and morality would be tested in the movie, who would ultimately be chosen by the heroine as her husband because he was a good human being. Preeti told me that she had never dated, that her parents had always told her they would introduce her to someone when she was of age.

I spotted the young man Prakash, our hero of the evening, in an opening in the crowd. He was tall like a reed, adorned in a sweater, a stiff collar shirt, and dress pants. His features were at once indeterminate and pleasant. He was intelligent and funny, and he talked and laughed easily with the older men who surrounded him in a circle, eager to like him.

People took food from the table in plates and ate standing up in various rooms. I remember my first cranberry sauce, turkey, cornbread, and chicken rice soup. At one point, Bina and Jodie came up behind me and poked me.

"Look!"

Preeti and Prakash were standing together in a private corner of the dining room, their faces burning as they spoke slowly and politely to each other while everyone stared at them. They were both eligible, good looking, from good schools, with good jobs, and from good families. What I remember more clearly than the young couple talking together is Preeti's father. I can still see the lines of desire on his face, the veins standing out on his grey forehead as his daughter was produced before the tall, lanky man by his old friends. A good boy. An eligible suitor. A decent young man who would marry his daughter.

At the end of the night, after the two Indian sisters had left with their parents, I stood at the foot of the stairs talking quietly with the last of the guests, including Prakash. It was decided that he would drive me home. He lived in the city and was driving in that direction, anyway.

He said he would wait for me to pack my things. Before I went upstairs, I saw Anwar Uncle and another elderly gentleman standing with Prakash under the staircase beside the rows of Bangladeshi pictures, drilling him in urgent whispers about what he thought about the 'girl'.

"So, what was she like? Did you like her?"

"Yes, she was very nice. Very pretty."

Bina and Jodie were chatting together sitting on Bina's bed under the fluffy comforter. I said goodbye, and they politely expressed their wishes to see me again. I carried my bag downstairs and bundled up in the bulky down jacket that hung around me like an impenetrable cylinder. I was so fat that semester that I couldn't walk properly. I used to wobble on the sidewalks on campus, lost, out of my element. I remember the acne, the sleepless nights studying, the uncombed hair, working in dining services and smelling of stale food when I rushed to class after work.

We stepped outside into the cold night. The snow was still falling. There was a thin white blanket on the ground. I said goodbye to my uncle and auntie, my family in America, who waved to me standing in front of the warm, delightful house. Then I walked with Prakash to his sedan parked a few feet away. My face and hands were freezing while my body felt too warm in the heavy grey jacket. Prakash opened the passenger door and I climbed in.

On the drive back, on highways I did not yet know, we chatted about comfortable things. Prakash asked me about my classes and subjects and teachers. I complained and joked; he listened. He also must have been a graduate of Penn. He had gone on to get a master's degree from the business school and was now working in the city at an engineering firm.

"Do you find your classes hard?"

"No, they're easy. A' Levels are much more advanced." I spoke in the usual arrogant way of international freshmen. "It's the social aspect that I find difficult."

"Yeah? What do you mean?"

"If I ask a question in class, the other students think I am being annoying, asking too many questions. They also think me arrogant for answering the teacher's questions. This is confusing to me. You're supposed to answer questions in class, no?"

Prakash laughed. "What else do you find difficult in America?"

I leaned forward to confide in him about what had bothered me in all my interactions with Bina.

"To tell you the truth, I find other South Asians born in America the most difficult. I don't understand ABCDs. They look like me, but they are completely different. I asked an Indian girl in my hall where she was from and she was very upset. She said she was born and brought up in Boston and I was being rude."

"You know it's not politically correct to say ABCD, right?"

"I know! Now I know."

At Hill House, we international students from the subcontinent used to go around calling *Desis* (South Asians) born in America, ABCD (American Born Confused *Desis*), scarcely understanding the connotations of the label, while they called us FOB (Fresh Off the Boat). "You're an ABCD, you would know," we would say. Or "What would an ABCD do in that situation?" I had no idea how offensive this was until an ABCD named Vandana in my suite told me so. Her admonition stuck in my head. I stopped using the expression after that. But we (the FOBs and the ABCDs) felt our mutual divide instinctively, that instant prejudice and mistrust of each other. I explained all this to Prakash, and he nodded, as if he sympathized with why I felt compelled to think of him as a confused *Desi*.

Perhaps because he was handsome, in his element, Prakash felt confident enough to reach across the divide and ask me questions about my lowly school life and listen attentively to my perspectives. He provided details about his own degree, company, and job. I might have told him about struggling in computer science class, about never having seen a computer or a disk before, about running around the halls with my suitemates in Hill Hall carried in the tide of a prank being played out by everyone else, splashing water under someone's door, screaming down the balcony, laughing loudly because everyone else was laughing, scarcely aware of my own body, my sense of self—where others stopped and I began.

Prakash only said, "It'll all work itself out in time. A lot of these freshmen aren't very mature. I made my real friends in my sophomore year. You'll find your crowd."

"Yeah."

"No, really. Just hang in there. You'll see."

The city lights of Philadelphia showed in the distance, spurring on a discussion about the meaning of the name Philadelphia, the city of brotherly love, and Schuylkill River (which Margaret had told me was a misnomer since kill already meant river in Dutch). We drove into the city, my destination nearing.

Then suddenly, in the dark, Prakash said, "I guess you could tell what was going on back there, at the party tonight."

I mumbled nervously that I knew a little bit about "what had been arranged." I was shy and awkward. Perhaps I tried to close off the conversation to save him embarrassment. But Prakash was determined to go on.

"She was nice. Don't get me wrong. She was very pretty. But to tell the truth, I couldn't marry someone just like that. I mean, I would have to live with her first. Try it out. I need to get to know her." He looked at me in the dark for validation. "You know?"

I chuckled nervously to hide my confusion. Everyone else at the party had assumed the marriage was a done deal.

"Somehow, I know that living with her wouldn't be acceptable," he said sheepishly.

"No." I shook my head in agreement. "It would be scandalous to suggest living with her."
I remembered Preeti's father at the party standing alone by the staircase, staring at Prakash with a look of longing and trust—a young man who would take care of his daughter. And Preeti, who had told me that she had been shielded carefully from men by her parents to be an ideal wife for a Bengali man.

I met Preeti and her sister again at another South Asian party during winter break that year, where I had accompanied Anwar Uncle. There were other South Asians of my age, loud and confident, students at Yale, Cornell, or Michigan, teasing one another about their college football teams. We were all gathered in one room on various sofas in front of a TV, pizza slices in our hands. Preeti came to greet me as soon as she spotted me by the long table laid with food. She was friendly, inquiring about my school days. But she looked sad. Her face had lost the flush of beauty and excitement from Thanksgiving. I became conscious that I knew something she didn't. Margaret Auntie had told me that Preeti and her parents were devastated by Prakash's rejection. But Preeti couldn't have known why he had rejected her.

"No, you couldn't ask her to live with you. That would be very bad," I had agreed with Prakash in the car that Thanksgiving night.

"I mean, I really liked her. I want to see her again and propose to her that maybe we could try it out first."

"She would be shocked! Her parents and all the other Bengalis would be shocked." I spoke in my clipped, South Asian, British-sounding accent, which must have sounded harsh to him because he was silent for some time.

With the snow outside and the heater warming up the interior of the car, we let the divide sit comfortably between us, in a companionable silence, a shared confidence. When we spoke again, it was to make small comments. As we passed through the familiar grid of the streets of West Philadelphia, we exchanged anecdotes about Penn.

Then we entered Penn campus and drove past the lighted windows of old buildings. Prakash parked on 34th Street to let me out in front of Hill House. "Have a great time, young one!" He smiled at me. "I hope you get good South Asian As, but also remember to have fun."

"Thank you so much for driving me back!"

"It was my pleasure."

He started the car. I thanked him again over the noise of the engine. Then I turned around to walk across the newly fallen snow and the long bridge to the doors of Hill House, crunching the ice underfoot. The wind bit my cheeks and the tip of my nose. Just before I entered the building, I looked back and Prakash was still there; he waved to me quickly before driving off.

Voices

The people I am going to tell you about are no longer around. They are all dead or their whereabouts are unknown to me. But they were there on that day, the day that I write about. It was a hot day in Mosul, like inside an oven for baking bread, like being surrounded by the *samun* bread baking fresh inside an oven burning on blazing red-hot fire. Hot like the cracking of watermelons, juicy and sticky and cool to a thirsty tongue.

My mother was having a baby, her second, my sister, in the house. She was surrounded by women inside the house, while she lay stretched out on the cool floor. We children were banished outside. Yusra was our leader, tall and soft like rose petals, and her two sisters, my age. They had all come over with their mother, and we had been together since the night before, since my mother's labor pains had started.

We had been told to get ice from the next-door neighbors. We called to them from across the wall, the family of Mal Allah. At last, one of the nine children of Mal Allah appeared with a large block of ice wrapped in cloth. He stood on a chair held steady by one of his brothers, while he passed over the block of ice to Yusra, who passed it to her sister Warda, who passed it to Najwa, who passed it to me. Cold like a sting it was, an unbearable, impossible sensation that made me want to drop my burden immediately.

"Oof!" I cried. "Ouch."

And we all fell over laughing as we did, too often. We carried the block among the four of us, Yusra yelling directions at us, under the vine-arched driveway, cutting across the lawn, through the rose bushes, and up the steps to the house, into the kitchen, past the wails coming from the closed living room door. The sounds made me uncomfortable, even though they weren't really cries, muffled, just a low moaning, but still, I wanted to stay as far away from them as possible.

"What shall we do next?" I asked Yusra.

Warda and Najwa looked at her also.

"We shall sit on lawn chairs and eat rose hips," she announced.

We followed her outside again.

"It's my job to keep you away from adult affairs," she said again importantly, as we plopped down on the metal lawn chairs with the crisscrossing plastic straps, all three of us on blue chairs, and Yusra on a red one. Sometimes I felt sorry for Yusra. Even then, I sensed I should feel sorry for her because she was so alone. She was older than everybody else, including her two sisters, whom she could box and tug and punish to stand still with their faces to the wall. If she told them to keep standing like that, holding their ears, faces turned to the wall, locked inside a room, they would still be there when she opened the door an hour later; but she could never be their friend. She could never be a part of their whispering intimacy, their quiet joint mischiefs soaking their dolls in colored water or painting clown lips around each other's mouths with their mother's lipstick.

It was a green day. The grass was impossibly green, and the roses—well, they were the roses of Mosul, red, orange, pink, and all the other impossible shades of a packet of crayons. And so, we achieved a degree of intimacy, sitting quietly there, biting on rose hips, Yusra's new hobby. One of the Mal Allah kids popped his head over the wall again and asked if we wanted watermelon. I shook my head quickly because that combination of images, watermelon and Mal Allah, always made me nervous. Mal Allah was our landlord, an old man nearing fifty, and often he would come over and sit with my father in the cooler night air on our lawn chairs and complain sadly about how his nine children always ate up all the food and never left any for him. In particular, he was very sad about watermelon. He would buy the biggest, fattest, juiciest melon in the shops, he said, and yet, there would never be any left for him to eat because his family was so numerous, and his children so ravenous and selfish.

"It's hot," said Najwa and Warda in one voice. We were wearing those cotton Chinese frocks, with the thin straps that fell off our shoulders, all different colors of basically the same pattern, the material gauzy and airy. Yusra's mother used to buy a trunk full of them in different sizes, knowing that at least one of her daughters would be able to fit or grow into any size she bought.

"Such are the advantages of a large family," she would say with a toothy laugh. And my mother would prod her with one fat elbow and say, "You should have more then!" Then the two of them would fall over laughing in their caftans. They usually talked like this by the cool interior of the water cooler, waxing their arms and legs with lemon and sugar.

"I am going to die, it is so hot," I said now, adding my voice to the complaint.

"That is because there are so many of us," said Yusra. "We should pull our chairs apart a little. That way, there will be more air for everyone."

"In that case," I declared, "I want to be the only person in Mosul, in all of the world, who is alive, so I can have all the cool and shade to myself!"

"I know!" cried Yusra. "I have an idea. We shall have ice cream. I have some money in my purse."

She always carried her purse on her, like a lady, and her purse, red with sequins, matched the red belts of her clogs. She pulled the chain of the purse and started to take out the assortment of dinars and filis. She put them in her cool palm and started to count them methodically. We watched her count, my eyes locked on the thin bracelet that beaded around her white wrist. She was impossibly beautiful, and yet she made me feel that I never wanted to be thirteen, ever. She made me so anxious about this gangly age that I watched my every move for signs of the Yusra-disease.
I think I felt this way because of my father, who would take me on his lap every time after Yusra's family left our house and say to me, "Now, Fatma, I never ever want you to speak in that nasal tone like her," or "Did you see how she kicks her legs in the air as she sits, I never want you to sit like that."

According to my parents, there was no end to her transgressions—she wore high heels or blew air through her mouth, interrupted the grown-ups to talk, to ask her father for a car lesson, grabbing his keys and going to sit in his Volkswagen, slamming the horn. And yet, she was beautiful, the thinness of her wrists and the plumpness of her pink arms bursting out of her perfect white dress. She made me nervous because I had only five years to find out what it was like to grow into her, experience what it was like to be Yusra, thirteen and awkward and alone.

"Hey!" she said. "How come I am two dinar short? Who stole my money?"

"Not me!" cried Najwa. "It was Warda's idea!" She sprang from her chair and ran barefoot into the grass. It always surprised me how scared she was of Yusra.

"Warda?" Yusra frowned in a grown-up way, waiting in that kind of silence that our mothers could create. She had some problem with her nose that made her speak in a grainy voice, as if being pumped out of narrow tubes, and this made her sound more ominous.

"We both did it!" Warda pleaded. "Don't hit me, please." She twisted her face to cry.
The crisis passed. Yusra's face became normal again, like a kid. "At least tell me what you did with the money," she said.

"We washed them in the water and they fell to pieces," Najwa cried from her distance.

"Al right, so we have only this much then and we have to make do. How much does each ice cream cost?" We went over the prices for cones and chocolate bars, trying to do the math. Finally, we decided we had enough money for four ice creams, and so we got up and rushed out the door. Then Yusra told us to make a neat line behind her and we walked gracefully with her along the street, past Mal Allah's house and Ali's house, past the Palestinian's house, turning the corner, then across

77

the street, to the little shop that I ran to at all times of the day.

"*Ashkadh hadha?*" we asked the shopkeeper, pointing to the cups and cones and bars. We whispered among ourselves and counted on our fingers. The shopkeeper slapped his cheeks with his hands and waited. Now I think perhaps he had just shaved on that day, and his face still tingled from the fresh sharp feeling of the razor.

"We shall have four cones," said Yusra. The shopkeeper rubbed his hands on the white shirt that stretched across his belly, and then picked up a scoop.

"I want the chocolate!" I cried.

"Me too," said Warda.

"I want chocolate," said Najwa.

Yusra got vanilla. We accepted our unwieldy prizes, which wobbled and already melted a little, dropping stickiness in between our fingers. I started to lick quickly, darting out my tongue. Licking and balancing, we made our way back, walking by the gutters, kicking stones in our path, past the gypsy girl who rode on her donkey, her gold necklace glinting in the sun. The sun was still hot, but the ice cream was just right, soft and cool.

When we were inside our driveway again, we stood in the cool of the grapevines, keeping out of sight of the grown-ups, lest they have some unexpected objection to our pleasure. Lick. Lick. Lick. We devoured our cones expertly.

Yusra said suddenly, "That's not the way to eat ice cream. You don't dart your tongue out like that. That's not dainty."

So she showed us how instead, and we practiced opening our mouths ever so slightly to bring away dainty portions, neither showing our tongues nor making any sound. Then we stood there and ate and ate and ate. This pleasure of eating, standing in the scant shade of the driveway, in the heat of June, just that constant source of milky sweetness cooling off the tongue, the mouth, the throat, was endless–it stretched and stretched and stretched, occupying all afternoon. The entire time we ate, I did not speak a single word. And then at last, it was over.

The afternoon sun began to subside, and still we sat outside. Nobody had asked asked us inside to eat, but the ice cream rumbled nicely inside each of us. We had pulled out a cool Syrian mat and were lying flat on it on the grass, tickling one another's toes. The faint cries of my mother made me start nervously now and then, as if some impending danger were at hand, and I shifted sides often. I longed for another ice cream, but there was no money. Then we heard shouting next door and sat up. What was that? The shouting reached ugly heights and there was the sound of scuffling, a woman's screams.

"Quickly," said Yusra. "Grab your chairs."
We each grabbed a lawn chair from the verandah by the rose bushes and dragged it across the lawn to the wall. Climbing up on the unsteady chairs, we peered over the wall. The two eldest Mal Allah children, ten and eleven, were choking each other with their fat hands. Their mother was between them wailing and trying to pull them apart. The sons were both large, and it was a monstrous sight to see the two brothers at each other's throats. Then the eldest Mal Allah boy picked up a sickle lying by the flowers and raised it in the air. We gasped collectively, following Yusra's example, our hands on our chests.

"I shall kill you! I shall kill you," cried the elder kid to his brother.

His mother grabbed him around his thick waist and whispered now, so softly that we strained to hear, "He is your brother." She must have been hoarse from all that wailing.

The boy broke down and started to cry. He dropped the sickle to the ground. His crying was even more disturbing than the fight itself. "He is my enemy, he is, mother," he continued. "He hates me. He took my kite that I made for so many days and broke it, mother." The boy wept and wept, and we watched fascinated. Then somehow the fight ended and the elder brother retired inside with Mal Allah's wife. We climbed down from our chairs.

"See?" Yusra said to me. "That's a lesson for you. When you have a brother or a sister, you have to share everything. You have sacrifice all your belongings and desires. You can't be a spoiled baby, the only child anymore."

"I'm not a spoiled baby," I protested, dusting my hands.

"My mother says all only children are spoiled," said Yusra. She took off her white ribbon and tied her hair again in a ponytail with the ribbon.

"I don't think I want a brother or a sister then," I said.

I thought of the elaborate dresses my father bought me from Baghdad or Kuwait, the dresses that my mother sewed for me on the Brother sewing machine, copying German patterns from Burda magazine, the surprises my father carried for me in his pocket every day when he came home from work, a balloon, a chocolate bar, a stamp from Sharza, just for me. The large parties my parents threw me on my birthday, guests filling up on the lawn, Coca Cola bottles nestling in the grass, as I tore the wrappings off my presents, amidst laughter and voices, all around.

"You will never have peace again when you are the elder sister," said Yusra. "Look at how much trouble these monkeys give me."

In the afternoon, we tiptoed into the kitchen and got out the ice from the freezer and a hammer from a drawer and began to break the ice. Yusra hammered while Warda, Najwa, and I collected chunks in glasses and then poured tomato juice over the ice. That's when we heard the scream. The full-throated scream of lungs with no bottoms, a cry of supreme command that commanded the air that blew through the house, perhaps all of the world, and stopped us all.

"Run! It's here!" cried Yusra.

We ran with our tomato juices after her, our wooden clogs clunking on the floor. The door of the living room was open at last. There my mother lay on the floor, and where were the cries coming from? Yusra's mother was cleaning blood with a bucket and a mop, her fat behind poking the air. Where was the baby? Was it mixed up in the blood, being swept away? Had there been an accident? My mother lay moaning, and someone covered her with our checked woolen blanket in the overheated room. We only used that blanket in the winter, when we all huddled together in the same room, upstairs, with a kerosene heater on and all the window gaps filled in with putty. My father would have to turn the heater up in the morning and make the room toasty like the crust of *samun* bread before I ventured out of my mother's embrace and the blanket's warmth. Then I would run directly to the cylindrical warmth of the kerosene heater and stand over it with my father, toasting my hands, my face, my behind.

"Look," said Yusra, pulling me to where a few of the women, my mother's friends, squatted on the floor. At the center of the circle they created was a shockingly large baby, larger than my talking dolls, being bandaged in swathes of white cloth. It was bundled from its shoulders to its ankles, its arms taped inside also. And all the while it cried imperiously, its mouth so wide that you could look inside its throat.

"Your sister," said one of my mother's friends. "Isn't she beautiful? Aren't you the lucky one?"
At that moment I felt the need to find my mother and have her see me. So I ran to her and knelt by her on the floor. She had her eyes closed, like she was trying to sleep.

"Ooh, ooh." She made these soft sounds as she lay there with her eyes closed, her face twisted like a crying baby.

"Mama, it's me, Fatma," I said. I wanted her to put her hand on my head, pull me to her chest, claim me as hers.

"Fatma!" called Yusra's mother. "Get off your mother."
But I threw myself on top of her and hugged her neck. "Fatma, get off! Yusra, get her off. Take her outside. All of you, go play a game or something."

So then I was pulled away my mother, and I went outside again with my friends, although now I wanted to be alone. I was sad in the way that you can't share with anyone. I didn't know why I was sad, but I didn't want all these people in my house anymore. It felt too crowded to me, and I wished that all the people would

82

leave and I could wait alone for my father to come back, the way he did in the evenings from the university, and then the three of us, my father, my mother, and I, could sit together outside on the lawn and eat tomato soup and khubz, roasted chicken, the dolma with the tomatoey rice and meat inside.

"Why are you sad?" asked Warda. "Don't be sad."

Warda was beautiful, she had a round face and straight teeth and she was the baby of her family. My mother said she was more loved than her sister Najwa because she was prettier. I wondered now if my mother would love me less, compare our faces to see who was prettier, the baby or me.

"Don't be sad," said Najwa. "Your father will be home soon."

"Are you a little jealous?" prodded Yusra. She turned her ankles this way and that; she was going to be a famous dancer so she had to exercise them constantly. "Are you worried about your future now that you are no longer going to be the only child?"

"What rubbish!" I cried savagely. "Nothing is going to change. My father will love me just the same. Wait till he comes home, only a few more minutes, and you'll see."

My behind was beginning to hurt from sitting on those plastic straps, my dress stuck to the chair, and my arms burned where they touched the metal. A morning of interminable waiting stretched and sheared, as we waited now for my father to return home. I wanted to have more ice cream. My tongue was dry. If only I could get money enough even just for one, I would run to the shop and eat it all by myself, in secret. Surely, my father would give me some money when he came home. The women who had come to help with the birth began to leave, one by one, shaking their burkhas free of wrinkles, Ali's mother pulling out a packet of cigarettes from the inside pocket of hers.

Then when the sun had smeared and bled into the sky, my father at last drove inside the gate and parked under the grapevine. He emerged tall and cool in an open-neck shirt and black trousers, a smile wrinkling his eyes.

"Baba!" I ran to him and barreled him and was whisked into the air. "Baba! It's here. The baby."
He put me down and went inside, and my chest felt heavy. I leaned against the car and concentrated on ice cream flavors; which flavor would I like if I could have another ice cream?

The sky was still colorful when my father came outside to sit with us on the lawn. He brought out a box of chocolates for me.

"For you, Fatma," he said. "Because today is a very special day for you. Today you have the gift of a sister, who shall be close to you for all your life."

"Baba, you brought it on your way home from the office, for me?"

"Share," he said.

I carried it back to my chair and lifted the cover. Somehow imagine that by this time, other children from the neighborhood had collected at our house, on the lawn. They had come to see the baby, and now they were all sitting on the lawn, and I was having to open my box of chocolates, my special gift from my father, in front of them. I chose one, white milk chocolate, my favorite, and put it in my mouth. Milk sweetened my teeth and tongue. The other children, all nine of the Mal Allah children, from the eleven-year-old to the one year-old sitting on his lap, Ali, Yusra, Warda, Najwa, they all stared at me.

"Fatma," said a faraway voice, "Share, ya habibi."

I chewed and kneaded the sweetness between the roof of my mouth and the buds of my tongue, I dug out remnants from inside my teeth, I opened the box again.

"Fatma! Share with your friends." I didn't look up, my eyes floated over the blurring chocolates. That which was waiting inside me all day, a taut string that stretched from my chest to my stomach, now began to break, and I felt tired and unable. If I have not mentioned this tension, this tight cord stretched inside me, I think I was not aware of it until now, in all of these hours of waiting. But now it pushed its way out, and I shivered and shook, and I began to cry.

"No, Baba, no," I said. "This chocolate is only for me."

"Fatma," said my father, all the love gone out of that tone.

I cried even more because I thought I was at last face to face with the inevitable, the loss of my parents' love. I began to wail and I dove to the grass and lay there with my face down, screaming.

My father pulled my head up and said, "Last time I am saying this, share."

I screamed in response and shook my hair to let it fall over my face. I scarcely knew myself or why I acted this way, and yet I could not stop it. I didn't feel the slap or my hair being pulled as I was dragged across the grass and left to lie somewhere, still on the lawn, but far away from the other children's voices, rising and falling in the distance.

Then slowly, thankfully, the Mal Allah children left with their mother, promising to come back later at night. I turned my face upward and opened my eyes slowly, and my father's face was bending over mine.

"Fatma, I'm sorry," he said. "My sweet. Forgive me. Come, I shall give you anything you want." He put his hand on my head and tried to smooth out the tangles of angry hair.

"Baba, I want some ice cream," I said. "I will share with the other kids."

"Sure, my love," said my father. Since only Yusra, Najwa, and Warda were left, he gave me enough money, for four ice creams, and sent me off to buy four cups.

The sky was dull now, a darkening gray, and I skipped and ran most of the way. I could think of nothing else but the ice cream. I could still remember that sensation of milky coolness on my tongue, the perfection of that earlier pleasure, and it consoled me that I could recall this pleasure at will at any time, every day, for all my life, simply by eating another ice cream. The night smelled of a breeze, and there was also the slight smell of burning paper, and I worried as I half-ran, half-walked, about what kind to get. I had had a cone earlier, and part of me really wanted to buy another cone. But I also wanted to try something different, perhaps a scoop of vanilla in a cup, a chocolate bar. When I reached the shop, and the fat shopkeeper was still waiting, his arms folded across his still stretched shirt, I was still confused. I could not make up my mind. I had only money for four cups. But if I bought a cone and a cup for myself, then there would only be money for . . .two more cups. If I got a chocolate bar and a cup? Okay, I would just get a cup. I felt more and more resentful about the constraint on my desire, the fact that

I had to buy four, and no less, that there were three others waiting for me back home.

"Girl," said the shopkeeper, "You could try the new combination, a scoop each of orange, vanila, and chocolate, three scoops, on a cone."

"Okay," I said. "Okay. May I see it?" I studied the flavors and the names again, carefully, my tongue filling up with hot saliva. "Okay," I said at last, after a long, tormented moment, "I shall get three scoops on a cone and three scoops in a cup."

I had given up the math, and it was too hard for me to think, so I bought the cone and the cup and walked home with my possessions. Perhaps there was still a way for four people to share two ice creams. I enjoyed my walk in solitude in the quiet night air, no moon, and sometimes I stole a lick from one cone or the other.

But when I reached home and slipped in through the metal gates; why, even before I entered, I heard the buzzing of hundreds of voices, and the lawn was just full of people. It was dark enough that I could stand by my father's Volkswagen and survey the scene without being seen. My ice cream melted slightly and I licked the scoops in each hand.

Then there was a figure beside me.

"Where were you? What took you so long?" It was Yusra, her face ghostly and so grown-up in the dark. "Look, we can't eat these now, there are guests here to see your baby sister. You can't eat in front of the other kids and not share. What will you do?"

I stared at her stupidly, wanting to explain how I had bought two ice creams instead of four, but she didn't even ask. She pulled me by the left elbow and dragged me to the aisle between the car and the wall.

"Listen," she said, "Stand here and finish these, then come out, not before that, okay?"

I nodded, not having any words to use, and I watched her as she faded into the lawn. For a moment, I felt as if she were *my* big sister. Then, hiding in the corner, I licked my ice creams in haste, trying to finish. My hair was plastered to my forehead, and my dress, perhaps long-warmed by lawn chairs, itched. The scoops dripped on my fingers, and milky sweetness filled every space inside me, from my throat to deep inside my stomach; coated my fingers, trickled down my wrists. I felt at once that the moment was interminable and that it was also too short. I gulped and swallowed and bit off chunks while voices swarmed around me, floated headless and bodiless across the lawn; voices floating in the air, so many people, all come to welcome my sister into the world. There was laughter and cheering as the new baby was held up in the air. And all I could think about, the only sensation I was aware of, was the ice cream that coated my mouth and shocked my teeth, then melted, again and again, all too soon. By and by, the lights went out, and the merriment came to an end. Then the people were gone, and no more voices were heard on the lawn.

Today I sit alone in Amman, eating boiled beetroot in my living room. Sometimes in Amman, they show the streets of Mosul on TV on the news, and I watch eagerly, but I can never make out any street that looks like mine. The streets I see all look the same, shell-shocked and explosively barren, with the American soldiers, covered bodies of children, and wailing mothers. I have heard of the Mal Allah boys going off one after another to the different wars. Some were killed, some captured now by Americans. And true to my father's belief, Yusra now walks the streets, and I hear distant rumors of her rape. Watching the ruins of my country on television, I ache to turn to her, or anyone, and share my loneliness.

Rental Car

Kakon had taken the red eye flight to Houston so many times that she knew the routine by heart. She rode the airport shuttle to the rental car office at Bush Intercontinental Airport as it was getting light outside and asked for the Hyundai Sonata that she had already reserved. It came in white as always and she had to fight against its flatness, one white car among many others, the same rental every time. She would have to push her way through another day away from her family, presenting herself to the company she was visiting as the expert polymer consultant, tough, confident, and aggressive.

The clients would be surprised that Kakon was not a middle-aged man with silver hair, and then they would be surprised again that they couldn't bend this young woman or talk down to her. Underneath her tender heaving breasts was a heart of steel.

As she lifted her red carry-on bag into the trunk of the car, Kakon's chest hurt and her blouse buttons popped again, reminding her of the fear that had been blinding her for the past week. She had a mammogram scheduled when she returned to Philadelphia.

When Kakon visited Houston on business, she

looked forward to seeing her cousin Dilruba Apa, who lived in the city with her family. They had moved to Houston from Bangladesh after winning a diversity visa lottery six years ago. It was still light outside when Kakon finished her work at the chemical company in Katy on the outskirts of Houston and swung the car onto Interstate 10, turning back to the city. She had spoken to Dilruba Apa several times on her cell phone during the day in between the site visit and the somber meetings at the client company.

The meeting had been hostile. The oil engineers had been defensive, questioning Kakon's authority, mumbling inaudible answers to her questions, even jabbing the air in front of her chest menacingly; but she was a senior engineer now, she had learned to handle challenge. She carried herself in such a way that people knew not to mess with her; if they did, she let them have it.

Her own balding colleagues had learned this about her the hard way when she had bid for and won a million-dollar grant for her research at her company. The senior men who were twice her age had tried to take her project away from her by plotting against her. This had lasted two weeks, until she had called them all to a meeting and blasted them.

Kakon had called Dilruba Apa three times that day, saying, "I am coming as soon as I take off from work here. You're going to be home, right?"

"Of course, my darling. Will I miss seeing my little cousin?"

Still, she wasn't quite so sure Dilruba Apa *would* be home. Over the years, Kakon had learned to anticipate certain things that came with Dilruba Apa's territory. Several times Dilruba Apa had kept Kakon waiting an hour where they were supposed to meet. Once, Kakon had driven to Dilruba Apa's apartment to see her, but she wasn't home. Kakon had sat at their dining table and talked with Dilruba Apa's overweight husband Mofiz Bhai, listening to him as he chatted about his gas station, wheezing and pausing for breath every few words. She had gotten into an intimate conversation with him about weight, a common ground they had discovered between them. The child was in bed, and they had turned the lights out, their shared pain forming in a pale blue light in the dark. Dilruba Apa had returned from the university library at one in the morning, marching into the room in her clicking high heels and turning on the lights; her usual gushing insincerity was intolerable in the blinding light. Kakon was suddenly tired and sleepy; she stood up, ready to drive back to her hotel.

There were other difficulties with meeting Dilruba Apa. If Kakon asked Dilruba Apa to come to her hotel, Dilruba Apa would say no because she didn't drive on the highway. If Kakon suggested that Dilruba Apa's husband Mofiz Bhai drive her, Dilruba Apa would plead that her husband was really tired from working at the gas station. Kakon had come to accept that the burden of desire was on her side.

It always had been, since Kakon had been a child, visiting Bangladesh with her parents on their annual vacations, dropping through a succession of airports as they traveled for thirty-six hours, carrying suitcases heavy with presents for their relatives in Bangladesh. Driving to Dilruba Apa's apartment now, Kakon remembered her other cousin Rezwan, Dilruba Apa's brother. Rezwan popped up in Kakon's mind from time to time in the middle of a busy day. They had had a deep connection. She remembered one particular visit to Bangladesh when she has been twelve or thirteen. Rezwan, who must have been about eleven or twelve at the time (he was a year younger than Kakon), came running in his smiling little boy eagerness, holding a glass jar of trapped butterflies as a present for Kakon. She closed her eyes to shut out the pain, and she forgave Dilruba Apa her unreliability and callousness.

Kakon thought that even if she didn't see Dilruba Apa today, at least Boro Auntie would be there at the apartment. Boro Auntie was Dilruba Apa's mother and Kakon's mother's elder sister. Boro Auntie had come to Houston three months ago on a visitor's visa and then filed for immigration through Dilruba Apa. Kakon genuinely wanted to see her. Boro Auntie would want to talk about Rezwan.

Now, driving, Kakon had another sharp image of Rezwan shoving sheaves of densely scribbled paper into her hands when they were both teenagers. The papers had turned out to be his shy budding poetry. His handwriting had been neat, small, tight scrawls in purple ink. His eyes had been good then, large with long lashes— like a girl's eyes. Kakon pressed the buttons on her phone, with one hand still on the steering wheel, and reached Dilruba Apa's cell phone.

"Have you gotten on the bus yet? Are you on your way home?" she asked suspiciously.

"In just a few minutes, my sweet," Dilruba Apa said, her voice melodious and intimate. "We'll talk all night, my baby sister," she promised.

These endearments had always attracted Kakon to Dilruba Apa; she had picked them up like a beggar child because she had been so starved for love.

Over the years, when Kakon was putting herself through engineering school, walking through campus sleep deprived, and then afterward when she started working as an engineer, when she had to work in group projects with masculine engineers with big heads and big egos who found it difficult to accept a woman among them, Kakon had developed her hard professional exterior. Then she had learned to be curt with Dilruba Apa also, calling her bluffs and her bullshitting. But somewhere inside a soft core had remained; it still opened up like a flower to Dilruba Apa's caresses.

"Get on that bus, Dilruba Apa! I'm leaving tonight, so there's no tonight, it has to be now. I'm leaving on a red-eye flight back to Philly. I know what a few minutes translate to for you! I know the vector transformation of a few minutes in your world!"

"Kakon baby, you can be *so* harsh!" Dilruba Apa uttered in shocked tones. "A hard-hatted engineer. Don't use your engineering words with *me*. I'm coming!"

Kakon took the exit for North Braeswood and found the apartment complex in which her cousin lived; very near to the crisscrossing lanes of the highway. She could pick up the hum of highway traffic sitting in Dilruba Apa's living room. The buildings carried a thin covering of highway dust like defensive armor. The interior was rundown and crumbling. Kakon parked in the parking space behind Dilruba Apa's building and called up to the apartment. Boro Auntie answered the phone.

"Kakon, baby, you've come? Wait, wait, I'll send Sonny down. No, wait downstairs. I want to welcome you properly, baby."

Sonny was Dilruba Apa's ten-year-old son, about the age Rezwan would have been when Kakon had seen him first.

"Boro Auntie, that's ridiculous," Kakon said. "I can take the elevator up. It'll be less trouble for me *and* Sonny."

"No, no, stay there, he's coming to bring you up."

"Okay, tell him white Hyundai at back."

As she waited, Kakon pulled out her laptop and luggage from the trunk. She didn't feel safe leaving any valuables behind in the car in this place. There was a bayou at the back, a ravine of thin water, and the smell of dog feces on the grass. The last time Kakon had visited, there had been signs on all the trees along the bayou and on the buildings about a recent robbery in one of the apartments. The rental car came with theft insurance. Even so, she made sure to park directly under the window of Dilruba Apa's apartment.

"Kakon Auntie, hello!" A large, heavyset boy waved and grinned at her.

"Sonny!" With a shock, Kakon recognized him as someone vaguely familiar, although she could not immediately place the resemblance. She had visited not three months ago, but in that time he had changed. He was as big as his father now–an enormous weight had descended on him, and he was wheezing as he came nearer. She gave him a hug. "Hello, big boy." Suddenly, she knew of whom he reminded her. She was remembering herself, similarly big at ten, just sinking into the onset of depression that would stay with her through years of hand slashing and therapy. She had never understood why her parents, who had pushed her so hard to study and excel at school, had let her get so fat. It was as if they had never actually looked at her beyond the grades, the admissions, and scholarships that they demanded constantly from her that would prove their success to the world. Looking at Sonny, she thought that this boy, the son of her Bangladeshi cousin Dilruba Apa, was more like herself than like her cousin; an American kid growing up with struggling immigrant parents.

Sonny led the way, holding the glass door open. As soon as Kakon stepped inside the building, the air became heavy with the smell of old carpet and trapped food. She felt breathless. She touched her buttons anxiously, afraid that they might start popping again on top of her tight chest.

"Aren't you taking me the wrong way, Sonny?" she panted. "The elevator is this way."

"No, Kakon Auntie. It's not working. Follow me."

"The elevator is not working? Okay."

She couldn't believe it. Her bag weighed the maximum weight allowance for a checked in suitcase; her laptop hung piercingly from her shoulders. She had not planned to climb stairs.

They took one flight of stairs, then another, a total of six flights to the sixth floor. Kakon fought for breath, pushing herself to keep up with the wheezing child, wondering nervously why she was breathless.

She had been reading about breast cancer and breast diseases for weeks now. Her daughter and husband had bookmarked pages off the Internet, saving articles for her in a folder on the desktop, and she had gone over these in the middle of sleepless nights of research, noting every symptom methodically with a ballpoint pen in a small notebook. Now she tried to remember, was breathlessness in any way significant?

Boro Auntie was standing in the middle of the living room with her hands on her hips, in a welcoming pose.

"Boro Auntie, you look so good! Let me give you a hug."

Kakon gave Boro Auntie a big American hug. She liked the sweet scent from Boro Auntie's clothes, and the change in her dress style. Boro Auntie used to wear soft wrinkled saris in Bangladesh; now she had on a smart tunic and pants, her head neatly covered by a scarf rather than the trailing edge of her winding sari, much smarter. "Boro Auntie, you look so American already. Good for you!"

"Kakon, you've gained more weight, isn't that so? Why are you breathless?" Boro Auntie asked, looking Kakon up and down.

Kakon made it a point not to change out of her work clothes when she visited Dilruba Apa. Dilruba Apa had remarked once that Kakon's knee-length skirt was indecent and that Kakon should wear a *shalwar kamiz* or *kurta* when visiting, something that Dilruba Apa considered more proper. Kakon hadn't changed for Boro Auntie either, but she knew Boro Auntie wouldn't dare to say anything to her about her clothes because Boro Auntie *knew* Kakon would speak back.

Once Dilruba Apa tried to tell Kakon on the phone that Mofiz Bhai said Kakon should wear longer skirts or *shalwar kamiz* or pants, something more decent that covered her legs. Kakon had replied, "Dilruba Apa, what is my brother-in-law doing staring at my legs? Tell him *that's* not decent. And if you want to insult me, do it on your own phone bill, not mine." Then she'd hung up.

"The elevator wasn't working, Boro Auntie. I guess I got some exercise for the weight that you say I gained," Kakon joked now.

Boro Auntie laughed. "The elevator works," she said. "Our Sonny just doesn't like elevators. He's afraid of them, that's why he told you they don't work!"

"Sonny!" Kakon raised her eyebrows admonishingly at Sonny, who had settled himself at the rusted metal frame dining table in one corner of the living room. He slid down on his chair and parked his feet apart, breathing as heavily as Kakon.

"Yes, he never takes the elevator," Boro Auntie was saying. "Come, sit. Sit down on the sofa here." The sofa smelled faintly of urine. Boro Auntie had started baby-sitting neighborhood children for pocket money; the room betrayed the set up: garish plastic toys lined the carpet by the wall, and a highchair stood beside the television set.

As usual, Kakon had to search beyond Boro Auntie's words to get at the truth. She knew Sonny was telling the truth that the elevator was out of order. Then why would Boro Auntie want to pretend that it worked? She remembered the constant hiding at Boro Auntie's home, the constant lying to cover up; sometimes she didn't even understand the point of the lies. Kakon's mother said that Boro Auntie was a pathological liar. She would have explained to Kakon exactly what was going on in Boro Auntie's mind now. Boro Auntie wanted Kakon to think that they lived in a nice apartment complex, everything in working condition, and the more to the contrary the evidence, the more at pains she would be to prove it; just the way Boro Auntie and Dilruba Apa had tried to cover up Rezwan's suicide.

Boro Auntie and Dilruba Apa hadn't told anyone about Rezwan's death for a long time. Kakon had found out accidentally a month after it happened. Rezwan was supposed to travel to America with Boro Auntie for his treatment; the plan was that he would just stay on in America like Boro Auntie had. Dilruba Apa would sponsor him for immigration also. One day, Kakon had called Dilruba Apa casually to ask when Rezwan was coming. A weeping Dilruba Apa had told Kakon that Rezwan had died suddenly and mysteriously in his sleep.

Weeks after that, the actual details trickled in, as Kakon's mother painstakingly pried the lies from the truth.

Kakon found out that, contrary to Boro Auntie's story, Rezwan had *not* died in his sleep. He had, in fact, hanged himself from the ceiling fan. It was suicide, Kakon's mother informed her with glee, a glee mixed with terrible sadness of course, but still glee competing with sadness. But every time Kakon called Boro Auntie in Bangladesh to offer her condolences, Boro Auntie insisted on the cracked telephone wires that Rezwan had died naturally from medication that the doctors had prescribed for his glaucoma. Meanwhile, Kakon's mother slowly revealed to Kakon the shameful details that Boro Auntie tried to hide. Police had come to the house! Rezwan's face had been bloated and his body smelled because they had not been allowed to bury him before an autopsy was done.

After Kakon heard the news of Rezwan's death, she was too depressed to let her husband near. She slept on the couch downstairs for a week, her back and shoulder bones descending into the indentations of the sofa. She had terrible aches at various points of her body for a long time afterward. During that week, she descended again into the all too familiar tunnel of depression from her teenage years. She had considered several desperate actions, including filing for divorce, because she just couldn't keep going. Every night of that week, she had remembered her own suicide attempts at one time in her life. There had been three in all, spaced three years apart. Now she was solid, successful, a patent-winning polymers engineer working for a top chemical company, married with a beautiful, large-eyed daughter. But for the first time in years, during which she had strung together success of every kind in a desperate attempt to live, she wondered again, what use was it trying to stay alive, to keep on jumping one hurdle after another, squeezing her body through one pain after another?

It could have been her instead of Rezwan, she thought. They had shared poetry as children; they had suffered from the same unseen lines in the world that only they could sense. There was something else that bound Kakon to Rezwan, a secret. When Kakon had visited Boro Auntie's home at fifteen, Rezwan had sniffed her bra hanging in the bathroom. She had found him there lurking in the dark shadow, standing barefoot on a moldy floor, one finger hooked around the strap, pulling down the trailing edge over his nostrils. Kakon hadn't been shocked or appalled. In fact, as she remembered it, she might have laughed out aloud about how he was a crazy kid. She knew he had done this because deep inside he was gentle, like a girl. He had always wanted to be just that, a gentle fragile girl who would not have to fight in the world.

Kakon had fought all her life not to be a girl, not to be sensitive, and not to be depressed, but after she found out that her cousin had killed himself, she wondered what it would have been like to give in to all her weaknesses instead of jumping through the hoops her parents set for her one after another. *It could have been me*, she thought. Lying on the couch downstairs all of that week, her marriage at a crisis, her husband staring at her through scared eyes from afar, she wondered, had Rezwan found a solution to his depression that she was not brave enough to face?

"How are you liking it in America, Boro Auntie?" Kakon asked now.

"Very good, very good. *Alhamdulillah*. You understand, the air is so fresh, and right by this apartment there is a beautiful bayou. Did you see it? Yes, can you believe this is such a beautiful apartment complex? Isn't it just very nice and grand?"

Kakon agreed energetically. The kitchen smelled of food, good food smells. Growing up, Kakon had greedily eaten her mother's food, the buttery *khichuri* and the *kheer* made with full cream; that had been the only happiness she had in her life. Her mother fed her but told her she was ugly and that she was nothing if she did not achieve the next thing in a long line of unending achievements. Kakon suspected suddenly that perhaps Boro Auntie was making Sonny fat with all her good cooking.

"Kakon, I cooked *pulau* for you and chicken roast and mutton curry, and some beef cutlets. Tell me when I should serve."

"Oh, Boro Auntie. Thank you! You've cooked so many things. It was very kind of you."

"Now tell me again, how big is your house? Dilruba said you live in a big house? How many rooms are in your house?"

"Tell me about yourself, Boro auntie. What are *you* doing nowadays?"
Kakon tried to deflect the question, which she was convinced was partly steeped in the jealousy that had always been there between their two families.

Sonny was making clicking sounds with his tongue as he worked on his homework. Every time she came to visit, she found Sonny parked at the dining table, doing homework. Apparently, he had gotten into the Vanguard program at a really good public high school. Dilruba Apa boasted that Sonny did homework till four in the morning and scored high marks on all the tests. Dilruba Apa stayed up at night with him and served him meals every hour as he studied at the dining table.

"Kakon, what can I say about myself since your cousin died? Does this life hold any meaning for me now?" Boro Auntie was speaking. Her vocal cords had grown old, and there was a furry quality to her words.

"Oh, Boro Auntie, I'm so sorry about Rezwan. Do you want to talk about it?"

"Kakon, if Rezwan had only grown up here like you and gotten the opportunities that you did, don't you think he would have shone like anything? I keep thinking about that. At least his eyes would have been saved, given the proper treatment."

Kakon let her aunt talk on, even though she didn't agree with her. Rezwan had not died because of lack of treatment; he had *killed* himself. He had suffered from advanced glaucoma, he was almost blind, but instead of going for surgery, he had gone for that rope in his room. Kakon thought he'd been too afraid to try, to fight for anything in life. But that would be difficult to explain to Boro Auntie. It would be hard to argue that she and Rezwan had had the same condition, only she had dealt with it differently.

"Your parents were able to give you everything, Kakon. You had nice clothes and a good education. Tell me, what kind of car is it that you're driving?"

Kakon wanted to protest that she *didn't* have a happy childhood. She'd had the same arguments with Dilruba Apa, who kept talking about the fancy party dresses with matching gloves Kakon used to wear as a child. The dresses, which were just cheap costumes bought from cheap department stores, had become legends in Kakon's cousins' stories about her. But her cousins didn't know anything about her childhood. Kakon's parents would drop her at neighbors' houses so that they could go to work. Her father was an engineer and her mother worked at a daycare center. They worked till late at night, and they picked her up from a different baby-sitter every night. They said they were earning money for her, sacrificing their lives for her. When they returned home, she sat in front of the television set, eating her dinner alone, while they prepared for the next day. Later, when she grew fat, her parents told her how ashamed they were of her. She never seemed to measure up, she never knew what they expected of her. She thought perhaps if she were really smart at school, if she went to a good university and became a doctor or an engineer, then her parents would be happy, and so she had started to excel at school, taking all the AP classes, getting into the debate team, working on the school journal. It wasn't until she was an adult and had become the engineer she'd worked her whole life to be, won awards and published papers, and patented her work, that she saw that perhaps her parents had just wanted her to be beautiful and simple instead. Or perhaps nothing she could do was good enough for them. But all her life she had groped blindly, to find out what was expected of her.

"Kakon," Boro Auntie said, taking Kakon's hands, "Rezwan looked like a prince when he died. His face was rosy pink! Like a handsome prince in a turban on the way to his wedding."

Kakon knew how her own mother would respond to these fabrications. She would snigger, she would point out that, actually, Rezwan's face was purple, distorted from the hanging, and that his body was already rotting. "Don't you think if he had been able to come here, he would have been a big engineer like you now?"

"Boro Auntie, I worked hard to be an engineer. Everyone in America is not an engineer. I had to fight for it."

"Come, come, come to eat," Boro Auntie said, ending the conversation abruptly and pulling Kakon by her hand to the dining table. Sonny had already taken a plate heaped with dripping curry. He was wolfing it down with a spoon as he worked on a page full of numbers. "You sit here, and I will serve you."

Kakon sat at the table with Sonny. "What are you working on?" she asked him.

"Homework."

Boro Auntie returned to the table with too much food. "Kakon, you have really grown a little fat," she was saying. She kept looking at Kakon from head to toe, as she had always done, as if by looking at her she could tell how well Kakon was doing.

"Boro Auntie, you say I am fat and then you feed me all this food! Is that logical?" Kakon laughed to soften the blow of her words. "That's too much food." She took the plate out of Boro Auntie's hands and marched to the kitchen to take some rice off.

"Kakon, you didn't say," Boro Auntie called after Kakon, "what kind of car did you come in?"

"Boro Auntie, it's *not my car*. It's a rental," Kakon explained again, returning to the table with a smaller heap on her plate.

"What color is it? How many cars do you have in the family?"

"We have two, Boro Auntie. Mmm, good food. Your cooking is just as good as ever. But this car I drove here in is not my car. I rented it just for this trip."

"And your house? Is it big?"

"What is considered big?" Kakon asked, chewing. "Ah, this chicken is delicious.. Did you put coconut in it?"

"Twenty rooms," Sonny said with the same seriousness with which he seemed to approach everything. "Twenty rooms is considered a big house." He walked back to the kitchen with his plate to get more food.

"Sonny is so smart," Boro Auntie said. "Rezwan was smart also, don't you think? Do you remember his poems? I saved them all."
Neither Boro Auntie nor Dilruba Apa had ever appreciated Rezwan's poetry. Kakon remembered Boro Auntie once calling him "stupid boy" and telling him to shut up when he tried to recite his poetry standing on a stack of cushions he had arranged on the floor of the living room of Boro Auntie's house in Bangladesh.

"When I grow up, I will have a house with twenty rooms," Sonny said when he returned from the kitchen.

"Kakon," Boro Auntie said, "when you leave today, I'll come down with you. I want to see your car."

"Boro Auntie, it's not my car. It's a rental car. It's a generic rental car. There were twenty others like it in the rental place." She could hear the rising frustration in her voice and stopped trying to explain. "Where's Dilruba Apa?" Some time had passed. Kakon's cell phone said that it was nine o'clock. "I have to leave soon."

"I think she missed the last bus," Boro Auntie said. "Then she has to wait for Mofiz to pick her up on his way home from the gas station."

"Well, Boro Auntie, I guess she stood me up again. I wonder if she does it on purpose." She carried her plate to the kitchen and washed it in the sink. When she returned to the dining area, she remained standing.

"What, are you leaving now, Kakon? Stay the night."

"No, Boro Auntie, I have a flight to catch tonight." She calculated the time. She could stay only half an hour longer safely without risking missing her flight. She had to return the car at the airport, check in at least an hour before the flight. "Bring on the dessert, Auntie," she said cheerfully.

Boro Auntie walked smartly to the kitchen and brought out the dessert, milky lumpy *kheer* in a saucer.

"Kakon, when I can't sleep at night, I keep thinking what Rezwan's life would be like if he had lived in America. He would have had a house and a car. We went to someone's house in Katy, Kakon. The houses were…mansions! Two living rooms! And expensive cars."

Kakon and her husband lived in the most expensive subdivision in Philadelphia, in a predominantly white neighborhood. They had a summer house in the Poconos where they went twice every year. Their two BMWs stood parked in the driveway every day, glinting silver in the moonlight. Kakon willingly imagined all of these things for Rezwan in his alternate life in America.

Perhaps at least he could have been a poet. He wouldn't have had to be ashamed of his poetry in America, his effeminate manners, his long-winded way of speaking in abstractions and images.

When they were teenagers, he used to write her letters. They were crazy letters, full of crazy dreams, like wanting to come to America, but she never believed he had it in him to take the plane from Bangladesh to America alone, live in a dorm by himself, live on a budget, work odd jobs for his education as she had throughout college. He had been putting on weight in the past few years, she had heard, he'd been sleeping with the manservant, he ate two dozen eggs a day, he took steroids for his depression which then affected his eyes. The rumors about Boro Auntie's home were as numerous as Boro Auntie's cover-up lies.

Kakon finished the *kheer*. She hadn't eaten the dessert in a long time, the rich sinful cream of it. She touched her breast and almost caressed it, thinking of the mammogram awaiting her, the onset of treatments in the country of the most advanced medical care, where Rezwan had failed to come. If it was cancer, had it reached her lungs, she wondered in a sudden panic. She would have to prepare herself now for yet another fight, with chemo and radiation and drugs and figuring out the right treatment plan.

"Boro Auntie, I have to go! Sonny, I'm sorry I missed your parents." She stood up and shook the wrinkles out of her skirt, trying to keep the disappointment out of her voice, the one-sided need.

Sonny nodded understandingly. "They're often late," he said. He turned on the TV to keep him company as he did homework.

Boro Auntie stood up gingerly.

"I'll come down with you, Kakon. Wait." Boro Auntie fixed her headscarf as Kakon bent by the sofa to lift her bag and the laptop. When Kakon stood up again, Boro Auntie had reached around her own neck and brought away a gold chain in her hands.

"Boro Auntie, what are you doing?"

"For you, Kakon. I'm getting old. It's a small present from me to you. Wear this."

Kakon tried to protest and became entangled in Boro Auntie's frantic insistence. It was getting late. She had to go.

"Boro Auntie! I'll take it. But I'll return it to Sonny's bride when he marries." She waved to him and he waved back. He was munching on the Toblerone she had brought him and jiggling his legs as he erased pencil marks in his homework.

"Kakon, I want to see your car. What kind of car did you say it was? It must be a very nice car." Boro Auntie had followed her out the door.

"Boro Auntie, come down if you want," Kakon said. "But it's not *my* car," she heard herself repeating inexplicably, even though she knew it was futile to protest. "My car is back home in Philadelphia. I didn't carry it on the plane here."

Boro Auntie followed her out anyway, immune to the sarcasm.

"I'll come to visit you in your city," Boro Auntie was saying. "I'll come to see your house."

"Boro Auntie, I'll send you an airplane ticket. You can stay with me for as long as you like."

Kakon walked to the elevator and pressed the buttons. The lights weren't on.

"Boro Auntie, the elevator isn't working."

"Who knows?" Boro Auntie said. "Sometimes they turn it off to give it a rest."

"Let's take the stairs then. Are you sure you can

manage?"

Boro Auntie took the stairs one at a time, stopping on each step with both feet, the way children climb down. Halfway down, she gripped Kakon by the elbow.

"Kakon, I have to tell you something."

The light on the stairs was dim, and there was the smell of old carpeting again. But Kakon could also smell Boro Auntie's sweet smell, of glycerine soap and talcum powder, that reminded her of her childhood. Those trips to Bangladesh had been happy times in Kakon's life, and now she kept coming back to Dilruba Apa's home for more.

"The night Rezwan died," Boro Auntie was saying, "he knocked on my door late at night. He was so excited when I opened the door. His face was breaking out in smiles. He had a newspaper in his hands. 'I can see again,' he said. 'It's gone! The glaucoma is gone magically!' But then he tried to read the paper, and he couldn't. Immediately, he was depressed again. He said he didn't want to take the plane to go to America and I began shouting at him. I kept shouting at him to make him listen. You know how he never listened. He never studied engineering because he didn't have the guts. He studied Bengali and disappointed his father. So I sent him back to his room, scolding him and telling him that he *had* to go to America. I called him a coward, a good for nothing. Then his face dropped. Kakon, I cannot bear to remember his face as he left to go back to his room."

"I'm glad you told me, Boro Auntie," Kakon said. She didn't know exactly what Boro Auntie was trying to tell her, but these were the first words of truth Boro Auntie had spoken about her cousin's death. She pictured his face again, pink perhaps as Boro Auntie had described it, pink with excitement, his eyes twinkling, his feminine nasally voice shouting in excitement because he had magically recovered his sight. Like all of Boro Auntie's family, Rezwan believed in magic, the lie of magic.

Outside, an almost full moon throbbed in the sky. They walked to the back of the building where the milky body of the rental car showed clearly in the moonlight.

"Here it is, Boro Auntie."

Boro Auntie touched the smooth metallic curves on the driver's side, running her rubbery hands along the door.

"I'll open it so you can see inside," Kakon said. She opened the door and Boro Auntie peered in at the leather-trimmed seats, clean pleasant dashboard, and power steering wheel. Now she was lovingly touching the generic synthetic car seat material.

"It's a very nice car," she said at last. "I pray for you, Kakon, that you can continue to be successful. If only Rezwan had come to America." She kept looking inside, at the car that would have been Rezwan's had he come to America, smiling as if she could see what his life would have been like.

"Well, Boro Auntie, I have to go."

The sounds of the TV carried down to where they stood, all the way down from the sixth floor, where Sonny worked on his homework. Boro Auntie stepped back.

"Yes, I also have to go back to Sonny. I have to give him *kheer*. He needs energy to do his homework."

"I'll walk you back up, Boro Auntie," Kakon said. She shut the door of the rental car, locked it with the remote key and followed Boro Auntie back to the apartment, where Sonny would be whistling now as he worked.

Borders

"Brother, please move your feet."

Faria glanced up from her seat on the Emirates plane to stare at the scene a few seats ahead. A very pretty, petite young woman with a boy cut and large eyes was speaking to a laborer seated beside her.

"Madam, how much more you want me to move? Why don't *you* move?" the man raised his voice.

His face was bearded, scruffy, his thin brown cheeks pockmarked by white and gray hairs. His eyes were small and shifty. He was one of the laborers traveling from Dhaka to Dubai.

Unfortunately, anyone taking a flight from Bangladesh to the US had to share a flight with the laborers to the Middle East until the stopover in Dubai. That was the only drawback to traveling via the Atlantic route and using one of the Middle Eastern carriers, which were superior in every other aspect.

Faria leaned forward with concern. Several other passengers looked up as well, turning toward the man and woman seated in Row 20. Faria recognized them both from Dhaka airport. The man was wearing a dark, smelly suit. His whole person was musty, his armpits, his breath all stinking. Faria had been standing in the line next to him and the other laborers at immigration at Dhaka airport. Her line had moved fast, while theirs, to the right of her, to counter ten, had been held up by complications, shady goings on, tough interview questions in raised voices, and furtive demands for hard cash. Faria had watched with some pity as the laborers had been shepherded by some sort of leader through the immigration line, obviously lost, with ugly looking bundles of luggage put together with rope and cheap black bags. Some wore tight jeans and T-shirts with random words like "I LOVE NEW YORK", bought at the garments surplus market. Others were suited like this man, reeking of men who did not take frequent baths, and cheap cologne. After the arduous, suspenseful theater at immigration, the laborers had hung out in the waiting area, sitting on orange plastic chairs, their faces taut with tension, chewing on blackened fingernails, with frightened eyes. But now, this man's face was twisted, his teeth bared at the young woman who had protested.

A pretty young stewardess of some European country, with blonde hair tucked beneath the uniform headdress, leaned over his seat and spoke to him in English. "Sir, is there a problem? Please give her some room. Your arms are on her seat."

"I bought this seat!" The man shouted apoplectically, spurting spit from his meat-red lips, and standing up from his seat. He was not so tall, about five seven, and she was wearing heels, so the difference in their height was not great. But her bright blue eyes retreated in horror.

"I'm sorry, sir, but it's against the rule…"

"Shut up! Shut up! Shut up!"

The laborers sitting nearby laughed and shouted encouragements in Bengali to the shouting man. A couple of them clapped. The back rows were filled with laborers, and the few families on the plane, America bound, were quite far, up in the front rows. Only Faria and the other female passenger had been left behind with the laborers. Faria shifted in her seat, wondering whether to intervene. She remembered that the same passenger had tried to light up a cigarette a half hour ago and been scolded by a male steward.

"Sir, if you don't sit down, I'll have to…," the stewardess began again, pursing her frosted pink lips.

"What? What? What?" the man barked, jumping up.

The stewardess recoiled back with horror, uncertain if he would strike her. Faria had half gotten out of her seat, when the British male steward, towering at over six feet, the same one who had confronted the man earlier, strode over.

"What's your name, sir?"

"Malik."

"Sit down, Mr. Malik!" The male steward shouted, his chin trembling with anger. "Sit down this minute. When the plane lands, we will report you to ground authority."

Mr. Malik sat back down demurely. Faria gathered her courage to stand up from her seat and approach the huddle around Row 20.

"Please, if it's possible, I'd like to exchange seats with—with this gentleman here and sit next to the young woman." She leaned toward the woman passenger and said in Bengali, "Is that okay? *Thik Ache?*"

The woman nodded gratefully.

Faria turned back to the English male steward. "Sir?"

In a short while, Mr. Malik was shouted at and persuaded to move down two seats, where Faria had been sitting. Faria brought over her large handbag and settled down, a little uneasily, in the rather warm chair Mr. Malik had vacated, still scented with his overpowering cologne.

She flashed a warm, friendly smile at the young woman sitting beside her. She had noticed her too at Dhaka airport. The pretty woman had arrived with a large family, a matronly looking woman wearing a wrinkled brown cotton saree wrapped all around her, across her shoulders and over her head, a thin elderly man who seemed to be her father, for he clutched her and cried every few minutes, a line of weeping women, and little children who hung on to her and cried and kissed her. She had cried along with them, hugging a little boy who may have been her younger brother to her waist and weeping tears over his back, extracting such bizarre promises from her companions as "Please tell me you will write me a letter every day" and "Abba, promise to take your medicine and don't strain yourself." It was a most tender and surprising spectacle of farewell taking, compared to the dry, businesslike way in which a distant cousin connected to the airport had brought Faria in through the VIP gate. Faria had first left home at seventeen and she had been living by herself for over a decade now, so she had watched the emotional scene with a voyeur's interest.

Afterward, Faria had run into the other woman several times in the duty-free area at Dhaka Airport, where they had waited for five hours, as the flight had been delayed. Faria had noticed her perhaps she'd because she was the only other young woman traveling on her own, or because she was striking, wearing a pretty little black polka-dot shalwar kameez. She had a dramatic face, like a child's, a button nose, soft pink lips, smooth pale arms, and long, delicate fingers. She had sat on the orange plastic chair reading a magazine, turning over the pages carefully, looking uncertain and distracted, wandering by the various handicraft shops, and stopping at the sweet shop to buy a sweetmeat.

"Thank you," the young woman said now, showing even white teeth. She could scarcely have been older than a child, Faria thought.

"Your name?" Faria asked in Bengali that had acquired a thick American accent.

"Polly."

"Apart from the two of us, the rest of the people on the plane are all men or families." Faria glanced around the plane meaningfully. "I'm glad to be sitting beside you."

Polly laughed loudly, as if Faria had pointed out something very funny. Her voice was surprisingly deep. "Where are you going, Apa?" Polly asked.

"New York. You?"

"New York."

"Well, then, we're even better buddies," Faria said.

They settled in their seats, relaxing their bodies, no longer worried about modesty. It was a relief to both the young women to be sitting together.

The first flight would take them to Dubai. About half the passengers would get off there. The rest were traveling onward to America, or Canada. There was a gulf of difference between the two kinds of passengers, and it was a strange irony for the two worlds to have to share a journey together. Faria always found it surprising, and a little disconcerting, how she felt closer to the people from America. She identified with the other young college students and the families who looked like her and dressed like her, and even the few white Americans traveling to Bangladesh. The America-bound passengers always huddled together on the seats at the airport, laughing together and talking easily in English. There was good reason to be wary of the male laborers bound for the Middle East. The young men pushed past the other passengers, including women and children, running to get the first seats on the bus. On the plane, they cleaned their noses with their fingers, smoked in the plane bathroom, stole the blankets by stuffing them into their cheap plastic bags, and called the stewardesses rudely as if they were lowly servants, crying one word demands, like water, water, while gesturing rapidly with their hands.

On the plane *to* Dhaka, there had been several other young women traveling with Faria. They had hung out together, exchanging life stories, and talking about their plans in Dhaka. Faria had been visiting family, but also doing research for her PhD on sex workers, meeting and interviewing sex workers in street settings. This flight back to the United States, in contrast, had no young women traveling by themselves, other than Polly and Faria.

"What do you do in New York?" Faria asked.

"My husband lives there." Polly's face turned pink to her ears. "I'm going to visit them."

"How romantic," Faria said encouragingly. She noticed that Polly's boy-cut hair had been freshly styled, probably at a salon, and plastered with gel. Her palms had fresh red henna on them, and she wore a thick gold bracelet on each wrist.

"Are you newly married?" Faria asked.

"No. Eleven years."

"Eleven years!" Faria cried. "But you're so young."

"And you, Apa?"

"Call me Faria. I'm a student, a graduate student at a university in New York. I was just visiting Dhaka for the summer."

"Are you married?"

Faria shook her head. The two women looked away from each other, falling silent for a while, as tired passengers do on the plane after talking for a while, caught up in their own thoughts, in their own different worlds.

At the airport in Dubai, Faria and Polly both checked their tickets and found that they had a layover of eleven hours.

"We should spend the time together," Faria said. She had carried Polly's luggage for her, seeing the young woman struggling. Faria had carried her own heavy luggage since she had left for college at seventeen. She was tall, big-boned, wide-shouldered, loud mothed, and brazen. She felt protective toward the younger woman.

"Yes, we could spend time together," Polly said. "I was going to go shopping outside to the market."

Faria exclaimed in surprise. She had never ventured outside the airport in Dubai, although she had passed through so many times over the years. "You're going to take the bus outside?"

"Yes. If they give me a visa."

They were standing in a long line of people with foreign passports. The immigration officials at Dubai Airport asked tough questions with stern faces.

Did you pack your bag yourself?

What do you do in America?

For how long have you lived in America, Sir?

Why does your face look different in your passport?

I can't find your visa here. Where is your visa?

Several of the adults seemed near crying with frustration at the questions, while the children bearing Barbie dolls, matchbox cars, and Nintendo games fell to the carpeted floor in heaps from exhaustion. Faria glanced at the next line, which was shorter and faster, and realized with a shock that soon, *she* would be in that line, for green card holders and US citizens.

At least, the huddle of laborers who had gotten off the plane with their baskets of smelly mangoes, bedding tied together with plastic rope, and synthetic black bags had disappeared into the city.

"Do you want to come, too?" Polly asked once they had finally made it through the immigration line. "I heard the market in Dubai is spectacular! They have the best gold in the world. I've always wanted to see it."

"No." Faria quickly shook her head. She had always regarded the airport as a stopover, to sleep, read, and recover from the previous leg. At most, she had wandered through the duty-free shops, looking at European shops with their different chocolates not available in America. "I'll meet you when you come back."

"Alright," Polly said. "I will see you later."

Faria gazed after her, surprised at this first-time traveler's sense of adventure, and went away to find a coffee place to recharge her laptop.

When the two women met again, quite by accident, they were both wandering near the Harrods in the duty-free area. Polly was laden down with shopping bags. In addition to the brown heavy bag that pulled her right shoulder down below her left, pinching her dress, several yellow plastic bags hung from her wrists. Faria ran up to her.

"Hey there!" "Hello," Polly said, looking around startled. For a moment, she regarded Faria with a blank expression. Then, recognizing her, she smiled and indicated her wrists, where the ropes of the shopping bags twisted and left angry marks. "Apa, I did a lot of shopping! I bought so much gold."

"Call me Faria," Faria said. "You look miserable." She pointed at the heavy carry-on bag and offered to take it off the smaller woman's shoulders.

"No, it's okay."

But Faria insisted and took the bag. Polly said thank you many times, gratefully.
"No problem," Faria said graciously, marching ahead. "Come on, slow poke, keep up." She looked behind affectionately at the weaker woman. "Shall we get lunch somewhere with the tickets they gave us?" She knew that without her, Polly would be lost at the huge airport.

"Sure," Polly said, using the polite form of you in Bengali.

"I was looking for you," Faria said. "I was worried for you."

"Oh, why?" Polly asked, a few steps behind her.

They found the Indian restaurant where they had all had tickets for lunch. Faria helped Polly to find her ticket and showed Polly how to use her ticket (she had misplaced her ticket, as unseasoned travelers often do, so Faria made her also check if she had her passport, ticket, and boarding pass to America).

Once they sat down with their trays, Faria asked, "So why is it that you haven't visited your husband for eleven years?"

Polly was digging into the food with her fingers. Lunch was generous: with Tandoori chicken, Naan, and various kinds of chutney.

"Long story," Polly said, but instead of telling the story, she said, "My husband really misses my cooking. He liked for me to cook for him. After we were married, every day, he asked me to cook this and that." Polly stared at the chicken bone she was biting. "This chicken is easy to make." She took apart the flesh at the bones and showed Faria where the spices had been inserted and how to fry it so the meat was cooked but not tough. "I make a good fried chicken that is his favorite. And various kinds of fried vegetables. He eats and eats. He says he missed his wife's cooking in New York, so I have to go and cook for him all his favorite dishes." Polly laughed with pleasure. A miniscule diamond stud glinted in her nose.

"How long were you married before he left?"

"One month."

"So he keeps in touch with you?" Faria asked, thinking perhaps the woman had been deserted after her marriage, as was too common among the women she researched.

"Yes, of course!" Polly laughed girlishly, using the back of her hand to wipe her nose, which was running from the spicy food. "He calls me on the phone every day to ask me how to cook this or that."

For no particular reason, Faria remembered the Bengali café she and Dan had once visited down in the Village. Of course, they hadn't known then that the owner was Bengali. The restaurant had an Indian name, and the menu touted itself as selling Indian food. But when the owner had come out, and started talking to them, he had turned out to be a Bangladeshi man.

Dan had asked for beer, and the owner had said that they did not have beer yet, but they had applied for a liquor license.

"Please, Apa, pray for us that we get it," he had said to Faria in Bengali.

Faria had been wearing a thin black tank top that hugged her body, and she and Dan, the Viking like giant Dan with his blonde hair and blonde eyelashes, had been holding hands. The Bangladeshi man had been wearing shorts and scratching his crotch. Yet, they did not judge each other, for the tank top, the American boyfriend, the shorts, or the liquor. Rather, they had felt a strong sense of camaraderie, speaking in their tongue in this foreign land, wishing each other mutual success in their different paths.

Still, Faria and Dan had laughed at the irony later: This Muslim man was going to sell liquor, and he was asking Faria to pray for him in their religion, in which alcohol was forbidden, so that he could sell alcohol. The two of them had thought this funny. It had become their private joke. They would tell it like a most amusing anecdote to friends. It never got old.

"So why did you open a restaurant?" Faria had asked the Bangladeshi man, as he had sat down at the table to talk to them.

"I used to be a taxi driver," he said. "And I really missed my wife's cooking. And I knew all these other

Bangladeshi drivers who cried to me, Apa. Imagine. Grown men with real tears in their eyes, because they too missed their mother's cooking or their wife's cooking. They dreamed at night of white rice and thick daal with onions and lemon. So one day I decided to open a restaurant, for myself and for them. Now, this restaurant stays open twenty-four hours. And these taxi drivers, when they get off their shifts, sometimes in the middle of the night, at one or two in the morning, when the other restaurants are closed, they come in here to my restaurant and sit here like it is their wife's kitchen, eating beef curry and talking with other Bangladeshi drivers about back home. I create a home for them here in my restaurant."

"So how long have you been living here?" Dan had asked affably, throwing his hands in the air to indicate the Village, New York, America. Even sitting down, he had towered over the shorter, darker man.

The man lowered his voice conspiratorially, leaned in, and whispered to Dan that he was ill-le-gal, still waiting for his papers. Then he drew back and grinned slyly, showing even white teeth. Like most immigrants who had started to do well, the man had acquired fat on his belly, face, and arms. He told them that he had come to New York on a visitor's visa, planning to stay behind. He had friends in the city who had written to him and who had promised to help him once he got here. Then he had disappeared into the folds of New York. He used to live with a distant uncle first, up in the Queens. Then driving a taxi for a company day and night, he had saved enough to buy a taxi of his own on loan. For two years, he had driven sixteen hours a day (no, really) to pay off the loan. He earned eighty thousand dollars a year, all his own money, to keep. Dan and Faria had joked later, falling of their narrow bed laughing, that *he probably kept his money under the mattress in cash, hidden away from the IRS.*

"So you still don't have papers?" Dan had asked with concern.

"No, still waiting. I go to court regularly. I have a lawyer working on my case. Please pray for me, brother."

The man spoke with dramatic flourish and self-importance, gesturing with his arms, winking, nodding his head, where his vocabulary could not fill the gap, and Dan and Faria had thoroughly enjoyed the visit and the conversation. They had talked of it for days, months, imitating him and laughing. He was such an oddity. He wore shorts and a Polo shirt, a thin gold chain around his neck. Faria had wondered how much of his home he had left behind, how much he had abandoned of his culture and his religion, along with the modest trousers he should be wearing. They shared an odd intimacy, this man in his shorts and Faria with her American boyfriend. Had the café sold beer, they might even have shared one across a table. So odd, they had said, discussing him, such an odd sort, so devout yet selling alcohol, so religious yet willing to do something illegal. New York was full of Bangladeshis, selling hot dogs on corners, suddenly emerging as a waiter in an Upper West side restaurant, a taxi driver piping up in Bengali. Faria loved these encounters, but she felt a world of divide between her and these men, who lived in dark corners, probably without documents. Faria and Dan used to walk the streets of Manhattan, Faria's hand in Dan's wool jacket pocket, discussing these things. In a few months, Dan and she would get married, nothing big, just get their license in court, then celebrate with a few friends in his parents' backyard in their Long Island mansion. Only once, when she had been telling a pharmacist, who had turned out to be Bangladeshi, in a drugstore high up on the West side, that she was graduating soon, the older man had asked, "What will you do after that?"

Faria shook her head, laughing, not wanting to say she would be marrying Dan, settling in with him. Then she would take some time off, taking advantage of her immigrant status to not have to work for the first time in her life. Then, when she had rested enough, she would apply for academic jobs.

"You should just stay," the elderly man had suggested, lowering his voice. "Just stay on. Nobody will notice in this big city. So many of us here."

Faria had smiled and got out of the store fast. She'd been so shocked by even the mention of such a possibility. That line that the men had crossed, that meant they belonged in two different worlds.

Now, at the airport restaurant, Faria stared dreamily at Polly, who was digging into the rice and yogurt with her greasy fingers.

"You must be happily married."

"We have one boy. He is ten."

"You have a child? A ten-year-old! You don't look it. I saw a boy with long eyelashes, about that age, hugging you around the waist at Dhaka Airport. Was that him?"

"Yes! When my husband married me, I was immediately pregnant."

"So why don't you move to the US? With your son?"

Polly hesitated. "My husband is illegal there. That is why. They don't want the child to visit. The consulate

people make me keep my child in Bangladesh and get a
visitor's visa so they can be sure I'll return. I left my son
with my parents. This is first time they gave me visa.
Every year before this, they refused. Too risky to let me
go there. I might stay behind. For ten years, I applied for
a visa and I got denied. But this time I tried again
because he cried. He said he misses having a wife. And
this time I got it."

Faria looked again at the young wife's face. For
the first time, she noticed the dark lines under Polly's
eyes, and she understood the tears at the airport now,
not of fright at leaving home, but at leaving her little
child behind, his little brown hands grasping at her. Polly
was going off into the unknown to meet her long-
separated husband, estranged, almost. What strange cold
world did he live in, how separated from her own sunny,
warm home of familiar trees and balconies and markets
and neighbors?

"How about you, Apa?" Polly asked. "Are you
married?"

"No."

"You didn't find time to get married? You were
too busy getting an education?"

"Ha, ha." Faria turned away, feeling faintly
offended.
She felt unable to explain who she was and her wide,
expanded world to people whose lives were narrower
and more straightforward than her own. She had even
felt it a lot of the time while visiting relatives and her
parents' friends in Dhaka. Never when doing her work,
though, when she went about the city on rickshaw,
talking to the sex workers on the streets, their clients,
their pimps in white shirts and jeans. But when she
talked to relatives or her parents' friends, people would

say things like, "Faria, get married before you become infertile." Or "time is ticking, you can't defy nature." She had only laughed uproariously at the rude comments of such people and made some rude joke as rebuttal. Her parents had tried to introduce her to several young men, who dropped in very awkwardly at the house and gaped at her.

"Shall we walk around and see what's on sale?" Faria dabbed her lips with a tissue and scraped back her chair, looming over the other woman.

"Oh, yes." Polly stood up, picking up her tray. Faria couldn't trust Polly, for the same reason she couldn't find common ground with her old friends and cousins in Bangladesh who always wore shalwar kameez, got married according to their parents' wishes. She could not trust them to respect her, or to understand her if she revealed herself to them.

Once her friends had taken her to drink local alcohol at a shady shop. They could have gone to a foreign party, the American embassy or one of the other foreign embassies, but they wanted to have an adventure. The local liquor shops were undercover so that there was no regulation at all. They could be drinking something that would kill them. She and her friends raised their glasses and cheered, drinking possibly to their deaths, laughing uproariously. They would sit and laugh about so many things that were beyond the pale, or illegal, in Dhaka, like driving as a woman late at night, walking on the streets alone late at night, that was perfectly legal in another country.

As Faria and Polly walked past the various duty-free shops displaying Lindt Chocolate and whiskey and matching luggage in front, Faria's tension melted away. Her shoulders relaxed. She'd been striding two paces ahead of Polly, but slowly she slowed down and offered to take Polly's bag again.

"Keeping up?" she smiled sweetly at Polly. Polly smiled back. "I'd like to see the gold shops."

"I thought you already went to the gold market?" Faria teased. She had a dry sense of humor and was good at making jokes. She teased everyone, men older than her, taller than her, patriarchal men in Bangladeshi NGOs, even her uncles and her father's friends who offended her.

"I bought some good bangles and earrings, but I'm looking for a necklace," Polly said.

"Sure."

Polly didn't know where the gold shops were, so Faria looked at the map. They were standing in terminal B. They would have to head back to Terminal A. They took a train, then walked the long airport past the shops selling nuts, candy, cigarettes, and liquor, to the gold shops. Polly studied the glittering displays under glass. She asked for pieces to be brought out, then asked expertly about karats, and designs, and prices. Faria looked on, smiling politely and suppressing a yawn. But she also felt her forehead tightening. She was getting married in a few months. She wasn't going to tell her parents till she was properly, legally, married, when they couldn't do anything about it. She wasn't afraid, she just didn't want any fuss from them. But had Faria told her mom, perhaps her mother would have brought out the gold she had saved for her daughter's wedding all her life. Looking at the matching sets of necklaces, earrings, and rings, Faria's eyes shone with this daydream, of her mother adorning her with *her* mother's necklaces, bestowing on her generations of tradition. She shook her head to get out of the temptation that must be in her

Bengali DNA to be attracted to gold like other Bengali girls and laughed aloud wrly. Polly turned around in confusion.

Dan's parents had no concept of gold. Their house was sparkling white, every room, including the kitchen. Everything was flat with the surface, marble white. Even the bathroom, as big as two large parlors, was white, with overhung mirrors on every wall and the ceiling, and a large famous painting that his mother had bought in a gallery in Newberry. The artist had been struggling when Dan's mother had bought it, an old boyfriend of hers, she claimed, but now he was famous, he had made a name. With each object came a story. The large Indian mask placed precariously on a coffee table in the dining room, from the Incas, the African drums in the long, white living room, the shard of glass by the pool, another piece of art, bought and shipped from Paris. Even the coffee cups had stories attached to them. Old restaurants they had taken her to, where even the sauce of the pasta tasted deep and complicated, sophisticated, cooked by a famous chef. They had a private plane, so they could fly off whenever they wanted their next adventure. Dan's mom said that sometimes on a warm evening in New York, they would think, why don't we eat in Alaska, and they would drive out to the hangar to get the plane and book a table at a restaurant in Anchorage, and there they would be, in a few hours, stealing out for a date, like two naughty kids.

Once, Dan had flown Faria in that small single engine plane. Suddenly, high in the air, he had teased, his voice rising in feigned alarm, "Oh, we're flying over Canada now! If there's engine trouble, I'll have to make an emergency landing."

Faria didn't even find it funny. Her face became plastic. "No, no, please, I can't be in Canada. I have an F-1 visa!" she had cried out, her eyes big with fear. All her sense of humor had vanished then. The loud, funny girl, the no-nonsense foreign student who gave everyone else in class a hard time. Now she was crying for him to turn around. How naïve, how gauche she had been. She liked to tell that story now to friends, of that old unsophisticated Faria, as if that were some other person in the past.

On another vacation, Dan and his parents had invited Faria to Texas with them, where they had a private ranch. After a few days at the ranch in Dallas, they had kept driving west, all the way to Laredo. They walked to the Rio Grande river. Standing in a park right on the border, they looked across the narrow river and they could see across to Mexico, where people stood by the water like them, some strolling, some fishing. Border patrol marched along the park with guns slung lazily across their shoulders.
"This is where people cross over," Dan's mom had pointed out with her long, slender ring finger, with the single diamond ring. Then she had suggested they walk across the bridge into Nuevo Laredo, check it out.

"No!" Faria had cried, her eyes darting, pupils large with fear, like a frightened wild animal. "I can't. I don't have my passport." She began gesticulating wildly with her hands, like a man who does not have full command of English. Again, she had lost her sophistication.

Her passport was always the first thing she seized during a fire drill, once during an actual fire with real smoke in the college dorm; this paranoia about carrying her documents with her all the time, to prove her legality, was something she would joke about, tell as an anecdote to make her friends laugh. But now she became the joke.

Dan's parents laughed at her affectionately. "Come on," DAN's mother said smoothly, fingering the pearls at her neck. "Nothing will happen." In contrast to gaudy gold and heavy brocade saris, Dan's very wealthy mother wore a simple T-shirt and shorts, her hair cut short to her nape. Her nails were clean and short. Faria looked up to her and had learned so much from her. Dan's mother had lent Faria books on gardening in New York, a book on the American West before their vacation. "Nothing will happen. When they ask, I'll say you're a US citizen. You're with us. You're practically my daughter." She pulled Faria close to her, the two women the same height, walking shoulder to shoulder.

And Dan's mother had been right. The border had been crowded. The immigration officers were exhausted trying to get through the long line.

"She's my daughter," Dan's mother had said. "We're US citizens."

"Welcome home, Ma'am. God bless."

No one even asked to see their passports [they were not carrying any]. Dan's parents had laughed and laughed at Faria later on. They would not let her forget. On the other side of the border in Nuevo Laredo, in one of the plazas, Faria had seen a sight she could not shed from her eyes. There had been little fat children in pink frocks playing, boys with their sandals off, chasing each other. One plump family, a father, mother, and their two little children sat with ice cream popsicles on the steps of a statue and ate, a family outing. A little girl in an embroidered white cotton Mexican dress flung her arms out, shut her eyes, and whirled round and round, as if, with those eyes closed, her world was large and endless. By contrast, when they had headed back, the border security guards huddled on the bridge were all suspicion, checking people's bags, looking savagely at their faces, accusing them of trying to cross over illegally, as if Mexico was barren, as if no one lived there or they only lived there to one day cross over to America.

Finally, Polly made a choice at the gold shop. She held a fat necklace around her throat and checked herself in the mirror, turning her face sideways and plumping her mouth, raising an eyebrow, then turning the other way.

"Do you like it?"

"It's nice," Faria said in a plastic way. She was no authority on gold. She wondered if she would ever fit in as a woman in Bangladesh. If she could even be accepted in that society as a woman if she didn't have any expertise in gold.

"My mother keeps all her gold at home," Polly chattered happily. "Once, when there was load shedding and we had no power, we live in Azimpur where the power always goes out, every evening almost for one hour, one day my mom brought out all the gold and started to sort them out, for lack of something to do."

In the end, Polly decided that didn't want anything at the shop and moved on. Faria followed her. With half her mind, she was beginning to wonder if she should leave Polly and go back to the book she had to read for school, or perhaps sort her notes from the research. Nut she followed along, for want of company, partly, wanting to protect the young woman.

Polly talked about her mom chewing betel leaves till tongue had grown red, her son playing football with the other boys in the field in front of their house, how she and her sister would steal green mangoes from her mom's pantry in the middle of the night and eat them with red chili and salt.

"Have you never shopped for gold, Apa?"

"Nope," Faria said.

"Oh. It was our favorite excursion. Even as teenagers, when we had no money," Polly giggled.

They passed several gold shops where Polly only took a cursory look and grimaced. "My cousins and I would go and make the shopkeeper take out gold bangles and we would put them on our wrists. They were too fat for our wrists, and the bangles would go *jhum jhum jhum*. Such a sound! Like rain shower. The shopkeepers would think we were real customers and they would treat us with Coca Cola. Then they would wise up and get very rude, and we would run out, laughing, our bellies hurting. We would double down laughing as soon as we got out the door."

"Oh, how we loved to go to New Market. We went to our favorite bookshops and bought the latest novel by Humayun Ahmed, and then we ate that spicy chotpoti and that's it, our money was gone! Otherwise, we would go to Gawsia Market across the street and spend hours shopping for fabric and then telling the tailor how to make our dresses."

They came to another shop, this one with more intricate designs in their gold, more Indian classical. Polly stopped suddenly, her eyes widening. Again, Polly made the shopkeepers get out several sets of glinting yellow gold.

"These are more sophisticated designs," Polly said. She explained to Faria how the gold in Dubai was pure yellow, whereas in Bangladesh it was softer, more fragile. She gave Faria a whole lecture in gold.

"My sister would like this design," she said, smiling. "I will buy her one for her wedding."

It seemed Polly's husband sent a lot of money home, allowing her to hoard gold not only for herself but also her younger siblings.

"I love gold. Polly closed her eyes and stroked the necklace the shopkeeper had put around her neck. "This one is called a *Sita Har.* It falls to the navel, see?"

"Why do you like gold so much?" Faria asked, her lips curling.

"It's the rule for all girls to love gold," Polly said, "It's the rule of the world."

At last, Polly had bought two necklaces and Faria had helped her calculate the conversion, and they walked back with their possessions, taking the train back to Terminal A. They had only two hours left before their flight. Polly kept talking about her mother and her younger sisters. Finally, they were seated at their gate. For once, Polly stopped talking. She rummaged about her many carry-on bags, trying to sort her things. Faria sat on the cold, sterile seat of the terminal train, remembering her visit. Things had been hostile, to say the least.

Once, when Faria had been headed out late at night, taking a taxi to meet friends, her mother had burst into her room.

"What are you doing?"

"Going out," Faria had answered rudely. "Why do you look at me like that? You look like you disapprove?" She was standing at her dressing table, with the long mirror, powdering her nose.

"I'm not looking at you like that. But society is," her mother had answered crossly, frowning. "It's not alright for women to go out at all hours of the night in our society."

The frowns looked like judgment to Faria so she turned away proudly, pouting in the mirror. "We need to take back the night then. I'm pushing back, so we have more space…"

"Everything you do, it's not acceptable here. A woman your age should be married. Should be going out with husband in your husband's car. Not out at two in the morning. Not going to foreign embassies. Smoking, drinking."

"Oh, I can't breathe. You make me sick. Give me some space!" Faria had cried, pushing roughly past her mother, and rushing out of her room, out of the tiny, suffocating flat.

That was how the entire summer had played out. She had felt sick, pressed in, as if her own childhood home wasn't home to her anymore.

Apparently satisfied with her packing, Polly sat back in her seat and asked, "So when will you marry?"

"Why do I have to marry?" Faria smiled coolly at the other woman.

"Do you have someone you want to marry, Apa? A boyfriend?"

Faria decided not to answer. Polly mentioned that she missed her son. Faria wondered idly if that man she knew, the restaurant owner in the Village, was the same taxi driver who was Polly's husband. The two women fell into exhausted boredom again.

Then a stewardess walked to Polly and told her could not carry so many bags on the plane. Faria tried to translate for Polly. Polly was in tears, begging, gesturing.

"I'm afraid those are the rules." The stewardess's lips tightened the way they did when speaking to laborers on the plane. She folded her hands in front of her dress and spoke very slowly. "One bag. Yeah? One bag. Not many."

When she walked away, Polly turned to Faria. "Apa, can you not take one of my bags? The heavy black one? After all, you've been carrying it all along for me."

Faria gawked at the audacity of the demand. She hesitated a moment before replying, just to gather how to reply to such a question. "The rules say that you can't carry someone else's bag," she said finally, enunciating her words, speaking firmly like the stewardess, "They'll ask me if I am carrying someone else's bags. I'm supposed to know everything that is in my bags."

This was exactly the kind of thing those other Bangladeshis in New York did, crossing this invisible line. Faria had never done anything the least bit in doubt–never taken a package to carry for someone without checking it first, never carried food, like other passengers did. She became sure now that that black bag was loaded with food for the absent husband.

"Please. It will help me a lot. I can't leave any of this behind."

"Well." Faria grimaced, extremely uncomfortable. "Can't you wear some of the things you bought? Like the gold, for instance. And–what else did you buy?"

"I'm going to see my husband after so long. He misses rice puffs from his village. And I'm bringing molasses. His books. I had to carry all. Please, Apa. You're carrying nothing on you. Look. Is that purse all you are carrying? You are allowed to carry one handbag and one carry-on bag, Apa."

Faria frowned. The incivility of the demand rattled her. She felt uncomfortable even sitting next to Polly, who seemed as if she would go on trying to persuade Faria.

Now she felt that she should really be getting back to her book, which she had intended to finish on the journey back. Faria stood up. "I have some work to catch up on. I'll just go sit a few rows down for a bit…"

She regretted wasting so much time with Polly. She really could have used the extra time on the plane to catch up on work. Or nap. She would definitely sleep the twelve hours it took to get to New York. She smiled politely. "See you in a bit."

They were interrupted by a man's voice at their elbow. "Sisters, didn't you both come from Bangladesh? Imagine seeing you again."

Faria and Polly both looked in surprise at the man speaking. He was the same pockmarked man in his musty suit who had been seated next to Polly on the plane from Bangladesh to Dubai.

At last, Polly spoke. "Bhai, I thought you were going to Dubai?"

"I worked in Dubai for many years," the man said amiably, "but this time I got a visitor's visa to USA. I have a cousin there. He will set me up in taxi business." He sat down in the seat vacated by Faria and fluffed his jacket. "Apa, sit down?" he said to Faria, as if expecting to settle down to a nice, long conversation with the two women. "You don't have to go to bathroom, do you? Then go and come back. My name is Malik. What are your names?"

He was all friendliness. He seemed to have forgotten their encounter on the plane. His thin, pinched face, and the sunken eyes of malnourishment had all broken into a bright smile.

"I really have to do some work," Faria said coldly. She moved away near the gathering passengers at the gate: Families with kids in shorts and GAP T-shirts, and women who had been in shalwar kameez so far suddenly changed into pants, people whose skin and bags and clothes all reflected an American polish.

Sitting far from the other two, pulling out her laptop and spreading out her book and papers to do some last-minute work, she noticed that Polly had not moved away from the man. The two had their heads together, talking conspiratorially.

When the airline started to board passengers, Faria heard an altercation at the gate. They had just called for passengers who needed assistance, followed by families with small children and first-class passengers. Faria usually waited patiently till the last zone was called, as she had no bags to stow away and she didn't enjoy the rush to get to the gate only to stand in a long line. She spotted the troublesome man Mr. Malik from the plane, in trouble again.

"Sir, it's not your turn yet to board the plane," the same stewardess spoke slowly to him, pointing at him with a finger. "Please go back to your seat till your row is called."

Faria shook her head and went back to her book. When she finally stood up to join the line, she saw Polly with her duty-free bags all piled into one duty-free bag standing in line next to Mr. Malik, who was, horror of horrors, carrying Polly's heavy black bag.

When they reached the gate, there was another altercation. It was astounding, really quite an achievement, how Mr. Malik seemed able to break the rules and get in trouble in possible way. He seemed alright with inserting himself in these situations too, immune to the insults hurled his way.

"Sir, this is two bags. Not one. This one on your shoulder. And this one. Yeah? Two. You need to make one bag."

Mr. Malik said, "Handbag. Handbag."

"No, Sir. Handbag is for ladies. This is too big for handbag. This is two carry-ons. Yeah?"

This went for five minutes, till the stewardess's eyes rolled back and Faria's ears were crimson. Her face burned with embarrassment for this man, on his behalf, actually, for the insults he had to endure from the stewardess, who kept raising her voice, jabbing at him, snarling.

But Mr. Malik kept standing grandly in front of her, as if he didn't understand English, or any of the insults; her words simply slid off his slippery suit. In front of Faria's eyes, he transformed into the hundreds of Bengali men she had encountered on the streets of New York, selling hot dogs in the cold, selling newspapers in the subway station, bravely navigating the city's grid system, its snow and cold and spiraling rent; selling Bengali CDs in Jackson Heights, songs she longed to listen to, opening shops, cafes, and restaurants where she ran to when she felt homesick, for samosas, paratha, chicken curry, milk tea. Brave men with taut faces, smiling at the unknown. Mr. Malik's gray stubble, the musty suit, and torn garments all appeared to define a man ready to take on the weight of the world. His old nemesis Poppy stood next to him smiling with the same stupid, plastic expression as him, as if they both did not speak English. Faria almost smiled at their daring.

On the plane, when Faria reached her seat, Mr. Malik was already seated there. He stood up as soon as he saw her.

"Sorry, Apa. Was just chatting."

"Well, no. You seem comfortable. I'll just—"

"Did you want to talk?" Mr. Malik gestured at the space between Polly and Faria.

Polly looked at her expectantly.

"Well, I have a lot of work…and I'm exhausted, so if you two want to talk, I'm sure…"

They exchanged seats (Mr. Malik had a great window seat a few rows down), and Faria settled in next to a young man with blonde curls who said he worked in the Middle East in oil, was traveling back to see his parents for a week, in Florida. They chatted for a while, and Faria took a nap for the rest of the flight.

At JFK Airport, Faria always hated the long lines at immigration. Inside America, she wandered freely, as if the land belonged to her, the fresh air, the mountains, the freeways. But at borders, she waited in line like a beggar asking for entry. She did not enjoy the unpleasant exchanges at immigration, the suspense, the rude, snide comments. On the way to Bangladesh, she had shown her ticket at the counter, she had kept asking, do you need to see my passport? The man had been nice, pleasant, chatting with her, and he kept saying, no, no need. Then suddenly, he realized she was not a citizen.

"Bring out your passport, Ma'am," he had barked.

"Well, I've been asking you if I needed to show you my passport," Faria had said coldly, lifting out her passport from her cavernous handbag with slow dignity.

The long line for people entering on visas wound round and round. Tired families with children inched forward a few steps. Faria saw a lot of people from the plane, a glimpse here, and then there again as the line shifted forward. She saw Polly a few times, lovely in the same Polka dot dress, cool and fresh as a bride, and Mr. Malik, still in his suit, looking solemn.

At last, Faria was up front at the immigration counter. She waited, holding her breath, remembering that in a few months she would be married, and she would have a green card. The next time she traveled, things would be different.

The elderly man checked her passport, glanced up at her face, matching the two pictures. Faria laughed to herself, thinking how that faded, ugly photo was woeful in describing her, all the spaces she had been in, the women whose stories she had listened to, all the things she knew about what they did for money, in the dark, all the fights she had had with her mother, all the philosophical conversations with friends. The officer asked her to pose for a photo and took her fingerprints. Then he stamped her passport.

"Welcome to the US." He flashed her a smile.

"Thank you."

Faria crossed the immigration line into America, feeling a great sense of relief. Now for her luggage, customs, a taxi home. Then she spotted Polly. The young, frightened woman was standing a few rows up, at another immigration counter. The immigration officer was speaking to her roughly. She was answering in faltering English. Her heart-shaped face looked small and sallow in the dim light. Her eyes were small and darting. The immigration officer became sterner. Faria stopped, initially thinking she would wait to exchange phone numbers with Polly when she came out, just so the young woman would have another contact in New York, and then, with growing alarm. She listened with growing horror to the hostile interrogation.

The immigration officer asked Polly where she was going, what her husband did, did he have papers. She heard scraps of their exchange, saw the sharp head nods, the jerks, the frowns, and the tense silences.

Faria remembered the stories Polly had told her, of going to New Market on rickshaws with her cousins, piled three on top of one another, to buy materials for curtains or dresses, in the back alley of the market, where a shopkeeper might pull a stool and say, "Sit, Apa, drink tea while I get this done." The shopkeeper's young son would bring around a tray of rattling teacups, filled with sweet milk tea. There would be happiness in the confines of the musty, airless shop. How could Polly's frightened face at immigration, her halting English, or her awkward passport photo speak of these worlds? Faria stood, her heart beating fast, her handbag weighing heavily on her shoulder. She even forgot what she was waiting for. Dan would be out of town, at his parents' house party in Long Island, but he would be waiting for a phone call from her. And Dan's parents had made her promise to call them too. She would have to switch on her cellphone, see if it was charged.

Suddenly, she saw Polly pass in front of her, with two immigration officials. Faria ran up to the group.

"Where are you going?" she barked in panic.

"Apa, they are taking me to a second immigration room."

Faria wanted to ask the immigration officials what was going on, but she didn't know if that would count as obstruction of their work. She gaped at the other woman.

"It's okay, Apa. My husband warned me about it. Happens to him all the time."

Polly's face was grey, young and lost like a child's face again.

In a flash, the group was gone, headed toward a closed room. Faria stared after them. They disappeared inside the room, and Faria could see them through the glass. She stood irresolutely for some moments, circled around, and then finally headed down toward baggage claims, along with the train of passengers hurtling forward. She felt bad. What would happen to Polly? Would she be okay? She kept walking with the crowd, down long corridors, down escalators, up again. She felt weighed down with worry.

At baggage claim, the belt went around and around, empty, creaking. Their plane's baggage had not arrived yet. Faria had just one small red suitcase. Others had pulled trolleys up, stationed themselves in advantageous positions. Children sat on the floor reading comic books. A young mother stood with her infant, trying to rock her to sleep. Faria stood daydreaming. Then the suitcases came cascading down. Faria was lucky enough that somehow, the red suitcase was one of the first. She hauled it expertly from the belt, landed it smoothly on the floor, and headed out the door to her home, the city in which she breathed comfortably, which flowed in her veins. Once she was outside, breathing its air, it was impossible not to be happy. Oh, how wonderful to be alive. Faria walked up the curb jauntily to where the yellow cabs were waiting and called a taxi home.

How to Break an Iraqi

This was 1976 and a hot summer in Mosul, Iraq, where my brother was waiting to be born. We had just moved to Iraq from Bangladesh because my father had a teaching appointment at the university. At school, I got into trouble with a Pakistani girl Samina because I had called her *Ullu ka Pattha,* and she had threatened to have her older brothers beat me up.

All the neighborhood girls met to play with beads on the roadside by the drains near Halwa's house. We brought out our tin collections of assorted beads and flicked them into a hole we'd dug in the mud. Whoever rolled the last bead in the hole won them all. I had taken apart three of my mother's necklaces for my bead collection.

When I won the game and gathered up everyone's beads with greedy fat fingers, Halwa asked me to show her my palm. Her own hands she held behind her back. I gave her my hand and she promptly gave it a blow with a stick that had magically appeared in her palm.

"Give those over, or we won't play with you anymore," she said, smiling brightly. Her eyes shone. She

144

was rosy faced girl, with curly brown hair and dimples.

"Collect them," she ordered the other two girls.

Nuha and Sada grabbed them from my palms, pushing them into their tin boxes. Beads scattered everywhere.

I lunged for Halwa, but she caught my arm mid-air and twisted it back.

"How does this feel?" she asked.

My eyes smarted. Sada and Nuha watched open-mouthed.

"Now?" She twisted it further back. I started to cry.

"Okay, go home now, game over," she said.

Nuha and Sada giggled nervously. I looked around wildly, surprised at my own powerlessness. Then I turned and ran all the way home.

We lived in a big, two-story house in Zahur with multiple roofs, a big lawn, and a driveway canopied with grapevine and lined with pear trees. My father was busy hosing the walls of the house with my two-year-old brother Abul.

"Where is my mother?" I asked.

My father turned off the hose. "She is at the hospital, having the baby. We're getting the house ready for her."

"Yeah!" Abdul cried.

"I want her!" I stared wildly. Images of Samina's brothers mingled with Halwa's laughing face in my mind. I rushed upstairs to my room and threw myself down on the multi-colored Syrian mat, crying. I waited a long time, but my father didn't come up. He called after me weakly a few times. My brother's wails pierced the air and I could hear my father rummaging around for the milk bottle.

My mother was gone only for a week, but she seemed a long time in coming back. In the mornings, I averted my eyes from Samina's gate as I waited for the school bus. Samina lived three houses away. Next door were the Palestinians, then the Polish boys, and then an Indian couple, and then Samina's menacing steel-grey gate, visible from where I stood. On the other side of the road, I watched Nuha's baby brother playing in front of their house, her older brother directing the trucks that dumped cement on their driveway in preparation to add two new rooms on the roof of their house. The school bus pulled up, and I climbed the steps slowly. Samina occupied a front seat with her cohorts.

"There's the name caller," she pointed at me. "I've told my brother Babar about you."

I walked unsteadily past her. Samina's brothers were big. They were teenagers, too old for our school, so they stayed at home. Samina said they would pay me a visit sometime at school. I lived in fear on the playground. While everyone played tilo-express and blind man's bluff, my eyes darted around, looking for them, as I peeled my orange and buried my nose in the pungent peels.

I had called Samina *Ullu ka Pattha* without knowing what it meant. I was practicing my *Urdu*. I had been bouncing up and down on the bus seat and joking around, but when I called her that Samina's face had frozen. Later, Samina had complained to our Kurdish class teacher Mrs. Hiyam.

"What does it mean? Is it a bad word?" Mrs. Hiyam asked.

"It means Son of the Owl, Miss."

Mrs. Hiyam raised her penciled eyebrows. "She called you the son of the owl? What's so bad about that?"

Samina was furious. Her face ballooned up. "It means a big fool."

The day before my mother came home, Halwa and Nuha paid me a visit. Their rosy cheeks dimpled when I opened the gates a crack, holding onto the bolt with one hand. They peered through the gap in the gate standing outside, their faces red in the dry sun, pushing back wisps of brown hair from their hot foreheads. I stood inside the driveway under the scant shade of the pear trees and the grapevine overhead.

"What do you want?"

"I hear you have a cat?" Halwa said, licking her lips.

"Yeah." I'd been going around telling people that. The more I said it, the more I believed the lie. The air was harsh and dry. I gulped my saliva to moisten my throat.

"Where's your mother?" she asked.

"She's coming back tomorrow," I said. "And so is Nancy Apa."

"And who is she?"

"She is bigger than you, and she will help with the baby, and she will beat you up!"
I'd been cherishing my fantasies of telling all to Nancy Apa and having her take revenge on my behalf. Nancy Apa was Hamid Uncle's eldest daughter, who stayed at home because she was too old to attend our primary school. Her parents sent her as a gift to all in need of some extra help.

"So, can we see the cat?" Halwa looked eager, her eyes bright.

I stood uncertainly, guarding the gate. My father was upstairs asleep with my brother.

"I heard she is beautiful?"

"She's silver gray!" I said. "She is mine and I feed her five times a day!"

"Oh, what do you feed her?" Halwa asked sweetly.

"Peanuts and flowers and carrots. Chocolate."

"Strange cat to be eating carrots. Ha ha ha."

Nuha laughed also.

"Well, she drinks some milk too, I suppose."

"You're a liar. You don't have a cat."

"No, I am not. Anyway, you can't see her."

"Look, your father is calling. Why don't you go to him?"

"No, he's not!"

"Okay, can you get Nuha a glass of water?"

I licked my lips.

"Oh, I am so thirsty," said Nuha.

I felt bad. It was a hot day. I knew their eyes twinkled too much, that they were up to something.

"Okay, wait here, Okay. Don't come in."

I stepped away from the gate, intending to bolt it down behind me, but they slipped in behind me. I saw them eyeing the juicy fruits dangling above our driveway. "Please go get water."

I strolled across the lawn to go inside the house, when I heard a mad dash behind me and turned around.

"What are you doing?" I cried.

Halway and Nuha shook the pear trees, filled their skirts of their dresses with pears, and ran away.

My mother lay propped on pillows in a cotton gown in the drawing room downstairs, her legs spread apart, moaning in pain. My new brother was wrapped in white cloth from head-to-toe. He was a fat baby.

"The nurses said he is a *Muslawia*," announced my mother.

"What is that?"

"That means he is one of Mosul."

"Okay," I said.

I walked around the bed but couldn't get a good view of my mother. I wondered if I could climb in beside her and hide my face in her tummy. She was sobbing, telling my father that he had left her all alone in the hospital. He was raking his hair with his long fingers, crying, "But I was looking after the children!"

I waited for Nancy Apa. She was six years older than me, thirteen, I think. Hamid Uncle dropped her off that night in his Blue Volkswagen. First, she looked at the baby, then she had rice and *daal*. I waited anxiously for her to finish.

"Can we unpack your bag now?" I said. She was going to share my room with me.

"Let's finish building the cradle first," my father said. "You'll like this, it'll be exciting."

"Okay," I said, wondering how long it would take.

It took a long time to build the cradle because there were some extra pieces and some missing parts. Nancy Apa seemed really excited. She only stopped to ask me how I liked my baby brother.

"You're a big girl now," she said. "You have to take care of two baby brothers."   I smiled and blushed. The stand was up, and they were lining up the wooden slats to build the crib itself, brows drawn together in concentration. I parked myself by Nancy Apa and thought about how she was going to solve all my problems. Finally, when I was yawning and there were still many pieces on the floor, the cradle began to swing.

"Okay, we'll figure out the rest tomorrow," my father said. "You can all go to sleep." He picked up Abul, who was wandering about holding a bottle.

I took Nancy Apa's hand and pulled her all the way up the stairs.

"Can you spell balloon?" I asked her as I took the steps two at a time. "And elephant?"

When she brushed her teeth by the sink upstairs, I stood behind her, and spoke to her reflection in the dirty mirror. I didn't want to leave her alone for a minute.

"Do you know any mean girls?" I said.

"Mean girls? No." She mumbled through the gaps in her toothbrush.

"What would you do if you met a mean girl? Do you know how to fight? Can you break her teeth?" Nancy Apa rinsed her mouth and closed the tap.

"Do *you* know any mean girls?" she asked.

"Samina," I said. "She says I shouldn't have called her the Son of the Owl. I was only trying it out to see how it sounded. She says her brothers will take revenge." I pulled at Nancy Apa's bracelet and wondered how to tell her about the darker story, the one that kept me up at night. I felt that I didn't have the words to describe my dread.

But when she was in bed beside me, sprawled out on the lilywhite patterns, I said, "There is this Iraqi girl in the neighborhood who is very mean. She beats me up."

"What nerve!" said Nancy Apa. "We have to do something about that."

By the night's end, I had told her the whole story and she had listened with sympathy. She promised to help.

"Snotty little girl," she said. "We have to teach her a lesson. We'll punish her like she never imagined."

The next day, Nancy Apa dutifully made scrambled eggs for my mother and triangular nappies for the baby. She adjusted my mother's pillows and added a few more pieces to the cradle. She picked up Abul and fed him toast and boiled egg. But all the while, when our eyes met, she winked at me. The time was coming. I followed her around the house with a pounding chest, chattering at a high pitch.

Finally, when the sun was high up in the sky, my father said, "Okay girls, time for a nap."

"We'll steal downstairs quietly," Nancy Apa whispered in my ear.

I did this on most days anyway, wandering alone in the shadow of the water tank on the lawn when everyone else napped, acting out the parts of kings and queens, and jumping around to switch positions, to appreciate the drama from its myriad perspectives. But today, we had a higher purpose.

"Look, here's the plan," said Nancy Apa as we parked ourselves on the hood of the Peugeot in the driveway. "You lure her in here saying she can have the pears. Then, when she is inside, we'll close the gate and trap her."

"Whee! What fun," I said, beating my sandals on the roof of the car.

We reached up to the arch and pulled at the sweet white grapes, mouthing them by the handful. Then

Nancy Apa wiped her hands on her pink dress and said, "Okay, go!"

I had to walk around for some time, but I finally found Halwa playing hopscotch with Nuha in Nuha's driveway. The air was colorful with orange trees and clumps of roses of every color. Sprinklers wet the grass on the green lawn.

"Do you want some pears?" I said. "We have lots of ripe ones."

They both looked up expectantly, but then their eyes narrowed.

"Why are you being so nice?"

"I want to be friends."

"Friends, huh?" They looked at each other, exchanging some secret information. I had only to wait for greed to filter in. They both stood up and smoothed their dresses.

"No, only you, Halwa, because I like you so much."

"Sure," said Halwa, grinning and coming forward, as Nuha fell back with a dismayed face. "Let's go." She followed as I led the way hurriedly. I could barely keep my chest from bursting. I pushed my hair back from my eyes and began to run.

"Hurry," I called.

Once we were inside the gate, I showed Halwa the ripe pears dangling tantalizingly above us.

"You can have as many as you like!" I said.

Halwa spread out her skirt and bent down to gather the ones on the ground. I watched her closely. Her pink cheeks dimpled in an angelic smile. She brushed a loose curl from her eye and grabbed at the fallen treasures with her small plump hands, gathering them in her dress. The dress was red, with a single pink rose at the collar.

Then there was a bang as Nancy Apa swung the gates together.

I ran to Nancy Apa and together we began to draw the bolts into the ground. Halwa started with panicked eyes. It took her a moment to realize that something was wrong. She ran to us, clawing at our dresses, screaming at the top of her voice to let her out.

"Oh, no!" I said. "You can't go. You're trapped."

Nancy Apa and I began to laugh. But the laughter was pierced by such pitying wails from Halwa that I looked at her face with new wonder. Gone were the rosy dimples as tears streaked down her dirty face.

"Let me go, let me go!" she cried with terror.

"No, you are trapped!" we cried again. "We shall never let you go!"

And we shrieked with laughter. There was no teacher to admonish us, no menacing elder brothers to stop us.

"*Ullu ka Patthey!*" I shouted triumphantly.

Then there was a voice behind us.

"What are you doing?" My father stood behind us in his pajama suit. His eyebrows were bushy from sleeping. I turned to explain to him.

"She's evil. She beats me. We're teaching her a lesson."

"Let her go."

"No!" I pushed myself against the gate, throwing my whole body against it.

"Come on. This is cruel. You're frightening her."

To my disappointment, Nancy Apa began to loosen her grip on the bolts.

"No! You don't understand. We have to get her."
"She's crying," said my father. "She's frightened."
"No!"

Nancy Apa moved away. Only I stood blocking Halwa now. Halwa pulled at my hands, trying to get at the bolts. Her nails dug into the skin on the backs of my hands. For a brief moment, there was confusion as the two of us struggled, both crying. Then, with my father's voice drumming in my head, I loosened my grip and let her slip out. Halwa ran down the street, sobbing.
"You bad girl," I called after her.

We left Iraq. All the foreigners left eventually. But Iraqis like Halwa and her family did not leave. Her name was not Halwa. I don't remember what her name was. I can't even remember her face. But at the moment she had freed herself, I had caught one last look of her eyes. And I had seen such despair as I shall never forget. I can see her now, standing inside the gate of our house in Zahur, her chest ballooning underneath her red dress. There she stands, pleading with me to let her go, racked with terror. And I say to her, forgive me.

Mita

Monica landed at the Zia International airport in Dhaka wearing pink bellbottoms, looking for a husband. Life in New York had suited her just fine, the glitzy job as a management consultant, more money than she knew what to do with, clubbing in the Village, midnight runs to Jackson Heights for *singara* cravings, except for this one overwhelming hole.

As soon as Monica stepped outside the airport building, the heat and humidity hit her. Beggar children clawed at her pants, calling her Memsahib. Coolies tried to carry her bags for her. A policeman walked up with a stick and thrashed it at the man till he ran away; Monica stood uncertainly, hands on hips, waiting to be swept up by a savior. She couldn't see her mother anywhere in the swaying crowd. She was about to panic when she spotted her driver, who took her suitcases and guided her to the car, which he had parked at some distance, a retinue of naked children following behind.

"I can't believe you wore Western clothes to the airport," Monica's mother said from the back seat. She herself was dressed in a silk sari wrapped around her thin body and wound across her shoulders and head. Thick glasses covered what remained of her.

Monica did not deign to reply as she climbed in beside her mother in the back. Dust filled the interior of her mother's non-air-conditioned Volkswagen as they bumped along Airport Road, narrowly escaping head-on collision with trucks traveling at breathtaking speed. Scooters and billboards warning of AIDS–the risk of making love!–rushed at the front windshield. Monica sat as far apart from her mother as possible, holding a scarf over her nostrils as a shield against the unknown particles in the atmosphere. Dhaka greeted her full of danger but also a certain promise: she would find a man and all her problems would be solved.

Monica first met Mita at a job interview at the S– Bank. She had been applying for random positions, anything related remotely to her training in economics. She wore an off-the-shoulder blouse to the interview and crossed her legs. The main interviewers were three elderly men seated across from her, on the same side of a long heavy desk. After introducing themselves, one of the elderly men gestured at the wall behind Monica. "And this is Mita Hossain. She's a journalist at the *Daily Ittefaq*. She'll be assisting us today with the interview. Is that okay?" Monica twisted her head to see. A young woman wearing a blue cotton sari was sitting in the shadows next to the red brick wall. "Sure."

Monica didn't get the job. She felt disappointed and surprised at this unexpected defeat, she who was so used to success. There had been some cute men who worked at the bank. When she eventually started working a month later at the research division of a non-government organization in Dhaka, one of her colleagues Jarina Apa mentioned the bank interview to her.

"You know Mita Hossain?" Jarina Apa asked. "I met her at a conference on poverty alleviation, and when she heard you had joined B–, she said that you had interviewed at a private bank. She said you're lucky you didn't get the job. It's a corrupt organization, she said."

"Really?" Monica said, remembering that woman's cool expression and wondering if Mita had somehow been responsible for her not getting the job.

Monica's job at B– involved research on microcredit, the rage among NGOs in Bangladesh. She followed the frame of any man who passed her cubicle on the seventeenth floor of the building. All day she sat in the freezing academic interior of her cubicle, surrounded by econometrics papers and annual reports. Sometimes, staring forlornly out the window at the hot street below, she felt that valuable time was passing while she pored over cold numbers.

On the pavement below, a garment worker's husband cared for their two children by the drains. The family had resurrected a tent out of tattered saris to protect the children from the noxious fumes of public buses. Their makeshift home bobbed like an island on top of rubble and the steel rods of roadside construction. Sitting at her desk, she read about rickshaw pullers in the economics papers on urban migration: how they came to the capital city to make a living out of uncertain fortunes, without skills, family, or any notion about what the future held for them. But when she looked out the window, the rickshaw pullers plying their cycles on the road awed her. As Monica stared at the writhing warm city outside, she half expected her future love to climb up out of the streets of Dhaka and appear before her at her desk, at any moment.

"I want to give you some advice," Jarina Apa said, coming up behind her.

Jarina Apa was petite and round-faced, with a beauty mark on her chin; she wore starched, ironed cotton saris to the office, a different color every day, with a flower stuck in her hair bun. She was married with two children, and Monica thought how peaceful, how wonderful that was—every day, Jarina Apa went home and served her husband rice and *daal,* and slipped in bed beside him at night.

"What advice?" Monica asked, flipping her thick dark hair behind her ears.

She had grown thick with Jarina Apa. The two ate together in the office canteen and sometimes slipped out to look at the clothes at the Western clothes at Westecs, Jarina Apa for her husband and children and Monica for herself.

"You shouldn't wear these Western clothes to the office. They grab the men's attention. They think you are *fast.* There is another woman I know who dresses like you. Mita Hossain the journalist. You've met her. You should hear what people say about her!"

"I dress as I like," Monica snapped, feeling the barb at her lifestyle, determining to keep her distance from Jarina Apa. "I don't care what people say."

Only, late at night, lying alone in her bed, Monica cared very much what people thought of her, a single woman at twenty-five, in a country where ninety-nine percent of the population got married.

Monica's mother threw many dinner parties at their old house in Dhanmondi, inviting relatives, friends, even distant, long-forgotten acquaintances.

To anyone who came to the house, her mother begged, "You people, why don't you look for a husband for her? As her guardians, you have a duty toward her."

Her various relatives sidled up to her, asking, "So Monica, you don't want to get married?"

"I want to," she said. "It's not that I don't want to. But there is no one."

Having gotten Monica to return home to marry, her mother didn't seem to be doing much in the way of introductions. Her cousin Samina's husband Imran Bhai showed her the biodata of two prospective husbands, both MBAs from Dhaka University, working at his pharmaceutical company. One of them was forty years old, paunchy, balding, with a large mole on his chin, and the other was the divorced father of two children. She returned them without a word, trembling with anger, thinking the gesture an insult rather than sincere effort. Samina's husband himself was a far cry from Monica's idea of a husband. He worked in the private sector (a dirty word to all those who worked in poverty alleviation), his conversation circled around money and real estate, and every Friday he played Bingo at Dhaka club while drinking beer, to help his career, he said.

On Thursday nights, Monica retired to the diplomatic mission clubs in Gulshan with her expatriate friends, grasping at the embers of their easy friendship, offered so unconditionally. She sat back in a chair on the lawn under a hazy summer sky, grateful for the respite, closing her eyes and inhaling the smoke of joints and cigarettes in the still air.

"You're so old-fashioned, Mon," they said to her.

"Cigarette?" someone offered then laugh easily when she refused.

"Married isn't everything," one of her friends said.

"You don't understand," she said. "Every Bengali gets married. It is our vocation in life."

"Ha, Ha, Ha," her friends laughed.

"My mother was married when she was fifteen. She was so young her mother-in-law used to oil her hair and braid it for her. And after she became a widow, that's it. Her life ended, and now she wants to get me married."

"You're such an innocent, Mon. A darling."

One of her friends dropped her back at her mother's house in Dhanmondi, late at night. The house was always dark inside, and damp. The plaster on the ceiling had flaked off, exposing the painful innards of concrete and reinforcement rods. Monica tried to go straight to her room without seeing her mother.

"Where have you been so late?" her mother accused now, coming out of her bedroom in a faded sari. "This is not New York! A decent Bengali girl shouldn't stay out late. Your reputation will be tarnished and then you won't get a husband."

Monica reached her room quickly, closing the door behind her and locking it. Inside, she sat on the bed and picked up a copy of the *Daily Ittefaq*. There was an article inside by Mita Hossain, the woman who had prevented her from getting a high salary job at a private bank.

It had been her mother's letters, bemoaning Monica's single state, that had drawn Monica back home. On many nights, she had sat on the floor of her apartment in New York listening to her mother's nervous plea on the phone.

"Monica, your time is running out," her mother's plaintive voice played on the phone line like a bow over string, "I'm growing old, Monica. I will die soon. You need to marry and settle down."

"Okay. Okay."

"If you don't marry now, when will you have children? Who will take care of you and give you shelter in your old age?"

She sat in front of the hall closet, crammed in the narrow space between the front door and the kitchen sink; her roommate ran the water in the sink, humming a tune as she washed dishes. Monica's head drummed with panic. She put down the phone and closed her eyes, but her mother's voice penetrated deep inside and stayed with her for days afterward. It was that voice that drove her back. Within months, Monica found herself quitting her job, packing, catching a flight home.

Jarina Apa had told Monica that Mita was a loose woman who lived a fast life since her husband had deserted her. *She had been with men.* There were plenty of rumors about the woman and Jarina Apa never tired of gossiping about her, sitting in the office canteen, while they ate rice and buttery daal with fried vegetables. Monica's pulse had quickened listening to stories of Mita's colorful life.

Now she arched her eyebrows as she read the article by Mita Hossain. Mita Hossain wrote about sex workers, who were beaten by their clients and husbands:

every man cheated them or lied to them; they could never trust the notion of love. Monica put down the paper and thought back to her evening. Her friends had laughed about her idealistic notions of love. Her friends in New York used to arch their eyebrows in the same way about her need to find a man, her sense of incompleteness. In someone so confident, so dazzling as you, they said, this is so unexpected.

Lying in her bed, on top of the floral sheets, Monica didn't feel confident that there was love in store for her after all. Would she ever meet anyone, would she ever know the sensation of love? Monica closed her eyes and began to dread that one day she would become one of them, the single Mita Hossain or an unloved sex worker.

A month after Monica's arrival in Dhaka, her cousin Samina invited her to dinner at her small flat in Dhanmondi. Salma had news, no wait, not on the telephone, she would tell her when they met. She would send her husband Imran Bhai to get Monica. When Imran Bhai came to pick up Monica, she was fully dressed, in tight jeans and a white shirt with frill and froth at the collar, high-heeled open-toed pink sandals. She had drawn a large serpent shaped *bindi* on her forehead and painted her nails blood red. She liked to dress up.

"Hello, Dulabhai," she greeted him as she climbed into the passenger seat.

"How is my favorite sister-in-law?" Samina's husband joked with her. "Khala, my salams," he called gallantly to Monica's mother.

"So have you found your ideal Bengali man?" he teased as the car negotiated the alleys of Kalabagan.

Open garbage lay strewn about on the streets. Monica rolled up her window quickly and Imran Bhai turned on the A/C, so the smells of Dhaka could not get inside.

"No, still looking," Monica said.

"Listen, you need to protect yourself, you need a man to protect you if you want to live in Dhaka."

"What do you mean?" asked Monica, arching her eyebrows.

Samina's husband laughed before answering. He had big teeth. He was a big man; when he opened his mouth, there was a gaping hole inside.

"Well?"

"I mean that a woman is like tamarind, hanging before men's eyes. Tempting them. You know how foul minded men are? That is why in Islam we like our women to be indoors, well protected."

"Well, Dulabhai, you must find me a man then."

"I already tried, two eligible bachelors," replied Samina's husband.

Monica closed her eyes at that painful memory but did not make a reply.

"Now I can offer you something even better."

"What's that?" asked Monica, turning to face him.

"I can offer you myself, your personal protector."

"What do you mean, Dulabhai?"

"I mean, my sister-in-law, we can have a special relationship."

Still Monica did not understand. She flipped back some curls with her blood red nails and asked again, "How do you propose to protect me?"

Samina's husband stopped the car on Mirpur Road near the Bikrampur sweetmeat shop and took her chin between his thumb and forefinger.

"What kinds of sweets do you like, dear sister? I can take you for car rides sometimes. We can go to a cottage in the hill tracts, in Bandarban. It is beautiful there."

For one cracked moment, with the heaving warm street smells all around her, Monica considered this future. Was this her destiny, the best she could hope for, an illicit love affair? It was a line, a clear, thick line as thick as the glass of the window that separated her in her office tower from the rickshaw pullers and nursing mothers and naked children on the living streets below. Monica had jealously guarded herself against crossing it all these years in America.

"My sister, you must take risks in life, live dangerously," Samina's husband spoke again, softly. "What fun is life otherwise?"
Monica slapped off her brother-in-law's hand.

"You had better take me straight to my cousin," she said, "and if you dare anything like this again, I shall speak to Samina directly."

Samina met her at the door herself, pulling Monica into her perfectly assembled drawing room. Big showcases stood crammed with porcelain dolls and glass curios Imran Bhai had brought back from his foreign trips. In the past, Monica had craved these possessions, imprinting them in her mind as the symbols of conjugal happiness, wanting a drawing room and a collection of crystals for herself. Now she remembered anecdotes from her colleagues at B— about the men who worked in the private sector, how they stopped at brothels in Amsterdam or London when they went abroad on business trips. She wondered if her cousin's husband too was one of these men.

She was barely aware of what passed in the drawing room, but soon Samina put her arm around Monica and ushered her into the dining room, where the table was large, glass top with a wrought iron frame. The glass was heavy, impressive, but the room had no windows. Monica felt suffocated. Her discovery of Samina's husband's infidelity and the precariousness of her own situation entwined together and plunged her into gloom.

"If you wait for a virgin, you shall never find a man," Samina lectured to her during dinner.
Her husband sang a Bengali song, "What use is it to light that candle of beauty, if noone comes close to you? Why collect so much honey in your heart, if there is noone to collect?"
Monica ignored him. "I can't bear it any longer," she said to Samina. "It is so lonely. When shall I get married?"

"Marriage is okay," Samina said. "It's all the same whom you marry."

"I must be the only adult woman in Dhaka who is not married!"
If it was really true that ninety-nine percent of Bangladeshis got married, it was a society where a single woman had no place at all.

Samina said, "Not the only one. There is Mita Hossain. Have you heard of her? There is a growing breed of single women. There, she's your role model."
She gave a little laugh at her own witticism.

"I don't want to be some Mita," she said angrily.

She finally met Mita again at a conference on poverty monitoring. It was her first presentation of her work on credit, and Monica was arranging her slides beside the overhead projector when she saw Mita.

Immediately, Monica remembered her from that interview at the bank. She was very dark, her features were sharp, etched in coal. She wore another wrinkled cotton sari, this one pale yellow. At her side was a tall man in a ponytail. From the corner of her eye, Monica studied Mita, the fluidity, the music of her movements, the glass bangles that ran up and down her wrists.

Mita was not wearing Western clothes, as Jarina Apa had led Monica to believe. And yet, Monica could see what Jarina Apa meant. There was a certain provocation in Mita's dress, in the plunge of the blouse's neckline, the way the blouse rode up her back, exposing a smooth dark expanse of flesh. Even the disordered sari, the state of dishevelment, suggested a dangerous familiarity, a sight for no eyes but an intimate partner.

Monica was showing photographs on slides of how credit from their NGO had improved the lives of the rural poor, especially women, photographs she had taken of their projects. Jarina Apa stood next to her, passing her slides as she needed them. She finished speaking and waited for questions.

"There's your role model," whispered Jarina Apa, gesturing toward Mita and giggling.

Some journalist was asking what B— had to say about accusations that their workers had taken away the livestock of villagers who couldn't pay back loans?

"I don't know about that," Monica replied stiffly.

"These stories are all anecdotal," Jarina Apa said defensively. "Perhaps one in a million cases. In fact, I can confidently say that B— has never done such a thing."

Mita raised her hand.

"Yes?" Monica nodded toward the woman.

166

"How can you sit there and protest that what we say is wrong?" Mita asked. It was the first time Monica was hearing her voice, deep, low, like a man's. "How can you congratulate yourselves on having done so well when you don't even reach the ones who need credit most? The poorest?"

"Whom do you want us to reach?" Jarina Apa asked coldly.

Monica was glad that Jarina Apa was there to answer the questions; she would not be able to face the brazen Mita Hossain on her own.

"The sex workers, for example."

Jarina Apa gasped, as did several other men at B-. Such unseemly words out of this woman's mouth.

Jarina Apa said, "But sex workers are hardly the poorest, Mita Apa. You should get your facts straight. Those women make *a lot of* money."

In another month, summer returned, the air became hot and cloying; Dhaka became so intolerable that Monica escaped to Nepal for a short trip. Her mother had suggested she should take someone along. "Like a man?" she had shot back. "Like my cousin's husband, for example?"

It was in Nepal, at Nagarkut, that Monica saw a perfect vision of romance. She had climbed a hill to catch the sunrise over the Everest. The guide at the hotel had urged her there, saying that it was a rare morning without clouds, she would get a clear view. There, on top of the hill, breathlessly taking in the fresh cold air, she saw a couple a little distance in front of her, sitting on the grass with their legs stretched out side by side before them. They had climbed higher than Monica.

They both wore Jeans and T-shirts. The woman was blonde, her hair long and loose. She sat straight, her back arched, her hands behind her on the grass supporting her frame, her shoulders thrust into the air, her cheeks rosy from the exertion. On her face was the expression of extreme happiness. Monica wanted to be this woman. She wanted the romance that would lend her this happiness. But no, love was not in her destiny. She would have to learn how to be a strong, bitter spinster. She determined to get to know Mita, find out what was in store for a single woman in Dhaka, how a woman coped, on her own.

Back in Dhaka, Monica called Mita at her newspaper office and asked her if she would like to come along on a field trip to a Mundi village in Mymensing. She needed someone to spend time with the villagers, collect some in-depth research, she said.

"I thought, since you're a journalist, you could get your own story out of it," Monica suggested.

"Yes, I've wanted to do a story on Mundi song and dance for a long time," Mita said.

Monica couldn't believe Mita had agreed so readily. She was excited. What would it be like, getting to know this Mita? She requisitioned a car from the office and Mita met her at B–. Later she wondered if she should have asked to pick Mita up from home. That way she would have seen Mita's apartment, witnessed how a woman lived alone in Dhaka. The very thought filled her with a romance she had not thought of before. She recalled again her own flat in Manhattan, how she had once traveled alone across the world at a young age, how fearless and excited she had been.

The road to Mymensingh was short but nasty. There were craters, many bypasses and detours. When a bus passed in the opposite direction on the narrow road, the car had to move to the slumped shoulder and wait. The entire way, the two women hardly spoke. But Monica studied Mita, her pearl-like teeth, her shiny hair and glowing, bright skin. She wanted to ask the other woman so many questions: Where had she gone to school, how many did she brothers and sisters have? The simplest, most trivial questions. She felt a strong desire to know Mita.

"Look," Mita pointed at the landscape through the glass window. "Isn't this country beautiful? So exciting."

Monica looked, but all she saw was the flat, monochromatic landscape of submerged fields, endless shades of sand and mud, the only color added to the landscape by the green plants around decaying huts and the colorful clothes on the backs of passing villagers. A bare-chested farmer wearing a lungi struggled with his cow under a darkening uncertain sky. Monica felt only desolation, hopelessness. She could not see what Mita saw. She remained silent.

At the Mundi village, Mita asked the villagers many questions while Monica sat back and listened. Mita would stay behind, spend a few weeks to collect the data Monica needed.
At one point, Mita asked the villagers she was interviewing, "What is the wine that you drink?"

"Do you want some?" teased the man of the household. "We can drink tonight. We can sing and dance."

Monica kept on taking notes, her heart beating fast. A Bengali woman who drank openly! What scandal.

After Monica left, Mita stayed behind in the Mundi village. Monica had hoped that when Mita returned to Dhaka, she would come to her office with the notes, that they would meet over tea in the B– cafeteria and talk. She had imagined all these scenes, conversations. But Mita sent the package to Monica's office by courier with a note inside in childlike handwriting in English saying that she was ill with diarrhea.

It was August now, and it rained daily. A full season had passed. Monica had seen countless biodata of men passed to her by her relatives, each one more dismal than the previous one. Monica slipped out more often to the clubs in Gulshan, willingly facing the humiliation at the gates of being able to get in only as a foreign national's guest, paying the hefty cover charge, just to be near her foreign friends.

Then one day she ran into Mita at the American Club, sitting next to that man in the ponytail.

Monica went up to Mita and leaned over her. "Who is that?" she asked, pointing at the man.

"This is my brother," said Mita. Then she laughed, unwomanly guffaws. "Let's say my cousin," she supplied with a smile.

"Is he your lover?"

Mita only smiled. Monica sat down at their table.

"Tell me," she wanted to ask. "Are you happy? Is this being single thing really viable?"

"Do you want some coffee?" Mita asked.

"No, I don't drink coffee."

"What, no coffee? I have not seen you smoke, or drink, and now no coffee. What an empty life."

Monica remembered Jarina Apa gossiping about Mita's endless string of lovers.

"Who is he?" she asked again.

The man stared into the distance, a beer bottle in hand, as if he didn't hear. Perhaps he didn't hear.

"Who do you want him to be?" Mita laghed. Monica noticed that her eyes were large, her skin like coal. "Definitions are tiresome, don't you think? A woman should not be constrained by definitions. They make her uninteresting."

"Uninteresting? Do you think being married is uninteresting?" Monica asked.

Mita opened her bag, took out a packed, and extracted a cigarette, inserting it in her mouth. The man in the ponytail bent forward to strike a match close to her face, lighting it up. Mita blew smoke in the air and smiled.

"Would you like to go with me to visit a brothel?" she asked.

"No!" Monica said abruptly. She had not realized till that moment how much she feared that place. Her whole life had been an effort not to fall to such a place. Mita smiled, curving her lips.

"My mother would not approve, I think," Monica said, blushing.

Mita said, "Do you always do what is approved? By the way, I am going back to the Mundi village in Mymensingh. Do you have any reason to come also?"

"Yes, I can come," said Monica. "I am applying for PhD programs in the US, so I am collecting some data in advance."

"What, are you leaving Dhaka already? Everyone comes to Dhaka just to get some work experience, some credentials, only to flee again. One should not try to tame Dhaka, I say. One should open oneself to Dhaka, experience it."

"I did not get what I came here to get," Monica said.

This time, Monica picked up Mita at her flat. She was surprised that Mita lived in Mohammedpur, not in the relative safety of Gulshan where foreigners lived. The flat was small, but there was clay pottery everywhere, artwork on the walls, tapestry trailing down divans. There were incense sticks on the coffee table, an ashtray overflowing with half smoked cigarettes, and Jasmine flower of the morning gathered in a clay dish. Monica reclined against the sensuous cushions on the floor, waiting for Mita to get ready.

They worked hard through the day, traveling from house to house in the middle of the Madhupur forest, collecting household information that would be useful as anthropological background for Monica's research, perhaps as a feature story for Mita. They interviewed the women on the fields, the idling men in front of a teashop or on straw mats in front of the mud houses: Mita asked the questions and Monica listened, writing in her journal.

"It's a matrilineal society. Women do all the work. Interesting, no?" Mita said to her, wiping a bead of sweat from her upper lip.

"You seem to find alternative lifestyles interesting," Monica replied.
As the day wore on, she felt an affinity with her interviewees and their narrowing lives. Even while she peeked hungrily into the vibrant domesticity of their homes, she heard stories of their deepening urgency and

despair. The government was driving the Mundi people out of their homes and livelihood cultivating the forestlands to clear space for eucalyptus and rubber plantations or logging operations. The forest was thinning. Only a few monkeys and colorful birds were left on the branches of the trees. The mud huts of the Mundi were in better shape than the homes of the Bengalis, but the thinning forest meant that their habitat would be gone in a few years. Monica felt naked, exposed, just walking among the sparse trees.

In the evening, they took shelter at a B– training center that had its own hens and ducks, a small pond with fish, a kitchen that served rice and *daal* and fresh garden vegetables. At night, they were given one room with a double bed. Monica waited while Mita washed in the bathroom.

She could hardly believe it. She was going to spend a night in the same bed with this woman who was a mystery to her, whose reputation she feared, whose fate she did not want. Here was her chance to probe.

At night, Mita turned toward Monica in the dark.

"So, you said you were unhappy in Dhaka. Why did you come here?"

"I wanted to find someone," said Monica.

Mita nodded matter-of-factly. She did not laugh.

"And you? You live alone? Are you not scared?"

"No, I know the people who live downstairs from me. I have many men friends."

"And you travel all over the country, for your reporting? Are you not afraid of danger, of men?"
Mita laughed, again that loud laughter exploding in the darkness, white teeth flashing.

"Everything bad that could happen has already happened to me," she said. "Nothing to fear anymore."

Monica wanted to ask Mita about her failed marriage, about the life of endless lovers, but she hesitated too long. Mita closed her eyes and began to snore gently. Monica considered her in the faint light of the full moon outside, studying her face. Then, overtaken by a strong emotion, she turned her back to Mita, and lay facing the cold, blank wall.

When they returned to Dhaka, Monica made no further attempts to see Mita: She had seen Mita at close range and never wanted to meet her again. *Mita was a temptress.* Monica could not forget the attraction of Mita's home, the inviting, carelessly thrown cushions on the floor hinting at frequent careless *addas* over tea and smokes. But she also could not forget the smile on Mita's face as she had slept that night at the BRAC training center, the way her face shone in the narrow beam of the moonlight; there was a smile on that face, and even light, and beauty, but also the deep, clear strains of sadness in the dark. Now Monica was sure there was only sorrow in store for Mita, the lonely ending of all people who did not stay within the narrow, prescribed bounds of society. She wanted no part of this life.

Instead, Monica made one last effort to find romance. Her cousin Samina took her to a reputable soothsayer in Old Dhaka who read her palm and pronounced, "You shall find your husband within the year."

One day, Jarina Apa walked into her cubicle and whispered, "Monica, you will not believe this, there is a new recruit in the department. A very handsome young man. He is from America like yourself, returned to serve the country."

Monica found him in the canteen biting down on a spicy *singara*: fair-skinned, bespectacled, and slender. She said hi. She had found him within a month of going to the soothsayer, right in her office building, high up in her tower.

By winter, Monica was married. She had been successful in finding a husband as in everything else in life. December was the perfect season for a wedding. The weather was just right, although it was difficult to reserve a community center, owing to the flux of weddings in that season. Only Monica's foreign friends wondered if it was all in too much haste.

"No, this is the way we do things in Bangladesh," she said.

She became a typical Bengali wife. She wore *sari*s and cooked omelet and chapatti for breakfast. Her glass bangles tinkled as she walked and dusted the television set. She even stopped wearing her flared bellbottoms. When her husband asked why, she said she just felt like it. She also decided to give up her plans of pursuing a PhD.

A month after the wedding, she woke up one morning in the bedroom she shared with her husband in her in-laws' home, feeling the need for an embrace. She adjusted her husband's arm about her waist, twisting her body repeatedly to fit into the crook, but she couldn't find the shelter she desired. Finally, she gave up and curled into a ball by herself, shivering in the morning chill of December.

In the summer, two years after she had first arrived in Dhaka, Monica attended a conference on sex workers. Her interest, B—'s interest, was in the role of microcredit in the sex workers' live: could sex workers branch off to other businesses if given credit? Who would have thought B— would one day work with sex workers?

Monica found herself amidst hundreds of sex workers wearing garish garbs, with pink ribbons in their hair, not all so beautiful. Most of the women were thin, weather-beaten, aged before their time, but sometimes, she saw a flash of young woman unimaginable beauty, laughter and freedom playing on a face. Monica stopped her thoughts right there. What was she thinking? *Desire for the freedom of a sex worker?*

She was sitting far away from the sex workers, in the front rows among the representatives from various NGOs, all interested in projects for sex workers now. Then Monica caught a swirl of white moving among the sex workers and turned her head to see better. There she was, Mita Hossain, sitting so close to the women, interviewing them and laughing with them, and from time to time pulling them close to her to embrace them. Monica frowned to concentrate. She was in that term in her pregnancy when she was out of breath, choking, almost suffocating. She watched a sex worker with her back arched, laughing loudly into the back of her hand. She had a thin, heart-shaped face, a long braid tied with red ribbon; she couldn't have been older than a teenager. Something about the young girl's gesture reminded Monica of that happy woman on a hilltop in Nepal with her lover.

The woman in Nepal had been staring into the mountains as she smiled, but Monica had never thought about where the woman was looking. Now the solitary peak of Mount Everest came back to Monica as if she were seeing it through that woman's eyes. The peak beckoned with the promise of solitude. Monica realized that she had not seen the woman's lover's face at all. In fact, she didn't know if the woman's companion was really a lover. The only thing she could be sure of in her memory was the woman's own happiness.

After the conference was over, Monica stood alone outside on the verandah, waiting for her chauffer. She kept twisting her head to catch another glimpse of Mita, wondering idly how she could have traveled so far only to discover that her salvation lay in the choice that Mita had already made. Then Mita appeared at her elbow. She was wearing a rumpled, off-white sari, a jute bag hanging from her shoulder. Monica felt happy; she felt that she wanted a friend, she wanted Mita to connect her back to the person she had once been walking alone in a thinning forest in Mymensingh. Perhaps they could discuss life, marriage, become friends, meet over coffee at Aarong sometimes to laugh together.

"Are you with B–?" Mita asked her, pencil and notepad in hand. "I wanted to talk to you about your NGO's project with sex workers."

"Don't you remember me?" Monica said. "We went to Mymensingh together."

Mita smiled politely, not interested. "I just wanted to ask you a few questions about B–'s plans. What do you think the sex workers need most?"

Mita Hossain was interviewing her, hand poised over paper.

"They need economic independence," Monica parroted mechanically. "Credit plus all the other support. Health, education for their children."

"The usual then, what all your beneficiaries need? The same solution for everyone?"

Was Mita teasing her? Why couldn't Mita remember her, recognize her? Or did Mita not find her interesting anymore, her round domesticated figure? Monica's eyes teared angrily.

"No," she said, putting a hand on her belly, trying to focus and give the teasing journalist a good answer. "I would say what they need most of all is to unite, organize, and articulate their own desires."
Mita wrote in her notebook. "Okay, thank you."
She was putting the notebook away in her jute bag now, preparing to go. Monica looked toward Mita hungrily, but the great expanse of her belly kept Mita at bay. There she was, moving away, disappearing into the crowd, leaving Monica behind in her bulky, aching body, standing alone on a verandah milling with teeming, hot bodies in colorful saris.

Construction

Muna went out to the roof where the construction was
going on. The men had finished building the two
additional rooms, leaving only a small section of the roof
still open. They had already just cast the roof slabs of the
two rooms; now they were plastering the walls.
Muna cupped her fingers around her thick spectacles to
squint into the sun. "Can you keep it quiet for just one
moment?" she shouted to the men. "My sister is calling
from London. I can't hear her."

They had been at it for a month now. There used
to be only two rooms on the roof; now the floor was
being extended to a full unit. Every day, Muna and her
two children returned from school in the afternoon to
resign themselves to the constant pounding of hammers.

"At least we shall have a bigger house at the end
of all this, Ma."

"Oh! My goodness, I didn't see you." Muna said,
turning to her eleven year-old daughter Nadiya, who was
kneeling on the leftover section of the roof by the
branches of the *boroi* tree, gathering the fruit in her skirt.

Muna went back to the phone. "You won't
believe it, Apa," she said to her sister, "there is dust

everywhere and there are workers at every window. Nadim is lucky to miss all of it because he is at work all day."

Even as she complained, she counted herself lucky for the blissful banality of her life. Her sister was recently divorced with two children. Muna had lain awake many nights worrying about her sister.

"Apa, give me your flight number," she said. "And your arrival time. I will pick you up at the airport."

She put down the phone and hurried to the kitchen to thaw the chicken for her husband Nadim's dinner. He had wanted to eat chicken roast and pulau for dinner tonight. She put the chicken in the sink and told the servant girl to grind some chili. She hoped that her house would be ready before her sister arrived. She imagined that the walls would be painted and the ladders removed before her sister arrived. She would put up the new beige curtains to match the new beige color of the new living room walls. Her home would be ready to welcome her recently divorced sister, who would be broken and in need of welcome.

There was another reason to get the work completed within a week. Her son Jhontu's fifth birthday was approaching. Jhontu's birthday was always celebrated, unlike Nadiya's, because of the bitter-sweet memory of his birth. There had been a twin who did not survive. Her husband Nadim had invited his colleagues from the bank to the party. It was not just a children's party but an official party, with much at stake. Nadim was being considered for the post of vice president, perhaps even a transfer to the capital city Dhaka from the Sylhet branch.

Muna dusted the dining table and called to her children to bring their homework. She was a teacher in the same school and kept a sharp eye on her children's schooling. The children were her responsibility. Nadiya and Jhontu brought their school bags to the table. The surface was crowded with pickle bottles and books and served multiple purposes. But soon there would be many rooms in their home, space for new furniture. Nadim and Muna had been visiting furniture shops on the weekends, looking at new sofas, beds, an entertainment center. Jhontu would move into his own room, so he would need a complete bedroom set.

Jhontu picked his nose and let his slippers drop from his feet. "Ma, I actually liked the old way our home was," he said.

Muna frowned. She and Nadim did everything for the children, and yet they never seemed to be happy.

"Don't speak like that, Jhontu," she said. "Your father has worked hard to give us all we have."

"I liked it because with the roof all around, there was so much light. And I could ride my cycle on the roof, Ma." Jhontu continued.

"Stop talking now," Muna silenced him. "Read!" She felt a headache coming on. Her glasses felt heavy as usual, sweating her nose. She pulled Jhontu's English notebook toward her and started looking over his class teacher's remarks.

"Shut up, Jhontu," Nadiya said. "You're making Ma sad."

At the airport, Muna almost missed her sister because she had been expecting someone in a crisis. A body pounded out of shape, whitewash and dust in the air. But the woman who came out of the gate with two children dragging matching pink suitcases was glamorous and eye catching. Apa stood smiling shyly, scanning the crowd for Muna. Her bright pink dupatta hung rumpled around her shoulders like the crushed wings of a butterfly just released from its cocoon. Muna waved to her frantically, fighting her way through the crowd.

"Apa, you look so young. Like a little girl. Like nothing has happened to you in the years in between! You...you look like an angel with her wings cut off." She hugged her sister tightly.

"It's so good to see you," Apa said, touching Muna's cheek.

"Look how fat I've grown," Muna grimaced, pinching at the excess flesh on her arms. Apa said no, no, although she was surprised to see Muna's glasses, how long had Muna had them?

"Oh, years, since Jhontu was born!" said Muna. "So you think I look worse? Because of the glasses?"

Nadim had sent the minivan from his office, so they could all fit in one car, with the suitcases. Muna was lucky that her husband's office provided everything. Soon, if he was promoted, if they could throw a good party on Jhontu's birthday, they would have even more amenities from the office.

Muna sat next to her sister in the minivan, pointing out her home as they approached. Apa rolled down the window to take in the view. Apa had not seen the house before because when Muna got married, Apa was already living in London. They pulled up inside the gates in front of the house. The men had finished working inside, now they were on rope ladders painting the outer walls of the two new rooms.

"Muna, you have a beautiful home," Apa said. "You are a very happy woman."

Muna looked with her sister. Indeed, the house was pretty: a two-story red brick building with trees all around, mango trees, lychee, coconut palm, and *boroi* tree.

"Wow, it's got a flat roof!" her niece cried. "We don't have flat roofs in London."

"It was bigger before," Jhontu said. "You could play football on the roof."

Apa was saying something. Muna strained to hear her above the clamor of the children.

"Stop, Jhontu!" she said. Then she laughed to her sister. "The boy talks too much."

Her in-laws lived on the first floor. Muna and Apa paid their respects there first.

The housed belonged to Muna's in-law. When they passed away, Nadim and Muna would inherit the whole house.

Muna's mother-in-law said to Apa, "Nadim comes home very late. He just works and works so his family can have everything they need."

"I'm sure he's a very good husband. My sister is very happy," Apa said quietly.

As they walked up the stairs, with the two pairs of children in train, Muna whispered to her sister, "My in-laws are paying for the construction. We could never have afforded it."

"You're so lucky," her sister said. "They're very nice."

But as soon as they reached the second floor, the walls reverberated with the sounds of construction.

183

"See what we have to put up with every day?" Muna laughed. "They should be done by now, but they've asked for one more day. Nadim is the lucky one. He doesn't have to face any of the commotion. By the time he's back, the workers have gone, and I have cleaned up the dust for the day. He comes home to absolute peace and quiet!" Then she added quickly, "Not that he has an easy day. He's tired from the office. But I just wish we could share our experience with him just one day!"

"Isn't it Jhontu's birthday tomorrow?" Apa asked. "May I help?"

"No, no, you just rest, Apa. And tell me about your sadness."

In the afternoon, Apa slept in the newly constructed guest bedroom. The four children busied themselves blowing up birthday balloons in the new living room with the new sofa and carpeting, Muna settled down on the floor of the kitchen with the servant girl and plucked the chicken, cut the beef into small pieces, washed the long grains of Basmati rice. She wanted the party to be perfect.

As she mixed the marinade of ground spices the servant girl had made, her hands deep in the mess of blood and raw meat, the hot spices penetrated a cut on her thumb. The gas flame whistled and lit up the walls, and she realized that she felt happiest in the kitchen where she was completely alone. She hoped that her sister too would be able to hear the happy hum of her home and be calmed by it. After an hour of this, she carried a jug of drinking water to the roof for the workers.

"Are you done yet?" she asked the men, setting down the jug and a glass. "You better clean up after yourselves," she said, pointing at the paint rollers and the ladder.

There were three of them, one a bit older than the other two. "We don't want to hurry too much," the older man said, wiping sweat from his brow, and coming to pour himself a drink with trembling hands. "If we don't do it right, and there's a defect, it'd be hard to trace later."

Muna lingered for a moment, watching them; realizing that the house was much darker than when it had been exposed to the sunlight from the roof. Jhontu kept saying that he felt like it was a jail now. Muna didn't let her thoughts continue. Instead she went into the living room to watch the children, and to admire her new living room with its rust brocade sofas and plush silk beige curtains, the new ornate lamps with flecks of cut glass, and showcases full of Nadim's achievement awards at work.

"Ma, do you want to blow up balloons with us?" Jhontu ran up to her and pulled her hand.

"No, I have work to do in the kitchen," she said. She freed her hand.

Jhontu's mouth twisted and he started to cry. "Don't you understand I am doing all this for your birthday?" she said, as she pushed him away and left. His sister and cousins tried to console him, taking him in their laps and kissing him. She felt that she could never please him, even when she did everything for him.

Later in the afternoon, the men finally stopped work and went home. Muna went to see her sister in the newly built guest bedroom. She found Apa lying open-mouthed on her back, her arms flung on either side. She was struck by the expression of contentment on on Apa's face. Had Apa found peace at last then, after the messy divorce? Her sister stirred as she stood watching.

"Ah, Apa you sleep so peacefully. If only I could sleep like that," Muna said, sitting down on the edge of the bed. "Tell me, Apa," she pressed, "Are you terribly unhappy? I haven't spoken to you at all. I feel so guilty."

"No," Apa said, sitting up. "I feel bad I'm not helping you. I am so impressed by you, Muna. You're so mature I can hardly recognize my baby sister."

"I was remembering her myself!" Muna laughed. "Your coming is reminding me of all these things that I had forgotten."

When they were children, Muna used to be the baby of the family, the spoiled one, demanding to have what she wanted immediately. She wanted to do everything Apa did.

"The rages you could fly into, your pigtails flying in the air!" Apa laughed.

Muna protested. "But I have learned to sacrifice since then. All the years that Nadim and I struggled. Can you believe, we started life on Nadim's meager salary from his starting position at the bank, and the two rooms that Nadim's parents gave us on the roof? It was difficult...but everything is good now."

"Your home is beautiful. This new room passes the test. I was able to get a good, restful nap."

"What are you reading?" Muna asked, noticing a book beside Apa, on the bed.

"Oh, just a novel. I've taken to reading again since...recently."

Muna picked it up, taking off her glasses to read the title. She hadn't read a novel in a long time. She was remembering how she and Apa used to have their hair oiled and looped into pigtails in the evening while they sat by the dim light of the kerosene lamp, reading at the table. Or they would lie on their arms side by side in bed, kicking each other, reading aloud romantic passages from their novels and giggling; the trees rustling their leaves outside the window.

"It's a new novel just came out in London," Apa said.

"Is it good?" Muna asked.

"Yes!"

"Oh! I want to read it too. Apa, do you remember all the books we had? That heavy trunk in Biswanath that held all our Shankar novels, and the entire collection of Ashutosh Mukhopadhyay?"

"Oh, yes. I wonder what happened to those books?"

She touched the sea green cover of Apa's book and remembered the last novel she had been reading. She had been trying to read it for years, each time beginning again where she had given up. Then a few months ago, Nadim had lent it to Rashed, his his best friend from college, and she never got it back.

Nadim called in the evening. "Are the workers gone yet?" he asked.

"Yes, they left a while back. Nothing to fear. You can come back now," Muna joked.

"Are the pots on the stove yet?" he asked. "Better be an amazing feast. Your best work. All the big bosses will be there, you know."

"Okay," she laughed, wiping her spice-stained hand on her kameez and imagining the perfect dinner she would have ready for him. She was proud of the parties she threw and the expensive dishes she cooked. No other housewife in Sylhet could throw a party like her.

"What's Apa doing?" Nadim asked.

"Reading," she said. "Listen, can you tell Rashed to return my Shankar novel if he's done with it? I hadn't finished reading it when he borrowed it."

"What? Calm down. Why this sudden interest to read novels? You should have your hands full with your sister here."

"Just do as I say," she said, suddenly bitter. "I have to go now. Can you pick up the cake on your way home?"

When Nadim returned at eight, the house was quiet and orderly. The hammers had fallen silent. Before they left, the men had cleared out the poking ends of paint cans and paint peelers. Then Muna had closed the door to the roof, and it was very dark inside.

"Please, can you go get the cake yourself?" he said. "I'm sorry, I was too tired to stop. It was a busy day at work. I've kept the car and the driver, so it should be no problem for you."

"Sure," said Muna. "That way, I can take Apa to see the town as well. We'll leave right away before the shop closes."

On the way to the confectionery, her sister said, "So your mother-in-law is not as bad as Mother had thought? She is building you an entire house."

"Yes, they want to leave us both the floors when they die. They have grown very sentimental in their old age," Muna said, adjusting her glasses. She needed to get them checked. They were blurry and slid down her nose.

"To the Happy Confectionery, where we ordered Jhontu's cake," she directed the driver.

She settled back in her seat as the white Toyota twisted through the winding streets. She didn't feel like repeating the truths that only her dead parents had witnessed. Muna had lain half-dead after the birth of Jhontu and the death of the twin, and her mother-in-law had turned her back on her. She never even came up to see Muna.

"One shouldn't speak badly of the old," she said, remembering her own parents, both of whom had died away from her in a remote village in Sylhet. In both cases, she had found out only afterwards, and she couldn't leave immediately to see them because of Nadim's work. At least she had been able to attend their burial, unlike Apa, who had been trapped overseas in a failing marriage.

"So tell me about Nadim," Apa said. "Is he very nice?"

"Men!" said Muna. Then she laughed. "I'm only joking."

"Only one thing hurts me," she said after a moment. "That we were classmates, you know. And now he is so successful, but I'm not doing anything. I didn't even finish my degree. All our other classmates, the women I mean, are somebody, you know. I wish I could go back in time and finish that degree. I feel ashamed sometimes to be the useless wife who just decorates the drawing room."

"Nonsense," said Apa. "You work so hard. You do everything for the children. I've seen you running after them."

"I didn't mean that either," Muna said. "I truly am happy, Apa."

Nadim ate an early meal, his favorite curry of fish head with daal that he had requested from work. He often called three or four times from work, to have his lunch delivered or order dinner, and Muna laughed at him. He excused himself and went to bed, shutting the door behind him.

"He's tired," Muna explained to Apa as she set the dining table again for the rest of the family. "He overworks himself."

Jhontu appeared. "I want to tell Baba that I hate the new house," he said.

"No, don't disturb your father!" said Muna, pushing him away from the door that Nadim had just closed. "Selfish boy! I have explained to you, Jhontu, we sacrificed everything to make this a happy home for you."

Jhontu ran away, bare legs flying. Muna turned to Apa.

"We had to struggle so much, Apa. Nadim would be at work till late at night and I would be alone at home. There were days we were so overworked we couldn't even exchange two words. How can this boy not be happy? How can he not feel our sacrifices?"

"He's only a boy," Apa said.

Muna told Apa to rest while she cleaned up. She helped the servant girl to wash the aluminum pots. When she hung them up on the wall, they sparkled with her reflection and made her feel happy. The children had made their beds in the living room and she could hear them shrieking with laughter. Something bothered Muna. She had forgotten to ask Nadim if he had asked Rashed to return the book. She had started reading the novel just before she met Nadim at Chittagong University, and once their romance had started, she'd never finished it. Where was the time in a busy life? Or perhaps she didn't read anymore because her eyes had gone bad after Jhontu's birth? As she worked in the kitchen, her mind kept wandering back to the novel. What was the title? She couldn't remember. She used to read it sitting under a *boroi* tree on the Chitagong University campus. She used to think that she would lend it to Nadim once she finished reading it.

When she came out of the kitchen, she found Apa snoring lightly in her bed and the rest of the children deep in sleep as well. She slipped into the master bedroom where Nadim was on the phone with his best friend Rashed. They had a habit of talking on the phone every night before falling asleep, to catch up about their days and their work.

"Who is it? Is it Rashed?" Muna asked.

"Mmm-hmm."

"Did you ask him about the book?"

Nadim laughed. "Hey, Muna has gone crazy about her novel. Bring it over tomorrow, if you remember." He turned to Muna, "He asks what the title is."

"I don't remember," said Muna.

"What, you don't remember? How is he supposed to find it then?" Nadim made an exasperated gesture.

He was reclining against the bedpost, his pale feet stretched out in front of him. Muna laid her head on the pillow, took off her glasses, and placed them on the night table, closing her eyes. She knew the conversation would last hours.

Some nights, she tried to interrupt with a cup of hot tea, hoping to distract Nadim. He drank the tea and continued to speak on the phone! But tonight, she felt impatient. There were so many decisions to be made about the party. How would they get the extra chairs, the plates? She waited for the conversation to end.

As she waited, she remembered the early days of their marriage, when they lived in one room on the roof of his parents' house. Nadim couldn't get enough of her.

In the winter, they would kneel by the far section of the roof, where Nadiya spent so much time now, feeding each other ripe fruit from the *boroi* tree, searching for that perfect taste between sweetness and sourness. When it rained, they would rush out to the roof to rescue the clothes drying on lines and get entangled in the bundles, laughing. On moonlit nights, they sat in silence on the roof, side by side on bamboo chairs; he stared into her face for hours. He would even sing to her.

"I am the night, you are the moon," he would sing.

In the morning, Muna's glasses shattered to the floor. Nadim was standing on top of the night table, trying to get down his CDs from the almirah for the party and he'd knocked them over.

"I'm sorry," he said.

"It's okay." She picked up the pieces and saw at once that one lens had shattered. They had been the old-fashioned kind, real glass lenses.

She called the servant girl to sweep the floor.

"It's Friday. The shops are closed. You can't even get new ones," he said.

"It's alright," she said. "My eyes aren't that bad. I can see without them."

All morning, she fried pakoras and chicken roast in the kitchen, letting the spit of oil and spices hit her hands, her face, her hair. The pan hissed and the gas line rumbled. The noises of the kitchen lulled her. Every now and then, Nadim would walk in and pace about, worried about the weather, her cooking, and the lateness of the chair deliverers. She calmed him, warning him to stand at the door, away from the mess of the kitchen, so he would not get spurted. "Ma!" the children cried, running up to her with burst balloons or decisions about tidying up their now separate rooms. She served breakfast and lunch to everyone, making sure to make Nadim's khichuri because he always liked khichuri on rainy days, and the skies looked overcast today. The house creaked and the windows waited for the coming winds.

"May I help?" Apa asked repeatedly, appearing at the door.

"No," she said, pushing Apa out. "I don't want you to see the dirt of my home!"

She had not been wrong that she could still see without her glasses. Her near vision was still good. As she busied herself in the kitchen, the things in her home appeared as a mixture of blur and clarity. The smashed glasses had broken her confidence; this one last thing crowded her head. It had started to pounded like hammers again.

"Ei," she called to the young girl who worked with her. "Can you get me some aspirin from that shelf?"

As she worked, she daydreamed about conversations with Nadim. She often made up conversations as she did housework.

"Do you ever think about our other little one?" she'd ask him. "The one we named Farhan for happiness before we buried him?"

"No," he'd answer.

"Well, I do sometimes," she would say. "I wonder if we fool ourselves. If we've built up too many lies around the pain, telling ourselves it was for the best. That all we have now makes up for it?" Sometimes she felt that she carried a heavier burden than Nadim, that everything affected her more. Now she felt pain all over. The servant girl penetrated her reverie with a bowl of freshly ground onions.

As the day progressed, her heart began to beat faster. Nadim went around arranging the hired chairs, and Apa tidied the drawing room, although each of them needed her help repeatedly. Nervousness set in. Try as she might, she could not lift the dense fog of grease and despair that sat heavily on her shoulders. She had to use all her resolve of cheerfulness to push herself through the last few hours. What was bothering her?

Rashed was the first to arrive, bearing a large present in gold wrapping paper for Jhontu.
"Hey, Muna!" he called to her. "Nice home you've got yourself."

He was swearing a shocking peacock blue suit with a pretty wife by his side, ten years their junior. He had married much later than Nadim. Husband and wife stood in the middle of Muna's drawing room, like immaculate models.

"You look better suited to it!" Muna joked.

Rashed's wife was a doctor. Apa had wanted to be a doctor, but their parents had married her off at nineteen to a man in England who had promised that Apa could continue her education. He hadn't kept his promise. Whenever Muna saw Rashed's wife, she remembered this about Apa, like a stab through her heart.

"It really is beautiful," Rashed's wife said. She held a tiny sequined purse in her hands, matching her pale silk sari. Her long face was perfectly made up, with shiny sparkles on her eyelids.

"Thank you, dear. You look beautiful."

Muna couldn't see very well. This bothered her now that the house was ready at last, and she could have enjoyed admiring it with her guests. Even without her glasses, Muna knew that beside the beautiful Mrs. Rashed she looked hideous in her hastily thrown on sari. Her chest had settled in a deep depression that she had not allowed in a long time. What was happening to her? She felt anxious and resentful. She was looking for something but could not recollect what.

"Did you bring the book?" she asked Rashed.

"Muna!" Nadim cried, surprised. "What childishness." He extended a hand toward Apa, who had just come in, in a Jamdani sari that reflected everything like the blue-green surface of a river. "This is my sister-in-law. Apa, Rashed is our classmate. And this is his wife Sheuli, she is a lady doctor."

Muna sat down shakily on the sofa, sinking into the folds. Apa sat down beside her. Muna gestured to the servant girl to call her in-laws upstairs. She told herself that she should take pride in how beautiful her loved ones looked—her husband, her sister, and the children.

She had gotten used to her own looks and all the little disappointments of life, but recently she had begun to have memories again, such beautiful memories. The *boroi* tree, which she had ceased to notice, she remembered again now. When she had first seen it, when she had moved into this house as a new bride, she had thought she would sit under it every day and read. She kept meaning to bring her library from Biswanath but she never got around to it, until her parents' death, and then it seemed useless to plot such idle pleasures, so she had given all their books away. She didn't know how that Shankar novel had remained. Perhaps because she hadn't finished reading it. Nadim was right, it was silly that she couldn't remember its name. There it was, in the shadows, taunting her. Her mother-in-law entered holding onto her father-in-law, leaning on a cane. He was weak from diabetes, steadily declining.

The bell rang again. The Vice President entered bearing presents for each member of the family. Nadim paraded the children in front of his boss, telling them to kneel down to touch his boss' feet for his blessings.

"Sir, do you want a Coke? Muna, quickly get Sir a Coke."

Muna hurried to the kitchen to get a tray of glasses filled with Coca Cola.

When she returned, the drawing room was full. She sank into the sofa again.

Rashed turned to her and said in a loud voice, "So Muna, you have a lot of time to read nowadays, it seems? A rich man's wife has a lot of leisure time, yes? Especially one that doesn't work!"

There was laughter. That was the way Rashed spoke: he had been a joker in college. He teased so much that he

196

offended all his friends. When he had first heard about Nadim and Muna, he had parodied a nursery rhyme: "Hey Cat, *chi chi*, what have you done? After waiting all day, you have caught such a small fish?" But Nadim always said, how could a joke rock you if the foundation was solid?

"She *does* work," Apa said quietly beside her, "she is a schoolteacher."
Muna turned to her, surprised to hear her sister speak up. Apa had been timid as a girl, too afraid to be alone in a room by herself. How far Apa had traveled from that past. How far they had both traveled from their childhood, where it was impossible to return.

"Oh, yes, I had forgotten," said Rashed. "Still, I would rather be a rich man's wife or a schoolteacher than have to toil away at work all day. What do you say, Nadim?"

Nadim smiled. Others laughed.

"Ah, Sheuli," said Muna's mother-in-law, who couldn't follow the conversation. "We are so proud of you for being a lady doctor. Our Muna never finished her degree. We told her to, so many times. I offered to look after the children. But no."

Muna heard a sound from the kitchen and worried if the servant girl had dropped the cake. She stood up and slipped out again to set the food on the new dining table. Her hands were shaking now.

The children vied for space around the dining table. They would really have to buy a new, larger table soon. The birthday cake had been placed at the center with the words 'Happy Birthday Jhontu' sprawled across the dark chocolate. The icing had melted a little so that the lettering was blotched, the greeting uncertain. Nadim had placed the Vice President by the cake, between Jhontu and himself. Muna made her in-laws stand on the other side of Nadim.

Apa pushed Muna to the front. "You go stand by Jhontu. I'll take pictures."

After the singing and candle blowing, which passed in a blur, Muna cut the cake repeatedly, crisscrossing to make perfect cubes, dishing out the portions on quarter plates.

"Are you alright?" Apa asked. "You don't look well."

"Muna, seconds please," said Rashed, shoving his plate under her face and grinning. "Looking for a fight still?"

Muna looked around the room and saw her husband and his colleagues, milling around the table, exchanging pleasantries. She saw the children carrying their quarter plates to the guest bedroom. She held a piece of cake on her knife, but something held her from lowering it onto Rashed's plate. Rashed had taken too much from her already.

"Give me back my book," she hissed.

"What's wrong?" he asked, concerned, in a low voice, leaning into her and placing a hand on her shoulder. Surely, he knew where she wanted to return? Surely, he remembered the trees and grass of Chittagong University, the woman that was Muna before they all became adults, bankers and wives, mothers and fathers, living in houses so enormous that their upkeep was suffocating? There had been a boroi tree on campus, and she wanted to sit under it and finish her novel. She knew him well enough to quarrel with him.

"Muna! What's going on here?" Nadim asked loudly. "What are you quarreling about?"

198

Then all the clatter and chatter in the room seemed to fade, even the shouting of the children who had carried away their cake to other rooms. Everything fell silent after the months of constant hammering. It was so quiet that Muna was surprised to hear the clear sounds of her own heartbeat, beating so loudly that even the children hurried back into the room.

Jhontu ran up to her. "Ma, what is it, Ma?" he said, pulling at her arm. He shoved his plate in front of her. "Ma, can I have another piece of cake? Ma? All the other kids agree with me, that it's no fun without a roof because we can't play football on the roof." His nagging voice, going on and on and on, pulled her down to the edges of her sanity, pulling up all forgotten memories to the fore.

"Here!" cried Muna, shoving the slice she held at Jhontu's head.

The cake smeared his forehead, and the knife she'd held it on grazed his cheek, drawing blood. Jhontu looked like a broken toy. He started to cry and tried to climb into her arms. She thrashed at him to get him away. Apa and the servant girl were pulling him away. Globs of chocolate and cream dropped from him. There was cake splattered on the floor. Nadiya knelt to gather the pieces of shattered cake in her skirt. Rashed wiped his blue trouser leg of sprays of icing, his wife bringing a tissue to help him. Nadim gripped Muna's shoulders to restrain her. Apa was trying to ease Nadim's hands away.

Her mother-in-law was saying, "Muna! Muna, have you gone mad?"

"Please take her away," Nadim said to Apa and the servant girl.

"Khala, come away with us," whispered the young girl.

Nadiya and Jhontu and her niece and nephew and her in-laws stared at her with their mouths open. Someone coughed. Apa led Muna out of the room.

Muna woke up several times in the night. She lay in bed alone listening to the yawning trees. Apa had taken her to the master bedroom and helped her to bed. Nadim did not sleep there that night. When Nadim had released her, her eyes fell on his wrists which ended in bony knobs. Nadim had once been very thin. He used to always look hungry. His stomach growled. She used to think his hunger very funny—this insatiable hole in his stomach. Back then, they used to say that all they needed to be happy was a solid foundation under their feet and a roof over their heads. The sky exploded; the rain, released from the clouds at last, drummed on the windows. She pulled the covers over her head and went to sleep.

In the morning, Muna heard the gates below closing behind Nadim's office car as he left the house. He did not come in to say good-bye. When she tried to rise, Apa entered the room and pushed her back down on the bed.

"Get some rest. You need it," she said. Then she left.

Muna lay in bed and cried, feeling helpless without her glasses. She had hoped that Nadim would have them on her table, fixed, when she woke up. After a long time, when the sun penetrated through the window and made the sheets hot and damp, Apa pushed open the door and came in again, smiling.

"Look what I have for you," Apa said, and placed a pair of chocolate glasses on the bridge of her nose. "I took a rickshaw to your optician." She laughed girlishly and pinched Muna's cheek. Muna reached up and held Apa's hand there.

"Apa," Muna said. "Sometimes I miss our parents so much."

Apa nodded. Muna sat up. The room greeted her with painful clarity. Every speck of dust shouted stridently for her attention. Even the sight of Nadim's forsaken nightgown crumpled on the back of a chair was painful. Muna stood up unsteadily and walked out of the bedroom, leaving Apa behind. She walked away from the children's chattering voices in the drawing room, out to the roof, now just a balcony, where she had locked up with the hidden tools of the construction workers. She let herself out onto the balcony and stood there for a long time, touching her face to the cold metal bars, staring out at the *boroi* tree which still stood, but would eventually have to be cut down to save the building structure.

Standing there, she took in the beautiful view of the house, the garden with its tall mature fruit trees, and the neighborhood beyond. She saw, as others saw her, how lucky she was, to own a house already, to be a senior banker's wife, to live the life that they had built together. Then the rain began to fall again and broke up her view.

Funny-Looking People

Masudul Huq pulled himself away from his blurred reflection in the window of the office meeting room and tried to understand what his colleagues were talking about.

"Look at those October leaves!" someone cried.

"They seem to be bursting through the glass," someone else said.

For some minutes, they all sat admiring the red, orange, and purple leaves, commented on their good cheer, a rare explosion of fall color in Houston.

"What are those trees? Maple?" Masudul Huq realized that after three years in the same city he did not even know what kind of trees stood outside the company building. The only October he carried in his heart was that of the soft green paddy bobbing in the receding water of the monsoon rains in Dhaka.
Now his colleagues were talking about something else. Masudul Huq couldn't latch his mind onto the conversation. Absent-mindedly, he pushed his chair back out of the circle, tilting it on its hind legs. He understood products, strength tests, the projects of the research division of the firm, but he always faded out when his

colleagues talked about other things, like baseball, the Houston Rockets, or swim lessons for the kids. They were talking about the kids again, Halloween, laughing about what costumes their kids were buying at Target or Toys R Us.

"What about you, Huq? What are your–you have two children, no? What are they dressing up as?" asked his supervisor Richard, head of the research division in toys.

"We don't celebrate Halloween, Richard," he answered. "My children don't even know what it is." He bent his head to flick a foreign object off his trousers. "You must, Huq." Several voices at once. "My kids just have a blast. It's the most innocent and fun memory of childhood I have!"

Masudul Huq waited for the focus to drift elsewhere. Smiling, he sat and removed himself mentally from the conversation. It had never been easy for him to socialize with Americans, but he had found the prospect especially difficult since he returned to Houston in the fall with his family and started the new job. He had made up his mind to settle in the US for a better future, brought his wife and children over, and the company had promised to sponsor him for immigration. All his plans were being realized. Yet, everything seemed unbearable to him suddenly.

Masudul Huq thought that his wife was the troublemaker. He had rented a house in West University before bringing her to Houston. He had settled his family comfortably in the large house. But there was something about his wife in this new climate that unsettled him.

"*Jaan*," she would say, munching rice crisps noisily on the sofa, calling him using an endearment, when he tried to speak to her about the things that troubled him. "You are getting too philosophical. I can't understand what you're saying!"

A well-meaning Bangladeshi family who had lived in Houston for twenty years had rented the house below price to him at six hundred dollars a month. They had also donated the floral blue sofa. He had accepted both gratefully because as a foreign worker he was underpaid by his company. But he never felt comfortable in the house.

His wife took their three-year-old daughter Meenu and two-year-old daughter Ritu walking around the neighborhood, bowing her head in greeting to all the white neighbors that passed. The other houses on the street were mansions with innumerable rooms, and towering columns; gaslight burned at the front entrance. Peering out from the half-lifted blinds of his bedroom window, he spied her trying to strike up a conversation in her halting English. He scolded her immediately when she came back, telling her that these people were prejudiced.

"Do you know what they think of us and our children?" he said to her as she plopped down on the charity sofa, irritatingly happy. "They think we are dirt, the color of mud."

"Oh, *Jaan*, the kids are so cute! So fair and big. And the dogs! Meenu and Ritu really took to the dog."

"Fatma!" he said. "Don't you know dogs are dirty in our religion?"

But she didn't know, she didn't seem to see anything he saw.

Since he had decided to settle in America, the complexities of their lives had been taken away. They had been transformed flat by some mathematical function. He remembered their house in Dhaka, with the scents of the jasmine and the night queen flowers, the cotton saris his wife wore in different colors, bright blue or bottle green, the checked blouses with raised colors and puffed sleeves, her oxidized metal jewelry. His barefoot children mixed green mango with chili and salt and smacked their lips. Masudul Huq felt that all these textures and subtleties of their lives were gone now. All he could taste was the bitter disappointment of seeing his family and himself through the eyes of America.

In this new climate, his children looked brown, scrawny, and undersized compared to the other children; his wife wore ugly chiffon or nylon saris which did not need ironing. They were boxed into the ugliest house on the road, in one of the richest roads in Houston. The grass was overgrown in their yard, but he didn't even own a lawnmower.

All four of them slept in the same room, on the single king-size mattress that someone had given them, as if too shy to venture out of the one room they had made their own. Not that there was any want of space in that house. There were four rooms, which stood empty like gaping holes, devoid of furniture. They used one of the rooms to hang their wash on clotheslines he had put up by hammering nails into the wall, Ritu's cloth diapers. He knew this was not a thing done in America, neither the cloth diapers nor the clotheslines. All of their secrets, the clothesline, the donated sofa, and their second-hand stained mattresses laid out on the floor of the other room, separated them from the world, filling him with both a sense of enclosure and a sense of shame.

Masudul Huq's loneliness had driven him home every summer while he had been a graduate student at the University of Houston. Year round, he longed for the sounds and smells of Dhaka, like the smoked pancakes called *pitha* at the roadside *paan* joints, the smell of drains, even old car exhaust releasing half-combusted fuels, that would remind him of himself and his angularities. He had gone back to visit three times in his three years as a graduate student, impregnating his wife every time, but only two children had survived. The third, the son, was born dead five months early and had to be buried in Azimpur graveyard in Dhaka, where the graves were turned every few years, so it was certain they would never be able to visit his again. Masudul Huq often thought of his dead son as the part of himself he'd left behind, that he'd been unable to carry with him to America.

"Surprise!" his supervisor Richard cried. "I have candy for you grown up kids." He plopped bags of Kit Kat in red wrappers on the table, a scattering of mini Milky Way fun size snacks and M&Ms.

The table filled up like a candy store. His colleagues were laughing, reaching across, prizing apart the wrappers and biting lazily.

"Hey, Huq, have some!" Richard gestured to him.

"I do not eat candy, Richard," he said. "I am no longer a child."

The chewing sounds made his hands itch. The wrappers promised the satisfaction of all his childhood sweet fantasies. He absent-mindedly jangled his thigh to close out the thought of how happy his own children would be at the sight of the offerings before him. But they contained gelatin. Masudul Huq had grown confident over the years about refusing things, even adopted a philosophy about it.

"You have to stand up for your identity," he would tell his Halaqa party, the congregation of friends who met to discuss how to raise their children with their values. "You have to assert it, even create it, because otherwise it will get completely trampled by the foreign culture."

When he was a student, he had learned to say at dinner parties thrown by his professors, "No champagne for me, thank you. I do not drink, Sir." At the office now, he declined Oreo cookies, explaining that they contained pig's lard. At the Halaqa meetings, he advised others that their children should attend Sunday school to feel the presence of a strong community, as well as learn about their heritage and their religion, because without that reflection of themselves in those around them they would be lost souls. They would always feel abnormal. He had a favorite story about how there were no mirrors in his house, not even in the bathroom, and so he always felt as if they were living in the darkness, unable to see their own reflections.

His Halaqa party had created a tradition of making their holiday Eid just as attractive as Christmas to the kids. Several families would get together and draw lots to buy gifts for the children and would set them around a tree at an Eid party, and the kids would each receive a gift, just as they would at Christmas. The boys could play basketball at the mosque, the girls have their own meetings about incorporating the head dress in fashion.

But his wife got in the way. Just two weeks after she arrived, she wanted to order pizza, and when it came it was pepperoni.

"Fatma," he said gently, "Pepperoni is pork, my dear."

"Oh," she said. She put her hands up to her small, heart shaped face, gaping in surprise, then fussed with the open box with fluttering hands. "Oh. Could we just pick off the pieces then?" she begged. "How can we let all this food go to waste?"

She walked the three-year-old and the two-year-old to the upscale Barnes & Noble on Holcombe road to spend hours browsing books in their children's section. They loved it. One day, she came back with a book that had the picture of a pig on it. She showed it to him, making bright eyes like his children and cupping her cheeks as he looked through.

"Fatma," he said, "There's a pig on the cover!"

"Oh!" she cried, her eyes wide. "I didn't notice, *Jaan.*"

The two daughters were already grabbing the book from him, turning the pages lying side by side on the sagging hardwood floor.

"But they don't seem to know the difference," his wife continued. "Oh, that is funny, *Jaan.* Isn't that funny that I did that, *Jaan?*"

Masudul Huq did not think that it was funny. He also hated being called by an endearment whenever there was trouble, because she did it deliberately to take away the gravity of the situation.

"Do you want your children to celebrate Christmas next?" he shouted, rising from the sofa.

He had never before shouted in his life. Fatma opened her mouth slightly, but she did not seem particularly affected. He was surprised at himself. He brushed past his startled children and out of the dark house.

That evening, he walked for a long time under the tall oak trees, remembering how tender he had felt toward Fatma when they were first married. Fatma's relatives and Fatma herself always said that there was no gentler husband than he. Although it was an upscale neighborhood, the sidewalk was uneven, broken by the roots of old trees, and there were few streetlights. Soon, he couldn't see his own hands in the dark. He started to cry, Fatma, Fatma! "If only you knew what dangers we face!" He whispered into the moist leaf-laden air. If only he could explain to her.

When he returned, Meenu and Ritu were in bed sleeping. He grabbed Fatma and shoved her tightly against his chest. She started to sob, and they both knew for whom they cried. Masudul Huq had never even seen his son, for whom his heart broke every night.

At night, he nuzzled her neck, lying low on the floor on the faintly smelly mattresses. Lying like that, he told her stories of the Bengalis who had gone awry, the wives who drank and smoked and the husbands who had affairs or left their wives for other women, imitating the lifestyles of America.

"We have to be very careful, Fatma," he said. "or our children could slide all the way down. We all have the human temptation. Specially men."

But Fatma only whispered in the dark, "They can't all be the same. I see our neighbors looking after their families. Playing with their kids. The grandparents come to visit."

His Fatma had never disagreed with him back home.

Fatma made a tall blonde friend, Serena, who came to their house with a red-faced gigantic kid to play with Meenu and Ritu. His wife said the child was an angel and wondered why their own children were so skinny. Serena was a young mother and lonely, so she often stopped by to ask Fatma, "Do y'all all want to go for a walk?" Sometimes, she picked them up in her red sedan to drive down together to a museum or a faraway city park. Soon, she was always over at the house with the toddler, casually dressed in a T-shirt and shorts, flinging back her bangs as she sat with the kids on the wood floor. Masudul Huq lowered his eyes when he entered his house to avoid seeing her bare midriff and veined legs. He went to his room whenever she came over.

In October, his wife nestled next to him and their two children at night, all huddled together for comfort in the silent big house. Fatma said that her friend Serena thought she would look nice if she got a haircut. And perhaps she could start wearing trousers. He closed his eyes in pain and did not say anything.

"*Jaan*? Would you mind if I cut my hair?" she asked, lifting her head and bending over him, the flower stud on her nose glinting in the dark. "You have become so stern, so strange. You're growing a beard, no?" He touched his prickly chin.

"*Jaan*, I found a picture of you as a student, and you looked so carefree then, so, so young, so American. You've changed. You weren't like this in Bangladesh. So serious. What happened to make you change?"

"Where did you find the picture?" he asked. He would destroy it, the evidence of his foolish fumbling years before he found himself.

"*Jaan*, did you ever have an American friend?" she asked. "I find them very interesting, easy to mix."

He didn't answer. A face ballooned up in his head. Yes, at one time he had thought friendship was possible. But he had been mistaken. He pretended sleep, shutting his eyes tightly.

His children hurt him even more than his wife. He couldn't bear their pitiful, excited faces as they ran up to greet him when he walked in the door of the derelict house. The lights on the front porch and in the hall didn't work. He felt an urgency of love for them, all the more tortured because they were like tiny mice scurried away in a dismal hole. He saw that they had lost all the color and freedom of their sun-filled days on the roof of the flat in Dhaka.

One day, they had gone to Hong Kong market to buy fish. The three-year-old, Meenu was in his arms. He hoisted her high to witness the way the fish were hacked, then sprayed with water from the hoses, the blood pouring down into the gutter. He was thinking that maybe these men who were fish-cutters now had been doctors and engineers in their own countries, China, or Hong Kong, or Taiwan, now reduced to cutting fish, as he was reduced to doing research on toys, a farce of a job.

Meenu put her face close to his and said, "Baba, they are funny-looking, right?"

She was pointing at the Chinese men. He asked her to repeat. His wife laughed, as if their daughter had said something clever. Meenu hid her face in his shoulder. But her words had hit him like that water spray. He felt wounded. Why would she think that these men were funny-looking? Funny-looking compared to whom? Why didn't she say the white people she saw at Randalls were funny-looking, since they looked different from her too? It was unthinkable to his scientific and observant mind that a child of her age could perceive herself as anything but the center of the world, and everything else a reflection of herself. If she had said *they're* funny-looking, she also meant *we're* funny-looking. What would happen when she would be in an American classroom, surrounded by white kids? What would she think of herself then? That incident bothered him for a sleepless night.

The meeting had come to a close. Everyone was saying, "Happy Halloween!" But Masudul Huq did not feel like repeating the greeting. He didn't feel like participating in a holiday that was not his. He asked Richard what the holiday was about. Something about saints, spirits, he couldn't pay full attention.

"Now buy some candy and get ready for those children!" Richard called to him as he gathered his papers. "Today you're going to participate in a truly American experience! Hey, take some of these for your kids. Sinful pleasures."

He pushed the pile across the table in Masudul Huq's direction. Masudul Huq backed away from the onslaught of the colorful wrappers sliding his way. It seemed to him that everyone in the room waited for him to pick up the candy. He could not help feeling offended.

"Go to the store and buy some candy to hand them out to the children."

"Oh, yes! Believe me, they'll come in the evening."

"Okay."

He nodded, while becoming obstinate in his decision not to celebrate something he didn't understand, was barely just learning about. Tomorrow, he would be interrogated on his participation in the holiday. Slowly, as he ruminated, the others filed out of the meeting room. Masudul Huq found himself alone in the room, with the falls leaves beckoning him from outside the glass.

Masudul Huq bent to pick up the leather box briefcase that he had bought at New Market in Dhaka, that looked funny now among his colleagues' sleek leather bags, and walked out to the lobby. The strategically placed mirror by the elevator showed his sallow, sunken reflection. He looked discretely ahead of him to avoid the secretaries wearing short skirts and bright lipstick.

"Bye, Sir!"

Pushing open the double glass doors, he went out to the parking lot, where the breeze fluttered the multicolored leaves on the carefully planted maple trees, and climbed into his battered Toyota. After shutting the car door, he sat breathing heavily, trying to compose himself. He felt depressed, alone.

He drove past Airline Drive, avoiding that street because of the women who waited, pouting, on the corners, making him nervous. Instead, he got onto I-45, but then missed the exit for the 610 loop so that he had to take another exit and make a U-turn to get onto I-45 in the opposite direction. He missed the exit for 610 again and then he found himself back on Airline Drive, where a tall woman in a leather jacket called out to him through parted lips.

He felt that the drive was already too long for his restless mind. Someone honked at him because he'd almost run them over as he tried to turn onto Holcombe, driving toward for the safety of his own street.

Finally, he was on Holcombe, in the silent car, the radio turned off, because he felt that there was nothing to listen to, just vulgar music. He let his mind drift back to Dhaka to calm himself. He thought of the clear sky of early morning, the clearing of throats, running water from the different flats, the sweet long sound of the Azan that made him feel alive.

He looked forward to discussing those days with his wife, but he knew that she would only upset him. Her memories were contrary. She would challenge him with the account of days they had watched plays at Mahilya Samity theater, listened to songs sitting on the roof of Art College, or lain on the grass together on the engineering university campus. He would have to protest that he did not remember those days.

He drove slowly past the Randall on Holcombe, remembering that his wife had asked him to pick up some onions; they had run out. But he was not going to venture into the store today. He did not want to go past the displays of candy, not even to buy for his children. He would completely ignore the day, defy the tradition. The temptations, he knew all about temptations. The temptation to give up one's own self, to be seen as others wanted to see you, wear the right clothes, drink the right drinks.

When he turned onto Vanderbilt, the sky had begun to darken. The gaslights had come on in front of the houses, swaying lightly in the breeze with the elegance of history and tradition. Carved pumpkins leered at him through the bushes. The children were already out, witches and fairies, cartoon characters he did not yet recognize, hanging baskets from their elbows; a swirl of moving lights in the darkness. He had to slow down. He drove behind them sheepishly, afraid of running over someone, afraid of all the masked and eerie children in his way. It took him a long time to cover the three blocks to reach his home, the apologetic, the dilapidated house on the corner.

The doorbell had stopped working, so he had to knock. When Fatma opened the door, he pushed his way in and locked it behind him.

"Baba!" his daughters came running to him, the two-year-old hobbling to follow her sister.

He put his arms around both of them and pulled them to his chest.

"Baba, Ma says it is Halloween, we can go trick or treating for candy," Meenu said.

He realized that they had been watching the street from the living room window.

"Close the blinds," he yelled to Fatma.

"Why? Can you take the kids out? They should join in, it's so beautiful. You know, one girl was dressed as Snow White. So pretty. . ."

"Baba, I want to be Snow White!"

"Why close the windows?" Fatma asked again, not moving.

"Just do it," he said.

He went around the house turning off the lights in every room. He had no notion that he was going to do this before Fatma had suggested the unthinkable, going trick or treating.

"Are you crazy, suggesting taking the children out?" he said as he shut down the house. "People kidnap children on these nights, poison the candies. Besides, it's a Christian holiday."

"Oh, I didn't know that," Fatma said.

His family was following him through the house, closing blinds and turning off lights in a flurry of excitement. He felt relieved that they followed him, fell in line behind him, especially Fatma. It didn't take much to give the house a completely deserted look. At last they reached their sanctuary, their bedroom. He sat on the floor with his daughters on each knee.

"Listen, we are going to hide out and pretend we're not home," he said to them. "Since we don't have anything to give them. Although I don't think anyone will come. It's hardly a nice house, and we don't know anyone. The doorbell doesn't work. No one will come."

"Baba, where should we hide?" Meenu asked eagerly.

Fatma didn't say anything, but she obeyed him. They crouched low, below the level of the windowsill. The two girls giggled quietly. Outside, they could hear faint bells, a mother calling to her child, a child's laughter.

"Come," he said to his children. "Let's lie on the mattress and tell stories in the dark. I will tell you a story about the prophet, how he survived on three dates only."

He lay down and pulled Meenu and Ritu onto his chest, and with Fatma leaning on his side, they formed a tent, a perfect enclosure.

There were knocks on the door.

"Happy Halloween!" a chorus of voices called.

216

Meenu started to clap, but he shushed her, and she was quiet. They waited in suspense. Fatma pushed herself closer to the window and peered out between the blinds, her head bobbing in the dark. He wanted to tell her no, but he didn't want to make a sound.

Such a long time passed that he was sure the party had given up and moved away.

"Trick or treat!" came the voices again. "Happy Halloween!"

"I can see them," Fatma hissed. She raised the blind a little, and glimmers of light streamed in.

In the gap she had created, he could see a band of children, three or four, with parents in tow. How long would they stand there? He noticed they were using the time to go through their candy. There was a golden-haired girl wearing a puffed-sleeve dress. Was this the famed Snow White? She was taller than Meenu, maybe five. And beside her, an older sister or a mother, young, plump arms cascading out of a T-shirt. Still wearing shorts in October. Masudul Huq was uncomfortable, but he couldn't help seeing, now that the blind had been raised, the round, smooth knees and pearly nails peeping out of pink flip flops. His face was at an awkward angle, and he was immobilized. He could not look away. His thighs began to grow hot and he felt his heartbeat quickening. He wanted to jump up and run, but his children sat on top of him, and he lay there, unable to stop the memories.

Masudul Huq remembered Margaret, his classmate in graduate school, a close friend. Margaret was one of the few people who asked him questions about home, his family, his country, and made him feel alive. They had been friends, and he had kept his

217

surprised eyes away from her midriff, her cleavage, the plunging plumpness of her bodice, until that project his final year. They were working late, their heads close together, doing strength tests. They had to stay in the department the entire night to finish the project. They had collapsed on separate couches in Cullen building, laughing, conversing in whispers. At three in the morning, Margaret stood before him and pulled violently at his pointed shirt collars.

"Masudul!" she called. "Get up. We only have a couple hours, Masudul."

She got out a wine bottle and the plastic cups that littered the lounge and offered him some.

"No," he said. "I do not drink."

"It's just wine, it's not bad," she said.

There was music on, some punk rock or something she had said, and he drank from his cup. It was sweet, but also slightly bitter. Masudul Huq watched Fatma's profile as he remembered this, the way Fatma tucked a tendril under each ear. That night in March, when he drank, just barely aware that he had a wife who waited for him at home, he looked at Margaret differently. The lines became blurred. Everything became possible. Her pants hung low on her hips, her midriff was baby-like, innocent, the back of her neck scented, almost the odor of baby milk. He wore Jeans and an open neck shirt, his hair ruffled and curly, his face brown, smiling, open, just as Fatma had seen in that photograph. "You're beautiful, Masudul," Margaret had whispered. Everything became possible because he had not closed himself. After that, and it was only the one time, he could not live with himself.

He began to cry in the darkness now, while the Halloween party waited outside, and his family hid in the darkness.

"Fatma," he called in a hoarse whisper, calling for help. "Fatma, I was with another woman."

"Oh, *Jaan*, look, they are trying to peer in through the spy-glass in the door, I wonder why they wait so long. They must be tired and don't want to walk."

Either she had not heard, or she didn't understand him. Masudul Huq lay there on the mattress, crying, his chest crushed under the weight of his two baby daughters.

"Why, it's my friend, that's why! Oh, no, she left." Then in the darkness, Fatma's body began to shake. Her shoulders rumbled, bouncing went up and down. She choked back a burst of laughter by holding her scarf to her mouth.

"What?" he asked.

"It's so funny," she said. "It's so funny! We're hiding from children! *Jaan*, it's so funny! You're so funny."

Meenu and Ritu began to laugh also. "It's so funny, Baba," Meenu said. "We're playing hide and seek."

The party outside must have registered the sounds; they stood with their ears at attention. Fatma stood up. Her nostrils flared when she tried to suppress laughter. Watching her at that height, he felt light-headed. The seriousness of their meeting had melted away in her laughter. He tried compose himself.

"I have to cook the rice. *Jaan*, do you mind if I turn the lights on in the kitchen?" She went away still choking, and he could hear her from the bedroom.

The party outside was beginning to disperse. Meenu and Ritu pushed themselves up suddenly and ran through the house, shrieking. He followed them. He tried to remember his own lectures at the Halaqa meetings. He tried to recall the philosophy with which he could hold the world fast. But he couldn't keep everything straight as he tried to keep up with Meenu and Ritu. He hadn't been able to think straight since the moment Fatma had lifted those blinds and dissolved the perfect darkness of his home, and then dissolved it again with her laughter. Her laughter mixed with Margaret's. And all he could feel, to his horror, was love. It encompassed everyone, Meenu, Ritu, Fatma, the children who had waited outside his home, even Margaret. He closed his eyes to shut out Margaret's open face, her laughter. But he felt only a warm feeling as Meenu and Ritu urged him on.

"Turn on the lights, Baba!" Meenu and Ritu ran ahead of him, bobbing up and down.

He followed, switching on the lights in every room in the house.

Meenu said, "Do you on the lights, Baba? I want to on the lights in the hall." The one in the hall didn't work, but never mind. Meenu and Ritu reached the front door and banged on it.

"Open the door, Baba!"

He wanted only to be filled by the love of his children. He opened the door, fighting with the bolt and chain. Then he stepped out of the wide open door, breathing hard. He felt a great desire to greet this Halloween party that had waited at his door. He didn't have anything to give them but he wanted to see them. The costumed children were already shadows in the distance, flashlights hovering in the air, little shadows and bigger shadows in the dark. He stared after them, disappointed to have missed them. One was a dog, another a chicken. They skipped and twirled, laughing that silly laughter that was Meenu's and Ritu's. His children joined him outside their door; together, they stood in the dark and watched the receding lights. In the distance, they could hear doorbells ringing and doors opening. Shouts of 'Happy Halloween!' Masudul Huq leaned against the wall of his house and stuffed his hands in his empty pockets, breathing in the night air. When he turned back to go inside, he could see Fatma through the dirty glass of the window—quietly setting the table.

Room Enough for Love

That winter, pregnant women in Lahore watched the BBC news anxiously, taking note of Farsi names for their future babies. Reporters spoke to refugees at camps along the border between Pakistan and Afghanistan: Abdellah Abdellah, his name meaning the servant of God; Shabnam, a dew drop; and Firoza, the color of the softest, most tantalizing blue. Now these people, with their beautiful names, sat around in the refugee camp, wounded, shocked, and dying. The child named Firoza faded softly, cradled on her father's knees, live on camera. The color on her lips was indeed blue, but an inferior shade, a disconcerting disappointment to her namesake.

Shahriar hoped that his own love in Lahore watched the BBC with the other women, thinking up names for their future offspring. Shahriar's love was a childhood friend, a good Christian girl named Mary back in Lahore. It was quite miraculous how the realization had come to him that Mary was his love. He had been working on a paper on the partition, making the argument that if the British colonizers hadn't cut up India with knife and fork, it was conceivable that

Muslims and Hindus would coexist peacefully today in the same land.

His fingers drummed the keyboard energetically. The next moment, his forehead pulsed with a hot throbbing. He drifted into a flu that lasted five days, emerging from his delirium to face the startling news that Kandahar had been bombed. For the rest of the fall, Shahriar slept out on the golf course under the icy moon and composed twenty *shers* in honor of the tendrils that cupped Mary's milky turmeric earlobes. He was a third-generation poet.

It suited Shahriar to be in love at such a time. As a future leader in politics, he was expected to take his due place by his fellow graduate students in the dark dungeons of the graduate towers, watching BBC and CNN and analyzing the waves of breaking news over nodding beer bottles. When he graduated and returned to his country–to his beloved Mary–, he expected to work in government, for a multinational development organization in Pakistan, or for a major newspaper. But now he stayed away from world affairs, hiding in the folds of development economics and Urdu poetry. He did not read the *New York Times*, the *Financial Times*, or the *Economist* at the Woodrow Wilson library. During lectures on the political state, he focused his questions entirely on the academic. The other questions, the bigger questions, fell by unasked, so vivid in his mind, and yet, as they dropped like the October leaves by the Graduate Tower, they became discolored and faded.

As winter approached and Shahriar walked on the icy path from the graduate tower to his classes, all the warring, starving, and dying people of the world seemed to rise up and hover in the shadows around him. He couldn't forget the face of Firoza, the child dying in front of a TV camera. In class, he was used to discussing ethnic conflict and nation states with cold detachment. But now, a single image of a dying child was about to break him and expose his rawness to his classmates. There were a handful of other scholars from the south, graduate students and faculty; Shahriar studied them carefully and began to imitate them, immersing himself in the intellectual, the beautiful, and the personal, closing out from his mind the ugly horror of the bombing of Kandahar. The goal was to attain peace, he told himself. Not world peace, just inner peace.

Slowly, the ice cleared, the weather grew warmer, and the year ended. It was dangerous for a Pakistani to travel on a plane that summer, even a Pakistani who was an American citizen (Shahriar's mother had traveled to the US during her pregnancy and give birth to him in an American hospital, thereby blessing Shahriar with an American passport). It was even more problematic for that plane to land in Lahore. But Shahriar had declarations to make. His love was waiting at home. He left for home with the blessings of his friends, a Danish doctoral fellow in music and an Irish beauty studying mathematics who had inspired him to sing many Hindi film songs against the haunting backdrop of the Graduate Tower. Urdu poetry, translated, acquired elliptical proportions, transfixing European classmates against the brick wall of the tower, their faces turned up to the moon, awaiting. He explained to his lady friends that the tower rose to the dark oblivion to meet his lady lover the moon. He flung himself into the oblivion.

He fell through tense borders, glad to hide behind his blue passport, his American accent, and the Princeton sheen. He handed all these documents over suavely at ticketing and security gates and laughed easily with the

224

officials. On the very day of his arrival in Lahore, he braved the heat and the dust and pulled up in his chauffeur driven car at Mary's house.

But what was this? Sitting coolly in the drawing room hung with heavy drapery, Mary received his proposal with an interrupting cough.

"Sherry," she said, "I have a fiancée, an American I met on the Internet."

"Oh," said Shahriar.
He focused on a decorative *paan daani* used to hold betel leaves and wondered if there were any *paan* inside that he could chew on. Then he tried to read to Mary the poetry he had written about her from so far away. He was sure that his verse carried a spell that was beyond all earthly logic. Mary stared with glazed eyes as he read. A servant came in and Mary stood up to serve him *Gulab Jamun* from a dinner trolley, handing him the fried brown sweets on a quarter plate with a silver fork and an embroidered napkin taped to the bottom. He found the intrusion of food painful and closed his eyes.

"You might run into him one day," Mary said eagerly. "He is at Princeton. His name is Michael Smith and he's an engineer!"

Shahriar fled the overstuffed drawing room, suddenly suffocating in its collection of dusty family photographs. He fled from Lahore to Karachi, then still seeking peace and not finding it, to New Delhi. He had obtained some money from Princeton to work on a book on the partition that summer, tracing a line from partition to the current political situation prevailing in South Asia. The grant had been awarded quickly and smoothly; it was the perfect time for a book on the region. Afghanistan had made the day for Shahriar.

At Delhi airport, Shahriar was received by a distant relative on that side of the family who had stayed back in India. Once again, he was able to hide behind his completely neutral and acceptable identity. His relative Mr. Qayum wore a safari suit over a large belly. His fingers were soft and full like a woman's.

"You look like me," Mr. Qayum said to Shahriar. The airport doors parted, and they plunged into the rasping, choking blast of the Delhi summer. Mr. Qayum's chauffeur carried Shahriar's bags. In the car, Shahriar intimated to his uncle his plans to write a novel. He had just made up his mind that it would be a novel, not a book of politics. His plans took up the hour-long car ride and gave him much comfort, the security of a world he could create and wander around inside when the world outside had turned upside down. They tried to speak about Afghanistan, but it was an embarrassing conversation because politically their countries stood on different sides of the issue. It was precisely the location of this embarrassment that had drawn Shahriar to India at this time. He wished to hide away in the crevices of this embarrassment, where no one would find him, where nothing to which he was remotely connected could follow him; where he would not be asked to speak his mind.

"Are you in search of your roots?" Mr. Qayum asked.

"You know," Shahriar said, "I hadn't thought about it before, but it will be an excellent project, especially since I will be living with you. I was going to write a story about the Partition. I can write it about my family. Our family." Shahriar had a warm full heart, and this heart now turned to Mr. Qayum, expanding and encircling him.

As the car sped on the road to home, Shahriar followed the mammoth trucks on the road that shuddered out of their hideouts at nightfall, lending the city the surreal quality of largeness and invincibility. He felt the full force of how tiny his hometown was compared to this powerful city. The car stopped at the gates of a house on a dark but wide street.

"This is Kailash Road," Mr. Qayum explained. Shahriar wondered how wealthy Mr. Qayum was. Mr. Qayum was a businessman, with ties to computers, trucks, and the movie industry. The driver unloaded Shahriar's bags, and Shahriar took the steps lightly. He was led into the drawing room. The room was crammed with end tables of every kind, from cherry wood to the bejeweled silver contraptions of Rajasthan. A large painting by an unknown painter hung on one of the walls. On the floor, between two sofas, stood a *paan daani*. Shahriar closed his eyes in pain because this drawing room resembled too closely one he had left only weeks ago.

"What is it?" asked Mr. Qayum, "You look miserable. Let me turn on the air-conditioner. It has been unbearably hot."
Shahriar turned his eyes away from the *paan dani* and sank into a chair. Mr. Qayum opened curtains and switched on the AC and removed the dust covers from the sofas. Then he rang the bell for a manservant to bring in a tray of ice-cold water.

The door opened again and an enormous woman moved slowly across the room and lowered herself into a maroon brocade armchair.

"This is our relation, Shahriar," Qayum introduced him.

Mrs. Qayum nodded her chin, pummeling her face with soft hands. "So hot," she said. "It's been unbearably hot. I hope your stay is comfortable. I'm very sick."

"Auntie, what is wrong? *Kuch serious tho nahin hain?*" Shahriar asked, leaning forward.

Auntie answered with a monologue on her gout and diabetes, which Shahriar tried to follow intently. Then she asked, "Do you know Michael Smith? He is also from Princeton. He visited us just a week ago. He was interning with Tata, so he put up here at our place. A very nice guy."

Shahriar could not breathe. He put his fingers to his forehead, which pulsated violently. Surely there could not be two Michael Smiths studying engineering at Princeton? He ran his fingers through his hair, sticky from the Delhi dust. The heat oppressed the air in the room. His sanctuary had been invaded. He had hoped to breathe deeply again and open himself to Delhi, but now he just wanted to be shown his room so he could lock himself inside. Mrs. Qayum warned Shahriar that the AC in his room might not work all night. Sometimes, the load was too much, and it stopped on its own. Then after some time it started up again.

"Unless, there is load-shedding," Mr. Qayum said.

"We have a generator, but we don't want to disturb the servants to turn it on at night," ," Mrs. Qayum said.

At night, Shahriar lay on the creaking bedsprings and practiced breathing, slowing down to take deliberate gulps. Michael Smith had flushed him out of Lahore and Princeton. Now he had been here in Delhi, in the very home of Mr. Qayum where Shahriar had traveled with so much courage and determination. Shahriar did not know where to go. He was looking simply to exist now, a refugee exhausted in his struggle for self-preservation. And now Shahriar could not even breathe.

Ten days later, Shahriar met an American on the green lawn of the Birla House, paying respects to Gandhiji. The mere sight of white skin made Shahriar's own jump in apprehension of the much superior specimen of Michael Smith. Michael's specter awaited him at every corner.

"Hi. I'm Olivia," said the specter, extending a slender arm.

"Can I tell you something, Olivia? You're beautiful."

Olivia was a Texan. She had blonde hair and a lingering, caressing accent. She was in the Peace Corps; she had just graduated from Berkeley.

"How tall are you?" he asked, bumping his head against her shoulder.

"Five ten."

"So what do you make of the concept of non-violence?" he asked, following her inside the museum, pointing at the narrow bed of Gandhiji.

Later, they walked to Olivia's house, not far from the museum. Her flip flops made a squelching sound on the pavement. He liked the squish squish squish. It had a comforting lilt to it.

"Listen, do you want lychee?" she asked.

They ate the fruits sitting on her front step, their fingers dripping the sticky sweetness. He read to her, from memory, the *sher* that he had written for Mary.

"These are beautiful poems," she said.

Emboldened, he told her about Mary.

"A tragic story. Like a Hindi movie."

"Yes," he said. "I have all sorts of questions now. Is a poet as useful to society as an engineer? Is an American a superior human being compared to a flawed pathetic Pakistani? Am I worthless, am I supposed to shrivel and disappear?"

"All valid questions," she said, laughing with a mouth full of even teeth. "Very sensitive. Like a poet. You'd make a good lover."

"How old are you?" he asked.

"Thirty-three."

"That's beautiful," he said. "A woman is not whole till she has gone through that arc, that last stretch from mid-twenties to the thirties. Those years lend her sadness, an edge, bitterness, a uniqueness. A bitter-sweet taste."

"Do you mean sexually?"

"Let's discuss this over a movie," said Shahriar.

Olivia became his fellow tourist. He took her to a milk stand at Connaught Place, where they drank from cold bottles of chocolate-flavored milk facing a dirty white counter, elbowing out the other milk lovers. And the Nagaland stall at Dilli Haat, where they belched after an over-feeding of momos. They went looking for Ghalib's house on Chandni Chawk, and returned unsuccessful, sweaty palms bleeding into each other. Olivia caressed his thick wavy hair with her large white hands. She wore tie-dyed T-shirts bunched up above her navel and spoke on global warming. She was idealistic, committed to human rights, peace; he began to feel that he had found the fold he was looking for.
In the morning, Shahriar could place his palm on his heart and feel the peace there. He could bear to look in the mirror and out-stare the fullness of his cheeks and

the wide girth of his waist. He could contemplate climbing out of bed, just to spend a few hours with Olivia. Her rain-drenched eyes drank in all his poetry and carried his words to a higher place, out of reach of the ugly world. One day, she was just a child who giggled over *masala dosa*. On another day, she would see a naked child pushing a van and cry. Shahriar had never seen such selfless tears.

When he walked with her, she hugged her wide, wide shoulders and skipped ahead, her eyes fixed on the stars. One day, while they sat in the general-seating section watching a newly released Salman Khan movie, he bent his head and whispered in her ear, "Your eyes are like wine, I am intoxicated. So help me!"

After that incident, Olivia grew cold and removed. He called her night and day, when the phone in the Qayum household worked. Once, he took a rickshaw to M Market and called from an ISD/STD shop, paying cash. When he had no luck reaching her, he went by her place with a bag of juicy red lychee. He found her sitting on the front steps, wearing white shorts and a tank top, licking a Kwality ice cream cone with her long tongue.

"I think you want to just sleep with me," she said.

"No!" he shuddered. "How could you say that? I put you on a pedestal. I simply want to write poetry about you, speak to you these lines, sing to you under the rain."

"Piss off!" she said. "I'm off men for the summer. Don't you get it? I have my own issues."

"*Yaar*, why don't you tell me?" he said, putting his arm about her shoulders. "You're my closest friend. I love you, *yaar*."

Watching the news, Mrs. Qayum spoke about how beautiful the Afghan women and children looked. Mr. Qayum also talked about how beautiful the Afghanistanis were, how cultured, how steeped in music and art. The family had been enjoying a midnight feast of sweet and savory snacks after dinner. Mrs. Qayum's cooks were good. The kebab was excellent. If Olivia would only speak to him, he could invite her to Mrs. Qayum's dinner table for some kebab. To think that he had to come to Delhi to discover the delights of beef. He would never forget Karim's restaurant on Nizamuddin Road. Shahriar tried to discuss Rumi with Mrs. Qayum, but she was too ill to stay up long. Olivia rang a few days later to say she was sorry for being so sharp. She was depressed about a former professor she had had an affair with a long time ago. A particular Pink Floyd song had reminded her of the man, and anyway he had been married, just having a fling, but she had been in love. Shahriar sang to her a Hindi song that might echo her feelings. She cut the conversation short but invited him along on a trip to Rishikesh.

When he met Olivia at the train station, there were two others who were going to travel with them. An Indian-born American graduate student from Harvard named Bijli who was a slender, dusky beauty, and a sour-looking thin journalist from the *Hindustan Times* named Sheethil. Shahriar managed to get a seat beside Olivia on the Rajasthan Express.

"I am like this train," she said to him. "Speeding by, witness to lots of scenery, desperately in search of love. Tell me, Shahriar, will I ever find it?"

"Of course," he said, meaning it. He offered to read her palm.

But when they got off the train at Haridware station, standing in a circle to discuss if they should buy return tickets now, Olivia turned her back to him again and expertly poised her towering backpack between them. The three others went back inside to buy the return tickets, leaving him with their bags. He stood alone watching a flood of coolies wearing fiery red clothes carrying blue tin trunks on top of their heads. Women with hoops on their noses and rings on each toe and tired fathers with kids parked on their shoulders flowed through the station.

It was a long time before the others returned with the tickets and the news that they would have to stick together and the tickets' dictates. It was a busy holiday season, and the trains were all booked. They found a tempo which would carry them all. Bijli climbed in after Sheethil, and Shahriar found himself squashed between Sheethil and Olivia. Olivia half-turned to the window so that her behind poked Shahriar; Shahriar felt comforted by this token gesture of intimacy.

The driver said to Shahriar, "*Aap movie actor je se Laagthahe.*"

"What did he say?" Olivia asked.

"He said I look like a movie actor," Shahriar answered.

"Liar," Olivia said, frowning and turning back to face the window.

"Well, that's what he said," Sheethil said in a deep, masculine voice and turned to the driver. "*Bhai Saab*, which movie actor does he look like to you?"

The driver said in Hindi, "Rajesh Khanna, when he was young."

Again, Olivia asked for a translation.

"Was Rajesh Khanna paunchy?" Olivia wondered, laughing loudly.

The driver asked Shahriar where he was from.

"Lucknow," Shahriar answered quickly. After all, he reasoned, his ancestors were from Lucknow in India, like Mr. and Mrs. Qayum.

This time, Sheethil frowned, asking him, "Why are you lying?"

Shahriar realized that he was facing India for the first time. Here he was, caught in a vehicle that contained two Indian interrogators, a journalist and a patriotic tempo driver. Bijli inquired what was going on, then supplied bright faced that her boyfriend had lied too during his stay in India. He was an American-born whose parents were from India, but he told every person he met that he was from Madras.

"That solved the language problem too. He didn't have to explain why he didn't speak Hindi!" Bijli laughed like the tinkling bells on a child's anklet.

"Yeah, *Yaar*," said Shahriar. "It's natural to claim many nationalities. And I don't even have a language problem. I blend right in." He laughed loudly.

"But what is it exactly that you're trying to hide?" Sheethil asked, facing Shahriar full body. "Why exactly are you in India?"

"*Aare, Yaar,* why are you getting excited for no reason?" Shahriar asked in an amiable voice.

"I don't like liars," Sheethil said. "And I don't like Pakistanis."

Shahriar closed his eyes and touched his throbbing forehead, trying to hide behind Olivia's shoulders. For the rest of the journey, Bijli spoke non-stop about her boyfriend. As the tempo climbed the hill, the Ganges raced with them, flew under them, then winked at them as they climbed higher. Shahriar thought of the Indian movie *Ram Teri Ganga Maili*, in which the Ganges had been made dirty by a violent and heartless world. Shahriar told the story wordlessly to Olivia's soft behind. He thought about how he wanted to be squashed by Olivia, out of his seat and out of the world. How he wanted to follow her to Simla and Agra and Fatehpur Sikri, hurrying behind her, being trampled by spiked pink heels, crushed, so that his blood would come charging out of his nostrils and ears. Oh, thought Shahriar. She never wears heels. She wears flip flops. As the climb became trickier, their driver became silent, the tempo jostled them, and Bijli discussed her boyfriend. Sheethil leaned in closer to listen until his ear was touching Bijli's lips. Their noses poked at each other. At last, Sheethil slid away from Shahriar, giving him room to breathe.

They reached a cottage on top of successive hills, with the town of Rishikesh far below. As he inhaled the crisp air, Shahriar's lungs expanded. Bijli had chosen the place out of the *Lonely Planet Guide*. The landlord wanted to know who was a non-Indian because he needed to register non-Indians in his book. But it was difficult for him to tell, just looking at them. Only Olivia owned up that she was American, yawned, slipped out of her flip flops and walked off in her bare feet. Shahriar wondered what Sheethil would do if he tried to register himself as an Indian.

They rented two rooms, one for the guys and one for the women, next to each other along a long verandah. Leaning out over the railing, Shahriar could see smaller hills below and a snake of a stream. He determined to take a walk by himself in the morning; write some poetry. Start on his novel. Sheethil and Bijli lay put down towels on the verandah and lay down, side by side, sucking on each other's hair.

Shahriar went into the guys' room and stretched out on top of one of the beds. When he woke up, the darkness was absolute. He climbed out of bed and stumbled to the bathroom, finding the light switch and turning on the light. Numerous cockroaches scurried away. When he came outside to the verandah, he found the others sitting around smoking. They had eaten in.

"Why don't you ask the guy to make you something?" Bijli suggested in a gentle voice.

Shahriar shook his head. He wasn't hungry. He sat down on the floor hugging his knees and looked up at the stars, bright in the remote sky. Olivia hummed a tune and talked about her professor, who was married and an ass, a bad professor too, didn't know his stuff, had been teaching from the same notes for years. She wanted to explore why would she waste herself trying to seek a relationship with someone so pathetic? But nobody was listening. Shahriar wasn't sure he was supposed to respond so he kept his mouth shut.

"So, Brother," Sheethil called to Shahriar. "What do you say about Kashmir?"
Shahriar tried to think of a *sher* that would deflect the question.

"Kashmir!" exploded Olivia. "Can we talk about something besides politics?"

They stared at her. Shahriar thought she meant the world trade center bombings, Afghanistan, the possibility of world war.
But Olivia continued tear-faced, "Why can't we speak about love?"

"Theatrical," Bijli muttered. Her thin shoulder blades stuck out of her dark tank top appealing for care.

236

Sheethil massaged them, saying "That woman's totally wasted," Sheethil hissed. "A woman in her thirties who doesn't know where she is going."

Shahriar wondered where Olivia had picked up these friends, with tongues as kind as hers. Olivia sat in her corner and cried in loud sobs. Shahriar realized that Olivia was drunk. He closed his eyes and tried to compose a poem about her sadness.

Bijli suggested that they sleep outside so they could watch the sunrise.

"I feel bad that you could not share it with your boyfriend!" Sheethil laughed.

Bijli agreed and lamented her boyfriend's absence with a long sigh. The four of them pulled the mattresses from their beds and pulled them onto the roof. Then they carried out bed sheets, pillows, and blankets. Bijli took the corner spot, and Sheethil lay down beside her. Shahriar lowered himself guiltily between Olivia and Sheethil.

"The *Guide* promises a great view of the sunrise from the roof," Bijli said. "That's where I got the idea." Shahriar closed his eyes, listening to their tinkling laughter and guttural woofs, feeling accepted in this mismatched company. He woke up to a brilliantly colorful sky and nudged Olivia, peering over her face. Olivia snarled and squinted.

"The sunrise," he whispered. "You'll miss it." He pulled her to a half-sitting position, then let go.

"My head," she said. "My back."

Shahriar said nothing. He watched the sky silently, trying to name the exact shade of ech color in his mind. When the sun shone fully, turning the sky an even blue, he turned to Olivia and said, "I can massage your back for you."

Olivia let him. Then he moved his lips to her neck and kissed it.

"You bastard!" Olivia turned around and slapped him. She pulled her blanket to her chest and scrambled down the ladder, the cloth falling away around her.

He ran after her and peered down from the edge of the roof to where she was standing on the balcony below. "Listen," he said. "If only you knew how much I care for you."

"You care?" Olivia laughed. "You self-absorbed fool! Listen, all those poems for that Mary, they weren't for her at all."

"No? Who were they for then?" Shahriar asked.

"For you. You, you, you. Always you. Just an excuse for you to flaunt your drivel. It's no good, by the way. Plagiarized, I'm sure."

"Plagiarized?" gasped Shahriar.

"Look around," said Olivia. "The world is going to pieces. There's more besides you. Face the world."

Olivia disappeared for the rest of the day. Sheethil, Bijli, and Shahriar explored Rishikesh town on their own, carrying light tote bags. Sometimes, they saw Olivia, flip flopping determinedly across the bridge or climbing up the hill to reach the temple, but they respected her distance and the warning in her glazed eyes.

High in the afternoon, the three wandered into a house of worship on top of a hill, admiring the beauty of the blazing yellow building. The grounds were large and filled with trees; the air was still and clean. Bijli took off her shoes and bent to pick up a clump of earth in her palm.

"Mmm, the smell," she said, sniffing. "So close to God."

Shahriar stood at a distance under a cherry blossom tree and twirled the Afghan hat he had bought at a market in Lahore. He had never been a religious man, but he considered that they were on a hilltop at a hill station, inside an ashram, as close to God as geographically possible. He felt a sudden need for God, for acceptance, eying the painted yellow hut with longing.

"Please! You must leave. I beg you!"

They were startled by shrill voice of panic. A tiny monk in orange robes had come out of the painted hut. He stood before them, with his raised hands clasped together at his temple. The horror was mutual. They stirred like sinners, joining their hands and raising them to their temples to return the greeting.

"Go!" he cried, as if very presence had soiled the holy place.

They backfooted out of the gates and fled, running, until they reached a stream. Bijli and Sheethil slid down to the muddy riverbank, laughing hysterically. But Shahriar stood aloof and unsmiling, startled by the rejection.

Back at the cottage, after they sipped their midmorning tea in porcelain cups sitting on the verandah, Sheethil and Bijli suggested that they should have lunch in town and explore the market there.

"I'm a little tired," Shahriar pleaded.

When they left, he lay back in his bed, stared at the whitewashed ceiling, and thought about the monk. He relished the monk's rejection. He tried to look at himself through the holy man's eyes. Certainly, Shahriar was impure. He drank and recited poetry to women. But he wanted to probe deeper. He wanted the monk to help him poke around inside his mind, which felt heavy and clouded, like a film of mosquito-infested stagnant water, unstirred for a long time.

For a long time, he had been so muddled that he didn't even know how he really felt. Did he really love Mary? Did he really mean anything he said when classmates at Princeton asked him what he thought about the political events unfolding around him that frightened him? He had only words for them. His poetry had been merely words to hide behind.

He had been shocked by the World Trade Center bombings, then he had been made speechless by the bombing in Afghanistan. Even if he had tried, he could not have expressed his sadness. Later, he did not even know anymore what he thought or felt. His mind was a blank, which made it easy for him to compose blank verse and translate Urdu poetry for his light flirtations with his women classmates. By noon, his room was hot. He spent another hungry day lying in his bed; he had no energy to get up for food. His forehead felt feverish, and he drifted off to sleep.

"Come on, get up. You haven't eaten anything." Someone's face was hovering above him in the dark room. It was Olivia, but her voice was strangely soft. Not like tinkling bells, but like the sound of rain, resonant with his pain, compassionate.

"Your forehead is hot," she said. "Beejli and Sheethil are waiting outside."

He sat up slowly, pulled on his boots, slapped out his wrinkled shirt and was ready to go. They took a three-wheeler down the hill, fitted tightly inside, to a marketplace in town that Sheethil and Bijli had discovered earlier.

They walked around the crowded market in the dark, looking for somewhere to eat. *The Guide* was not very helpful. Olivia declared that she wanted a *thali*, a tray of vegetables, daal, and rice, with bread. Bijli craved spaghetti; she was homesick, she said. Shahriar was ready for a three-course dinner. Finally, they sat down at a dirty table inside a shop called Maharaja. A waiter came and began to wipe down their table with a dirty washcloth.

"Where are you from?" the waiter asked.

"From Lucknow," said Shahriar. "We're all Indian here, except for the memsahib."

"She is white, I see," said the waiter in Hindi.

"A white woman sticks out like a sore thumb anywhere in South Asia," said Sheethil.

"Shut up," said Olivia calmly. "I know your country better than you do, you snob. How many villages have you visited? How many hungry people have you spoken to?"

"I'm a journalist," said Sheethil.

"Journalist, huh!" said Olivia. "You call yourself a journalist? I've read the stuff you write, pure drivel. You just attack people because you're an insecure ass." Shahriar felt sorry for Sheethil. He was beginning to like him, after being rejected together by the monk. He imagined sharing a few lines of his poetry with Sheethil. At least, Sheethil would not need any translation. The waiter began to take their orders. When the waiter left, Sheethil turned to Shahriar.

"So tell me, what do you think of your country's role in Afghanistan? Don't you think Pakistan is a bit hypocritical? I mean, you call the Afghans your friends, then you let the Americans bomb them and park them across from your borders, and you let them die."

Shahriar was going to say he couldn't argue with that, especially because he was very hungry and sorry to lose a friend over politics. Their food came. Shahriar dug his fingers into the heaped, fragrant *pulao* with fluffy, buttery rice, and it occurred to him that he hadn't really eaten properly since the last time he had been sick at Princeton. He was suddenly filled with hunger and gusto. The fever was leaving him, and his mind cleared.

"My friend, are you evading my questions?" Sheethil spoke with his mouth full of rice and daal. "What's the use of your visit if we do not have bilateral talks?"

Shahriar turned to Sheethil. "All right, my friend, I'll answer you."

"Start first with what you think of all the bombing in Afghanistan," said Sheethil. "Why you are in India this summer?"

Shahriar thought that he did not have many words in him anymore. He closed his mouth and opened it again. "I have been very depressed about Afghanistan," he said at last. "Often, I think about Firoza, the child they showed on BBC, dying slowly away in the refugee camp."

"Firoza? Who is Firoza?" Bijli asked. "This spaghetti is horrible. They don't know how to cook spaghetti here."

"That's very poetic, but never mind poetry," Sheethil said. "What do you think as a Muslim? As a Pakistani? A student of politics? We are trying to have a political discussion here."

"A Muslim? A Pakistani?" repeated Olivia. "Huh! He is neither. He has an American passport!"

"What are national boundaries? God can chase you anywhere," Shahriar said, thinking of the monk who had chased them out. "The answer to your question, my friend, is that I am in India as a lover lost and fleeing. But my rival seems to have preceded me here by a few weeks. He was here, he walked here, and I still walk in his shadow."

Shahriar felt an enormous sense of relief, having spoken those words about his jealousy of Michael Smith. His head, which had been stuffed and low on oxygen, had cleared up. He stretched his legs under the table and relaxed his arms behind his head, fingers clasped around his Kabuli hat; he felt warm and satisfied. He had no more words now.

Olivia turned to him and said, "I'm really sorry about that Michael Smith. I'd throttle him for you if I could get my hands on him. And I'm sorry about what I said about your poems for Mary. Your love was real." She put her arm around him awkwardly, in a rare gesture of solidarity.

Shahriar smiled. He had loved Mary and written poetry for her when he had been most frightened, and he thought this a beautiful act now, the most he could do in this world–make love and write about love, even made up love.

When they walked outside, it was raining. The market was wet and dark. Water had collected in the alleys. The rain flew down at an angle, carried by a cold wind. Bijli waved her strawberry umbrella in the air till a three-wheeler flew up to them and sputtered to a stop.

"Where to?" asked the man in Hindi, cutting out the engine.

Two other men occupied the back seat.

"But you have passengers already," Olivia said in English.

"No problem," said the man. "They are my friends. They will sit with me in the front." He had a handlebar mustache and shining eyes.

Olivia looked dubious.

"Look, it's almost midnight," Sheethil said. "Let's take it. We won't get many others."

They climbed inside, too tight again, sitting shoulder to shoulder, turned slightly at an angle to fit. The three-wheeler started its ascent up the hill. The men in the front began to sing popular film songs; Shahriar hummed along softly. The rain splattered the sides of the taxi and bounced off the tin roof, drumming to the singing. Bijli and Sheethil made room by moving closer together, dissolving into each other, then layering themselves on top of each other. As the three-wheeler climbed up the hill, the rain grew louder and more menacing. The three-wheeler slipped occasionally. The night was pitch black all around them. The men laughed and sang louder. They sang on top of one another, crossing out their individual voices in destructive sound wave patterns. The three-wheeler sputtered up the hill, made sharp turns around and around, on the narrow road on the edge of the cliff. Several times, it felt like they might fly into the air, fall all the way down hundreds of feet.

Bijli started to scream. "Stop! Go slow."

One of the men was holding a flashlight. Why was he holding a flashlight? The answer dawned on Shahriar.

"This thing has no lights," he observed quietly.

244

Bijli buried her head in Sheethil's hairy chest.

"They're drunk," Olivia muttered, her face white. She pushed her head out of the back opening of the three-wheeler into the rain to see, her drenched hair plastering her cheeks.

The three-wheeler swerved, then slipped, sliding backward some distance. Bijli screamed again. The car had stalled. The two friends of the driver got down with the flashlight to give it a push. Push, push, push, they chanted. It sputtered to life. The two men climbed inside the three-wheeler in their wet clothes and laughed. "Didi, are you scared? No problem." They had climbed in backwards so that when they started to sing again, a sad romantic song, they sang to an audience. The three-wheeler climbed blindly and wildly into the dark oblivion.

"Stop! We're going to die!" Bijli sobbed.

Now the driver turned around to face them, taking his eyes of the road.

"It's all right," he laughed; his mouthful of white teeth glinted in the dark interior. "Don't worry. We all take care of one another. Everything is okay up here, on top of the world. Room enough for everybody."

The three-wheeler blasted through another devil's elbow, perhaps headed straight off the cliff. But Shahriar felt safe in the pitch blackness, with the three drunken drivers in charge, in a blind three-wheeler. Here, the world was a beautiful place with enough love for him and for a little girl named Firoza who lay dying on her father's knees. It was snug and warm inside the car. Olivia turned up her lovely head and observed the men calmly. Sheethil brushed Bijli's hair with soft, gentle strokes of his hand. The driver sat half-turned toward them, his neck twisted away from his body at an impossible angle, seeking communion.

Sraboni

"And now, dear audience, for you is being presented tonight's eleven O'clock full-length Bangla feature-film, *Under My Husband's Feet.*"

A young woman wearing a black georgette sari spelled out the feature next on the program on Bangladesh Television. A smile played about her chocolate brown lips.

Sraboni lay on the sagging divan in the living room, her face throwing distorted shadows on the wall. The servant woman, Putulir Ma, sat on the carpet at the foot of the divan, her forehead pressed against its wooden leg and her large feet tucked beneath her printed red cotton saree. Watching the old Bengali movies was their nightly ritual, for which Sraboni called Putulir Ma out of the servant quarters.

On the screen, the hero, played by Alamgir, came home drunk on three nights, swaying from side to side in a dark shiny shirt that glittered even in black and white. He was having an affair with a wealthy woman. His wife, played by the actress Shabana, confided to a friend that no matter what her husband had become, he was still her husband. "My place is at my husband's feet," Shabana

247

said. "Don't you know that a woman's heaven is under her husband's feet?"

The movie came to an end. Putulir Ma sighed. Sraboni inserted a thumb in her mouth and stretched one foot.

"Apa, don't you have college tomorrow?"

"Hmm."

"Apa, Putuli's father, he was a very handsome man. He looked like the film star Alamgir." Sraboni sat up straight; the muscles in her stomach tightened. She only knew vaguely that Putulir Ma had come to work for them after her husband had deserted her, leaving her child at home with her mother. They called her Putulir Ma, meaning mother of Putuli, because she had a daughter named Putuli, who was now fourteen.

"Really?" she said and changed sides, hugging the pillow underneath her belly. "He was so tall and muscular from working on the fields, his body shining. But his face was round and fair like a well-to-do person. He loved me very much, Apa. He never raised a hand to me ever. He was a very meek and gentle person."

"So, then what happened?"

"Apa, he used to go to one house for chatting, and the woman of the house decided she wanted him for her daughter. She used to send the daughter out in front of him, tempting him. She did it all on purpose, Apa."

"He left like me a crazy man, Apa, like one possessed," said Putulir Ma. "He wanted me back so many times afterwards, Apa, but my brothers never consented. No need to go back to him ever and lower yourself, they said. Apa, I raised Putuli myself, as you know. Putuli says, you did the right thing, Amma."

Sraboni did not speak. She stared at the television screen, feeling the pillow against her stomach, and her chest hurt.

"On the day he left me, Apa, Putulir Bap moved through the house like a mad man, throwing pots and breaking glass," Putulir Ma said. "I barred the door so he would not leave. I'll kill you, woman, move out of my way, he screamed. I said to him, no, you are not in your right mind. Don't leave. Here are your wife and child in front of your eyes. Stay with that girl as long as you like. But don't abandon us, you are mistaken. At this, his eyes went bloody. He never beat me in my life before that day," she said. "He never even raised his voice."

"I'm so sorry. You're like family to us. This is your home now," Sraboni said in an emotional voice.

"Apa, every time I look at you, I think of you as my Putuli, my own daughter," Putulir Ma said to Sraboni.

Sraboni blushed and stuck a finger in her mouth.

Sraboni and her friend Hena sat together on the grass under a large rain tree of Dhaka University campus. The April air was heavy as it hadn't rained for days. Sraboni wore a short-style shalwar kameez in a large-flower pattern fabric–she had had two outfits tailored in this latest fashion, in red and blue.
Hena pointed out a tall young woman in tight clothes buying snacks at a street side cart. "She's a *bad* girl." He had a long face and expressive eyes, a wide mouth, all of which she used when she gossiped.

"What's she done?" Sraboni asked.

"She's having an affair with a young faculty member in Physics."

"What's her name?"

"Majeda. She goes to his house when his parents are not there. But he has been telling stories to all his friends, so now everybody knows. Men don't respect these types of girls who are willing to have a physical relationship, you know."

Sraboni made a round O with her mouth as chewed on some American bubblegum Hana had brought her. Hena had a brother who lived in America. American bubblegum retained its elasticity much longer. Sraboni tore clumps of grass between her fingers, considering the taste of the orange flavored gum in her mouth before announcing, "Sheuli wants to introduce me to this boy in Statistics. He is doing his MA."

"Statistics?" Hena made a face. "The people with the lowest HSC marks get into Statistics. Would your parents approve?"

Sraboni blushed and shrugged at the same time.

"How're you supposed to be introduced?" Hena asked.

"I have his email address. I'm supposed to write to him. Sheuli suggested since you have email, I could use your computer…"

"Why do you have to date? Your parents will find you a nice man. I myself would never do such a thing. My mother is going to find me a groom settled in America, when I graduate."

"I don't have the patience to wait so long," Sraboni laughed.

"Listen, Sraboni, you have to make sure your parents meet him, make it official before you go out anywhere with him. Otherwise men can just play around with a girl like she's a throwaway."

"Madam, I haven't even sent the email yet! When can we do this?"

When they entered the classroom, Rafiq Sir was already lecturing on the wave-particle duality of electrons. He had drawn the elaborate diagram of an experiment on the blackboard. Sraboni frowned and tried to grasp the concept, both a particle and a wave, both here and not here. Heisenberg's uncertainty principle. If you try to locate the position of a particle exactly, the velocity becomes infinitely inaccurate, so that you can never pin it down. Even if you set up an experiment to calculate the exact position, Rafiq Sir was saying, the very act of observing it would change the reality. Sraboni thought about this. Like a human heart, unpredictable, as they said in the songs she practiced singing at home. She tried to write a list of all the Tagore songs that carried the same sentiment.

The bell rang. Sraboni stopped thinking about Tagore songs and looked around for Hena. Rafiq Sir was packing his books. He was telling the girl from the English medium school to stop wearing skirts to class. How many times did the girl have to be told? Had she no shame? Sraboni herself wore skirts only at home. She walked to Hena's desk.

"Do you want to go in my car?" she asked. "My driver's here, I think. Then I can, you know . . ."

Hena smiled and winked, fixing her scarf around her head. Her mother made her wear it so that the political-type cadre students wouldn't dare to tease her. Some other classmates huddled in a group, and Hena stopped to chat with them. Everybody was lingering. Sraboni was impatient; she had never used email before. What would she write to this boy? Sheuli had said she would bring his photo to class today. But Sheuli had cut class again!

"Did you hear about the first-year girl Majeda?" one of the boys was asking the group gathered around them. The girls made faces and uttered shocked expressions to show that they had heard the gossip.

"Is that the girl who visits her boyfriend in his bedroom?" Sraboni asked. She was bored.

Hena was still gathering her books. Sraboni caught sight of Sheuli coming in through the door.

"Sheuli!" Sheuli registered Sraboni and pulled her to a corner.

"Quick! Give me your class notes! Here, I brought you the envelope with the photo. Have you written to him yet? He's very handsome, as you shall see . . ."

Sraboni took the envelope stuffed in her palm and placed it carefully inside her jute bag.

One of the women said, "Don't you think this Majeda ought to be expelled? She is creating a bad name for all female students at the university."

"It's indecent!" Hena said. "What will the boys think of us girls? They will think we're all like that."

"Disgusting!" Sraboni said. "I would never. I would kill myself and die of shame."

Hena lived on Road 28 in Dhanmondi in a one-story bungalow with a front lawn. In the drawing room, a large photo of Hena's American immigrant brother greeted all visitors directly as they entered through the front door. The photo had always made Sraboni giggle, until a year ago, when she had started university and Hena's mother had suggested to Hena the possibility of a match between Sraboni and her son. Now the laughing face made Sraboni shiver with a peculiar excitement.

In Hena's bedroom, the phone rested by the head of her bed. Sraboni could not understand why Hena never managed to answer it before her mother. They closed the door behind them and shook off their sandals, piling barefoot onto the bed, giggling. Sraboni looked around for the computer. When was Hena going to turn it on?

"Badshah!" Hena called to the little boy who worked for them. "Bring us tea!"

"Apa, milk tea or raw tea?"

"Raw tea with ginger!"

"Apa, sugar or no?"

"Your servant boy can talk!" laughed Sraboni. She sat down at the computer and stared at the giant screen. "Is this the On button?"

Badshah entered the room without knocking and said, "Apa, can you get the tea leaves down for me? I can't reach." He wore a red flannel shirt tucked into perfectly pressed khaki shorts. His hair was neatly parted at the left and smoothed down the sides of his tan face. "The boy has enormous eyes. How beautiful," said Sraboni, in English so Badshah wouldn't understand. "I can see he is spoiled! He is showing off!"

Hena left for the kitchen. Sraboni remembered the envelope. She pulled it out, then paused. Perhaps she should open it with Hena. Or perhaps what was inside was for her eyes only. She caught her shadowy reflection in the computer screen and smiled, let the envelope lie, and looked over at the cylindrical box of snacks on the computer table. Pringles. She'd seen them at Gulshan Market once.

"Hey, are these from America?" Sraboni asked when Hena returned.

"Yeah, they're like potato chips. My brother sent them. Have one. They come in different flavors."

Sraboni took one. It was very good. She wanted more.

Hena tinkered with the computer. Sraboni tore open the long yellow envelope and pulled out a typed biodata. She unfolded it and a picture fell out onto the mosaic floor. She picked it up and stared at the perfect look-alike of the cricketer Imran Khan. Were those eyes really blue? She felt her thighs contract.

"What's this? Allah, I see this is a real prince, Sraboni!"

"Okay, is the computer ready?"

"Why don't I type and you dictate to me? First, you need to insert some poetry or poetic reference. You also need to tell him what you look like."

"What *do* I look like?" Sraboni asked, nervous now.

"Like the perfect match for our handsome prince. Ha Ha Ha."

Sraboni began to dictate. "Write. I am like Tagore's Ordinary Girl in his poem *Sadharan Meye*. My complexion is dusky, like that of any other Bengali girl. My eyes are large, and I am small and thin."

"Say you have a nice figure!"

"*Chup*! And you're supposed to be so proper!" Badshah trying to balance tea and biscuits on his dancing tray.

"Sraboni, make sure your parents meet the boy. So he doesn't dare to think of this as just a fling," Hena said.

"You said that already. Don't be boring."

Sraboni showed Putulir Ma his photo as the maid oiled her hair while she sat at her desk studying.

"Apa, he is like a prince. But a big heart is more important than looks."

"And that is what you have learned from your marriage, Putulir Ma?" Sraboni teased.

"Apa, I think my husband left me because the other woman was beautiful. And in Bangladesh, there are always other women more beautiful."

"But to leave a young wife and child! The logic doesn't enter my head. Do you really understand it?"

"Apa, when he left, he said 'Why should I stay with you, woman, look at your feet, just look at your feet. Have you ever seen such ugly feet?' Apa, his words still ring in my ears."

Sraboni felt sad about the labyrinth of the human heart. She didn't want to think about Putulir Ma's husband anymore. She closed her eyes and thought instead about Rashed Zaman, five foot eight, age twenty-six. Once Putulir Ma had tied her hair, she pulled away and went to sit by the harmonium on the floor, pulling off the dust cover to sing. Her father liked her to practice for at least one hour a day. He had named her Sraboni after the rainy month of Srabon, the month of Tagore's death anniversary. He was a romantic.

Hena had printed out Rashed's email and brought it to class. Rashed wanted to meet Sraboni. Sheuli advised going to a public place, like the Aarong café. Hena would accompany Sraboni' it wouldn't be proper otherwise. Sraboni wore a blue silk saree and attached a large bunch of fresh jasmine flowers to her hair. He would meet them by the Banarasee sari section in the store.

"That's a good omen. We can finish shopping for the wedding today, if you like." Hena laughed.

"*Chup*, you naughty girl!"

When he entered the floor for women's clothes at Aarong, they recognized him at once by his cloudy grey eyes. Sraboni felt that she had known him all her life. The glass bangles tinkled on her wrists which were shaking from her nervousness.

"Let's go upstairs to the cafe, then?" he smiled widely.

He ordered for them both at the counter of Aarong café and paid, although they tried to protest. Hena and Sraboni chose a table by the window, looking down on the intersection at Manik Miah Avenue below. Sraboni watched the big trucks chase the three-wheeler baby-taxis and rickshaws out of the way.

"I'm sorry I was late. Did I keep you waiting?" He was looking directly at her.

Sraboni blushed and shook her head. She was surprised at her own sweetness, she had not realized she was such a heroine. "Do you watch cricket?" she asked, to make conversation.

"Cricket? No, I have no time for sports. I'm always studying, why do you ask?"

"Because you look like Imran Khan."

It was Friday morning and Sraboni lingered in bed. Hens clucked outside their house in Kalabagan, and some children screamed as they jumped into the pond. They were lucky enough to rent a house in a circle of residences at the heart of the alleys, with a large open meadow in front and an actual pond where the neighborhood kids played. Putulir Ma had called her twice to get up, reminding her that her music teacher was waiting. She put her hands between her legs, feeling the warm sensation of her thighs, and thought back on her dream of the night before.

"Sraboni," her mother called through the closed door. "Your music teacher is waiting. Eat your omelet and start your practice."

She had been speaking to Rashed on the phone daily for two months, discussing Tagore songs, Bengali poetry, and the latest English movie video releases.

"Do you want to go to Madhumita cinema to watch the Indiana Jones movie?" he had asked. She thought this the perfect opening.

"Please come to our house tomorrow," she said in reply. "I will make chotpoti. Do you like chotpoti?"

Every night, after Sraboni put down the phone with Rashed, she spoke to Hena. Either she called, or Hena did, wanting to know every line, ready to interpret. Hena said Sraboni should prepare her parents for the meeting. Sraboni warned her mother that a boy was coming to the house. Her mother told her father while he was watching BBC in the family room, and Sraboni heard him asking her mother, "Is she going to marry him?"

"Who knows?" her mother said, making Sraboni shiver with excitement.

When Rashed entered the drawing room, Sraboni stood up to gret him, smoothing her hair nervously. Sraboni's mother had suggested they should receive him in the formal drawing room rather than the TV room they used every day. Rashed sat down on the maroon velvet sofa, fingering the threads on the maroon cushion. The sun streamed in through the window behind him, enveloping him in light. He wore a checked shirt buttoned to the collar, tucked into tailored black trousers. His shoes were polished a shiny black. His face looked thin and earnest.

"What does your father do?" Sraboni's father asked. He wore his best kurta and straddled his left foot across his right knee. His big toe peeped out of his best leather sandal.

"He is not living," Rashed answered.

"Oh!" Sraboni's mother said. "And your mother?"

"She is also dead. They died in the liberation war."

Sraboni smoothed her hair, feeling deep affection for this earnest boy. He was much darker than in the photo, he was shorter than Imran Khan, and his hair was dusty.

Putulir Ma wheeled in a dinner trolley with chotpoti and pakoras. Sraboni and Putulir Ma had cooked the snacks together, amid many jokes: "Apa, are you cooking your first meal for your future husband?"

When Rashed stood up to leave, Sraboni's father grew very solemn and announced, "I have only one daughter, you know. She is everything to us." Sraboni cringed from tension. Was that kind of talk premature? But Rashed gave her a sweet smile as he left. They exchanged no words, but his enormous eyes nodded to her in a gracious embrace. They walked all the way to the road. Then he turned and called a rickshaw in the Kalabagan alley.

Sraboni was on the phone with Hena that evening. She had called twice to get through. Hena's mother had said, *she is at Maghreb prayers, don't you pray?* Sraboni giggled: Why was Hena's mother so concerned about her prayers, did she still think of Sraboni as her future daughter-in-law? Putulir Ma was stretched flat on the floor of Sraboni's room. Sraboni lay on her narrow bed. Putulir Ma had back pain and Sraboni had given her Napa to ease the pain.

"Oh, my God, Hena! I am going to die!" Sraboni said when Hena came to the phone.

"Why?" Hena asked.

"I'm so happy. But also afraid. I mean, I had never thought any man would like me. Why would any man like an ordinary girl like me?"

"If you are ordinary, then you are like all the other girls. If all girls are like you, then who else would a man marry? It's physics, my dear, pure and simple logic."

"But I'm so scared." Sraboni said. "I think I'm affected by Putulir Ma's experience. Her husband left her. That has always made me feel afraid of men."

"Why are you suddenly so anxious?"

"I think I'm in love, Hena!"

"Nonsense. Keep your head. With men, always keep your head. And listen, you are educated, your Putulir Ma is not. No man will dare to leave *you*. Much less an average student from Statistics. Oh, sorry. Didn't mean to insult your lover boy."

Rashed met Sraboni at Madhu's canteen. Sraboni had not eaten at Madhu's canteen before, when she hung out with Hena and Sheuli, because Hena's mother would never let them frequent such a low-down place. Sraboni eyed the students around her. Everybody looked like a political student leader, the cadre type, with scratchy beards and shift eyes. Heavy smoke filled the air. Rashed lit a cigarette. Sraboni drew her legs together, her bangles tinkled. Her father never smoked. The smell of smoke was new to her, exciting.

"So how are your studies?"

"Good." Sraboni kept her face half-turned toward the other tables.

Rashed motioned to a little boy. The boy walked up to the table. "Would you like some tea? The tea is very good here," Rashed said.

"Yes, Okay."

Sraboni took a small sweet sip from her cup. She never drank tea because it was bad for her complexion. Also, her music teacher said it was bad for her voice.

"Are you politically involved?" she asked.

"What do you think? Yes, of course. Someone whose parents died in the liberation war? How could I not be?"

Sraboni drank some more tea, she didn't know what to say. She didn't know anything about politics. She did not read the morning paper that her parents pored over.

"Which party?" she asked. He smiled with his eyes again.

"You're always asking questions, so serious! You tell me, which Hindi movies have you watched? Who is your favorite actress? I mean, who do you think is the hottest?"

"The hottest? I have never had such a conversation with a boy before!"

"Come on, now!"

"Well, who is it for you?"

"Smita Patil."

"Oh, but she is so thin. And, and, she is dead." He leaned forward and looked at her frankly then, saying, "She looks like you. And you're here, very much alive." His fingers stayed on his cup, tapping soundlessly on the rim. Long thin fingers, darkened at the tips by tobacco stains.

Putulir Ma's brothers visited her one Friday afternoon, while Sraboni and her mother were watching a Bangla film on television. Sraboni's mother made them wait outside the door. They were big broad-shouldered men, and one could never tell what intentions lay hidden in their hearts, she said. Putulir Ma talked to them standing outside in the Kalabagan alley and then hurried back inside, leaving her brothers still waiting outside on the street. She found Sraboni and her mother in the family room.

"Khala," she said to Sraboni's mother, leaning against the wall beside the TV, "Please let me go home for a few days. Putuli's father has been visiting my mother's house. He demands to marry Putuli to an uneducated man in the village. A political type powerful man. I am afraid. If he has his way, Putuli will never be educated."

"But Putulir Ma, how can we get by without you?" Sraboni's mother protested. "Find a replacement, and then you can go."

Putulir Ma wiped her eyes with her large hand and hurried out of the TV room. Sraboni inserted her thumb in her mouth and focused on the television screen.

Putulir Ma mopped the floor under Sraboni's feet with a rag, getting on her hands and knees. Sraboni raised her feet and planted them on her chair to get them out of the way. She leaned forward at her desk, writing his name over and over again. He called her his Malati, referring to Tagore's poem about the ordinary girl. They met at Madhu's canteen, or at the chotpoti carts parked on the street near the national museum, where he slipped her a single kadam flower, the first of the season. Once he took her to the Children's Park and they went on the rides together. When they came down from the roller coaster, she fixed her dupatta quickly and placed a hand over her heart to calm it. But he pulled it away.

"How many children would you have?" he asked her.

"What?" she said.

"Say, if we were married, how many children would you like to have?"

"I don't know. How many would you?"

Sraboni smiled now as she remembered the scene. He had called just now, asking her to visit him in his hostel room.

"No respectable girl goes to a boy's room in the hostel!" she'd laughed.

"But I have no other home to invite you to! You know I would like to entertain you too, cook chotpoti for you?"

She had laughed. "Don't you have any relative's place we could go to?"

"Relatives? But then I would have to explain who you are!"

"Who *am* I?"

They'd both chuckled.

Now she wrote his name again inside her solid-state physics textbook; she knew that she would visit him.

"Have you found someone to take your place yet, so you can go home?" she asked Putulir Ma happily.

"No, Apa," Putulir Ma said. "I have to write a letter to Putuli. Will you write it for me?"

"Sure," Sraboni said, drawing the bar over the triangular R in Rashed.

Sraboni had become a regular visitor in Rashed's room at SM Hall, standing stiffly in front of the sunlit window, leaning by the table piled with books, but never sitting down on the only place to sit, the narrow single bed. One day, he suggested that they should go to his uncle's house in Rayerbazar. The uncle, Rashed's mother's brother, had raised him. On the rickshaw together, though they tried to sit apart, their thighs touched. Rashed let the hood down and lit a cigarette. The rickshaw weaved its way through the alleys of Rayerbazar, traveling at great speed, plunging deeper and deeper into the endlessly winding, narrow alley. Sraboni hated Rayerbazar. The narrow alleys made her nervous; she felt like running away. They brushed past houses that encroached on the road; the raw legs of cows dangled in front of the butchers' tin-shed shops. There was the smell of blood, everywhere, making her want to vomit. "This is where the massacred people, in Rayerbazar, during the liberation war," Rashed said quietly beside her.

"Did—your parents die in the Rayerbazar massacre? Where they killed people and threw them in a mass grave?"

Rashed nodded.

"How could the Pakistani soldiers do such a thing? Don't you think they were evil?"

Rashed turned to her as if he couldn't understand her. "Evil? No, I don't think they were evil."

"Then how could they do such horrible things to us Bengalis?"

"Because they could. Simply because they were more powerful and they could."

Sraboni felt enormous affection for the orphaned boy. She touched his shirt sleeve very softly so that her fingers barely brushed the fabric.

When they reached the narrow green house, he knocked on the door and a guard opened it. There was an older maid and a small servant girl, but his relatives were not in.

"They wouldn't be," Rashed explained, turning to Sraboni. "My uncle and aunt both work. But they will be back soon. It's almost four now."

Sraboni nodded happily. He showed her family albums—he had been a thin boy with enormous eyes. He always seemed to be slightly outside the family circle in the photos. Sraboni wanted to ask if he had been treated well by his uncle's family. When they had finished looking at the albums, she wiped the bead of sweat from her upper lip, and hugged her arms tightly across her chest. Rashed put the albums back in their cabinet and touched the back of her hand very lightly.

He closed the bolts on the door of the living room. The living room separated the house from the servant quarters. They walked deeper inside the house and walked into a bedroom, where he switched on the fan and opened the windows.

"My room," he said shyly. "Sorry it's so hot."

A crooked table stood in one corner beside a narrow bed. A dirty white mosquito net still hung over the bed, nailed to the wall in four places. Sraboni stood at the door for a long time; the hot air crackled with static electricity. The sky grew dark and the rain fell outside the window in weighty pellets. The rainy seasons had started. Sraboni put a hand on her abdomen; she felt heavy with blood. She felt that she was floating between two worlds, neither here nor there.

Rashed took her hand and she sat down on the unmade bed under the mosquito net. In the space they created in the tent of a blanket, anything was possible. She gave herself up like a doll as he disrobed red, pulling the kameez over her head, her arms outstretched.

They lay together in the curtained room. Rashed was watching the clock. At 4:45 PM, he stood up and dressed, tightening his belt buckle. Sraboni closed her eyes and tugged on her clothes under the white sheet. Then Rashed opened the doors and went outside to the servant quarters. Sraboni could hear him telling the maid to get new sheets. Now that she had lost the tautness in her stomach, the last vestiges of recoil, Sraboni wanted to sink into the sweetness of the heated cotton. She didn't want to get up. But the maid was coming.

After that first time, she visited him in his hostel room. She liked to lie in the direct path of the sun's beam, gathering up the heat with her naked body. Then she rolled over, entangled in his white blanket, announcing, "Hiya! I'm a ghost! I shall haunt you for the rest of your life." She snatched his cigarette from him and took a pull, exhaling the smoke slowly through her flared nostrils. Was this the kind of love Putulir Ma had at one time, in her youth? She felt her spirit mingle with that of the young Putulir Ma, rising, held adrift in the angled beam of sunlight.

She no longer joined in the conversations about Majeda. Rafiq Sir announced to class one day that Majeda, the first year girl in Physics who had been sleeping with a professor, might be expelled.

"She's pregnant," Hena mouthed to her.

After class, Sraboni went to meet Rashed at the hostel, but he wasn't there. She felt the guards eyeing her idly outside. The pavement hit hard through her thin sandals. There was a kadam tree inside the compound. Sraboni wondered if Rashed had plucked the flower he had given her from this very tree, but now the kadams were strewn about on the ground, ripped from the tree in the repeated onslaught of the rains. She went by Madhu's canteen and waited at a table in the smoke-filled interior, listening to a conversation about how the big powerful parties swallowed up individual students. Someone was saying that the ruling party had rounded up some political students at one of the hostels. Which hostel? She strained to hear. Rashed did not show up at the canteen.

The sky had grown dark and she thought she had better leave before the nightly torrents of rain started. She walked to her car and told the driver to head home. She was worried for Rashed, bothered by rumors about student political leaders being arrested. She had no way to call him because there was no phone in the hostel room. Putulir Ma nagged her to eat her lunch, but she pushed past her and locked herself in her room. In the evening, she took a chance and called Rashed's uncle's phone number. He went there sometimes, and she had called him there before.

The maid answered the phone. "Rashed bhai?" said the nasal maid. "Rashed bhai is getting engaged today. It is his engagement party today."

By midnight, Sheuli had uncovered the entire story and called her.

"I'm sorry, Sraboni. His uncle arranged the marriage. She is the daughter of a businessman. Her father owns some garment business. Rashed says he had to marry out of obligation, and also because he has no future as a statistician. This girl's father will set him up in business. He says he wouldn't have been able to provide for you."

"But when did he decide?"

"Yesterday. It all happened yesterday. His uncle told him yesterday, he met the girl, and he decided."

Putulir Ma called for her through the locked door, asking her to come to dinner. Also, was the red kameez dirty, should she wash it?

"Go away!" Sraboni cried.

She called Hena. It was past midnight. Hena's mother answered the phone.

"Don't you sleep?" her mother asked. Hena picked up the other phone on the same line.

"It's okay, Ma, you can hang up now," she said to her mother. She sounded distraught. She said Badshah had left suddenly, and their house was in a mess. "My mother and I have been washing clothes and scrubbing pots all day! Did you want to say something?"

"No, that's okay." Sraboni let Hena go that day without breaking the news.

"Good night," said Hena. "I'm very sleepy."

With daybreak, shame filled Sraboni. She inspected her dark hands and her callused feet in the bright light of the morning, thinking that she had to tell her parents. She told them quietly while they were watching a Hindi movie on video.

She said, "Rashed is marrying somebody else." Her father switched off the TV and cried. "You have filled my heart with shame!" he shouted. "How could a girl openly date a boy and then not marry him? We told everybody that you were going you marry him."

"Why are you crying?" Sraboni's mother snapped. "I am going to my sister's house now. We will get our daughter married within this very year. Why cry over a useless graduate of statistics? Men! They make me so angry, thinking they own the world. It's not like she lived with him."

She walked over to the divan and pulled Sraboni into a hard embrace. Sraboni trembled because of what they did not know.

When Sraboni called Hena, Hena's mother said she was taking her afternoon nap. Besides, there was an exam the next day.

"Aren't you studying for the exam?" Hena's mother asked.

Sraboni called Sheuli, who said not to blame herself because orphaned children were twisted, especially someone whose parents had died in the liberation war; Rashed had to be pretty mixed up in the head. Besides, who could resist the temptation of marrying someone who had been educated in America?

"She was educated in America?"

"Yes, she actually lives in New York. She's an artist or something, very creative."

Sraboni hung up and flung the cordless phone across the bed, wanting it to crash to the floor and break into pieces. Instead it fell over the side and was caught in the thread of the bedcover, where it dangled and rotated slowly. Sraboni threw herself to the floor and began to

268

beat her head against the hard mosaic surface, wishing she could escape her overwhelming ordinariness. Then it came to her. Hena's older brother. She would marry him and move to America. She would wear her red kameez and he would like her instantly. Slowly, she picked herself from the floor and walked to the corner of her bed. She stooped to disentangle the phone, checking to see if it was broken.

She decided she was going to Hena's place, she would ask Hena about her brother. Sraboni's mother had taken the car to her sister's house. But Sraboni would go by rickshaw. She would wear her red short kameez, let her hair down to her waist, and travel with the rickshaw hood down.

Sraboni hunted madly for her red kameez, flinging all the contents of her dresser on the floor. Then she walked out of the room, the phone still in her hand. She would call Hena's mother and tell her she was coming. She marched into the kitchen, phone in hand.

"Putulir Ma!" she called. "Putulir Ma!"

Putulir Ma emerged from the bathroom with two wet strands of cloth, red and blue, strung together.

"Apa?"

"Putulir Ma, where is my red kameez? How come I cannot find it?"

Putulir Ma held out the contents of her hands.

"Apa, I was just washing it. It has become stained. The color has run from the blue Kameez into the red one."

Sraboni could not believe it. She stood staring at the ruins of her new clothes. She ran to the sink and let the tap water run over the fabrics, but each lay permanently stained. She moved closer, until she was level with Putulir Ma's chin.

"What have you done?" she hissed.

"Apa, it was my mistake. Sorry."

"How dare you?" she cried, her voice rising. "You fool of a woman! Don't you know how to wash clothes? Hmm? Don't you know? How dare you?"

She prodded Putulir Ma on the elbow, pushing her, wanting her to return everything to normal. The kitchen was hot and suffocating. Both the stoves were burning. Sraboni felt fire shooting through her head.

"Apa, I made a mistake. I am sorry."

"How dare you, you woman?" Sraboni cried helplessly, almost in a tender voice. Then she rushed at Putulir Ma with the cordless telephone and hit her on the shoulder, three times. Putulir Ma ducked, hiding her head. Sraboni was enraged. She threw the phone down on the floor and reached for Putulir Ma's oil-streaked hair, pulling hard, till it came away in clumps in her fingers and made her cry.

"You leave now, this moment, do you understand? You don't have to wait for my mother to return. I order you to leave!"

"Apa, I have worked in this house for so many years. Is it fair to make me leave at a moment's notice?"

Sraboni felt exhausted. All humanity had been drained from her. She turned and left the hot kitchen without another word.

Walking past the living room, she saw he father sleeping in front of the TV, his mouth open in a helpless gesture of defeat. She went into her bedroom and locked the door. Then she lay down on her bed, pulling her knees up to her head to curl into a ball, and fell asleep. When she awoke and pushed the curtains apart, she saw that the sky was dark outside. The trees were wet and the drainpipe was dripping water; it had rained while she had been sleeping. Sraboni ran to the kitchen to find Putulir Ma. But she was gone. Sraboni searched for Putulir Ma's belongings, the red printed saree and the orange batik saree, the black bag, the blue comb. There was nothing. Sraboni walked back to the family room. Her mother was back.

"Where is Putulir Ma?" her mother asked.

"I don't know," Sraboni answered, throwing up her hands. "I had an argument with her. I told her to go."

Sraboni's mother didn't say anything immediately. She closed her eyes and fell back on the sofa. "How will I do all this work? How will we get another maid? Can you turn up the fan speed?"

"May I take the car to Hena's house?" Sraboni asked.

Hena's mother opened the door to Sraboni. Her sari was wrapped around her waist and she had a dustpan in her hand.

"Hena is still sleeping," she said.

"She's expecting me. We have to study for a physics exam," Sraboni lied.

Hena woke up in a long blue maxi that her brother had sent from America. She rubbed her eyes and said, "Allah, what time is it?"

"You know about Rashed and me," Sraboni accused her. "Why haven't you called me?"

Hena sat up and swung her feet to the floor.

"Well? Don't you feel bad for me?"

"I'm sorry," said Hena. "But you will be all right. He's the one who'll be forever stained. It says so in the Koran, the wrongdoer is the one who can never forget."

"I don't think I shall live past this," said Sraboni.

"Tell Auntie to look for a husband for you. If you get married, you shall forget all this soon."

Sraboni sat down on the bed. The cover was sheep white wool, like Rashed's sheets. Now that she was here, she didn't know how to broach the subject.

"Your brother. Is he still– is your mother still looking for a wife for him?"

Hena just looked at her.

"Didn't she say she was thinking about me for a match? Could you please ask her if she still thinks it's possible?"

Hena stood up and started to search for her slippers.

"Do you want some tea?" Hena asked. "I have to make it myself, though."

"Please. Speak to me."

"Listen, Sraboni, you're not in your right mind. You are still in shock."

"But you just said, you think I should get married soon."

Hena was walking out the door, saying, "My brother is too young to marry yet." But then she stopped at the door. "Actually, I will be plain. You are now someone who has had a relationship. I can't knowingly marry my brother to someone like that."

Sraboni looked away and let Hena go out of the room, to make tea or whatever. Stained by a relationship, and Hena didn't even know half of it. Sraboni wondered if she should tell Hena that she had had a physical relationship with Rashed. Like Majeda had with a faculty member. She looked across at her image on Hena's computer screen, searching for a clue to the horrors she was capable of.

When Hena returned with the tea on a tray, Sraboni was crying.

"Why are you crying? Listen, I'm sorry about what I said. It's only how my mother would think, if she knew . . ."

"Hena, I'm not crying for myself. I hit Putulir Ma. I hit her because she destroyed my red short shalwar kameez. Then I told her to leave. And now she is gone."

Hena passed her the tea and sipped from her own cup. Sraboni remembered Putulir Ma's tea, the sweet tea that Putulir Ma made with condensed milk.

"Please! Say something!" she cried. She drank noisily and inhaled to clear her stuffed nose.

She watched Hena, the dainty fingers on the teacup, so composed, so angelic.

"Hena, you're so perfect. You must be disgusted by all the wrong things I've done. You're so principled and good."

Hena stood up, standing in front of Sraboni, with the computer screen behind her.

"Sraboni, do you remember Badshah, the little boy who worked for us?"

"Yes."

"He left because I hit him. He stole—I thought he had stolen—five hundred taka from my desk drawer. I asked him about it and he kept denying it. So I beat him for lying and stealing. I kept slapping him till he fell on the floor. He went to bed without food. Later in the morning he was gone. My mother says he left because I hit him."

Sraboni was glad it was difficult to call Rashed, since he had no landline phone in his hostel room. She didn't want to become like a ghost stalking a past lover. She decided she could call just once. She dialed his uncle's number. Rashed was saying Salam Alaikum.

Sraboni gathered her breath and said in a rush, "It's me. Your ordinary girl. Your Malati. Don't worry, I am not calling to haunt you. I just have one question. How could you do this? I feel like I never knew you. Are you a good person?"

Rashed said, "I don't know, Sraboni. I'm just an ordinary guy. You decide."

Sraboni put down the receiver and went to the verandah, leaning against the wrought-iron railing and staring outside at the neighborhood. It was raining again, noisily. Water had gathered everywhere in puddles, and the boys from the nearby cottages were playing football barefoot in the mud.

Sraboni went back to her room, resting her head on her elbows, and lay awake in the dark listening to the heavy sounds of the rain outside. She felt haunted by Putulir Ma. How would Putulir Ma feed Putuli now, send her to school? How was she feeling now, how heavy was her heart?

Sraboni spoke into the dark, "Putulir Ma, I know why your husband beat you up. Why he left you and married again. Because he could. Simply because he could."

She closed her eyes, trying to conjure up Putulir Ma in her mind, the bad back, the limp, Putulir Ma sitting at her feet by the divan, cleaning under her chair as she studied. But the image was blurred. Putulir Ma's features began to fade in her mind. Sraboni wondered about one question, that she had never thought to ask the maid whom they had simply referred to as the mother of Putuli. She wondered what Putulir Ma's name was.

The Father of the Nation

A big red banner hung on the whitewashed wall of the seminar room of the NGO, announcing the seminar topic of the day: the trafficking of women and children from Bangladesh.

The NGO C– had arranged a meeting in its staff house for all the organizations that worked with the poor: UN members, non-government organizations, activists, university researchers, the press, and even members of the government. People would have sighed about yet another meeting on an old issue, yet all the members of the consultative group on trafficking respected Dr. Rashid Uddin. He was like a father to them. There were about twenty people in the room. They sat in a semi-circle, on black leather sofas, with a small assembly of chairs up front, by the banner.

At the beginning of the meeting, Dr. Rashid Uddin promised that this was going to be an action-oriented group. The objective of the week-long seminar was to find an area to work on, to mobilize for. This was positive talk indeed in a tired seminar culture. The haggard faces leaned forward, and the eyes brightened a little.

"As you all know, trafficking has increased alarmingly in just the last decade," said Dr. Rashid. "It is the greatest evil facing women and children."

He quoted some statistics. Then they briefly broke for tea. Some of the lesser souls from the national NGOs followed Mary Hogwarth from the World Bank to the tea table. Mrs. Tinni from the UNDP crumbled her pistachio sprinkled biscuit into milk tea and tried to look bored, fixating on a point in the distance. She had already decided the only persons in the room worth her attention were Dr. Rashid and Mary Hogwarth. After ten minutes, everyone drifted back to their sofas, sinking into the soft leather with their smoky teacups.

"We are the most powerful people in the nation assembled here today," said Dr. Rashid. "Surely we can put an end to trafficking if we put our minds to it."

This began the meeting of the most powerful people in the nation.

"First," said Dr. Rashid, "Let us inquire into the cause. Why has trafficking increased? What makes us susceptible? That will lead us eventually to the solution, the answer to the question, how can we stop trafficking? It's as simple as that."

Mr. Toufiq of the Labor Ministry thought that trafficking had increased because of 'the greed of the village women'. "They will go with anyone anywhere in search of money. They want more. Their eyes glitter with greed, for this thing and that. So the way to stop trafficking is to re-educate them in values."

Reema Rani of the *Daily Ittefaq* agreed. "These village women," she said, "they are greedy and also uneducated. It is their ignorance that makes them susceptible to traffickers. They don't have the brains to understand that the man who promises them a ticket to the land of their dreams in exchange for their land and property is tricking them, selling them into prostitution and slavery. The solution is to provide them with information at every step."

"Yes," said Mrs. Tinni of UNDP, nodding sagely. She crumbled another biscuit into her teacup. "This is all true," she said. "But I think it is the lack of community mobilization that makes them susceptible. We must spread advocacy by mobilizing the grassroots through local NGOs. The UNDP can fund a project like that."

Mary Hogworth put up a finger and the entire room turned toward her respectfully. "Much as UNDP's intentions are appreciated," she said, "it is the crime network that we must stop. The World Bank is lending Bangladesh 10 million dollars to track the trafficking chains and step up border controls."

There was some confusion. Many voices spoke at once, angry at the implications of the previous speakers. Dr. Rashid tried to motion for quiet. The servers in uniform refilled the tea flasks and laid out some spicy singara. C— was famous for its spicy singara. Mrs. Tinni of the UNDP felt the entire length of her fat belly rumble and list toward the table.

Dr. Rashid coughed.

"We mustn't forget that poor people have a right to aspirations just as we do," he said. "Don't we line up in front of the US Embassy for immigration? Don't we marry out daughters to "suitable" husbands we have never seen in the US or UK? Do we call ourselves foolish or greedy or uneducated then?"

These were all old arguments and all the old faces in the room rolled their eyes at each other and jumped through the same hoops. Each felt her blood course through her veins in the thrill of the intellectual argument. Mrs. Tinni wondered if her SUV was back to pick her up and if she might not stop at Hotel Sonargaon for lunch on the way back to the office.

At last, the most powerful people stood up and ambled toward the spicy, hot *singaras* laid out in the break room next to porcelain cups filled with milk tea. Mary Hogwarth burnt her tongue and her eyes stung. These C– *singaras* had given her diarrhea only a month ago. She ambled up to Dr. Rashid and inquired of him if any trafficked women were being brought in as representatives, 'for of course they had a voice too'. This was the age of participatory development, she said.

After the second tea break, conversation drifted to the most frequent destinations of cross-border trafficking, ranging from India to the Middle East, and the most frequent modes, from being sold off by a wicked husband to willing parties who paid to have themselves 'trafficked'.

Sona Banerjee from Naripakkha sat in the back and took in   the conversation from all angles. The speeches in the front of the room and the counter whispers from various rows in front of her. As she listened, her bulbous mouth billowed out and her nose with its glint of gold grew very large. Several times, she smoothed the edge of her wrinkled cotton saree with her long-nailed fingers. She pulled at the edges of her blouse sleeves. Finally she raised her hand.

"Dr. Rashid, Dr. Rashid," she said. Sona had a meek voice and she sat in the back row. She tried a little louder. "Dr. Rashid."

Mrs. Tinni was expounding on the definition of trafficking, she thought it was the act of crossing anyone, man or woman, of or against their will, illegally to another country. Mary Hogwarth was arguing with her on the fine points between voluntary migration and forced or tricked crossings.

"DR. RASHEEED!" Sona surprised herself. She was standing upright, her wrinkled saree a straight taut line at attention. The room was utterly silent. Those in the front rows craned their heads to stare at her.

"I have a story to tell," said Sona, "if people would care to hear. It is a rather long story. But when you have heard it, I want you to tell me, in the case of this one trafficked woman, which factor played a part. Was it greed, or lack of education, innocence, or ambition?"

Not many years ago, Asha Devi and her husband migrated to Dhaka from their village home in Faridpur looking for a better future. They were both only eighteen. They lived in a tiny straw hut in the Mohammadpur slum close to Geneva camp. Asha enrolled in a skills training program and that is how she came into contact with the credit-lending NGOs and Naripakkha. Asha's husband Kumar was a tall man with powerful muscles in his arms and thighs, so he soon found a job as a rickshaw puller. But Asha's husband was really an artist.

All his life, Kumar had worked with clay, molding it into various forms. He came from a family of potters, the special line of potters you know those who supply the statues of the gods to temples. But times were hard in the village, and few were interested to invest in statues. In Dhaka, Asha hoped to resurrect the family business out of Kumar's talent. She told the credit NGOs that she was interested in learning how to market dolls and curios. She brought in Kumar's work to our offices and showed it to many of us, hoping to impress the NGO staff and find herself a market.

One day, she hit upon the right door. One of the junior staff at an NGO I will not name had connections to the Prime Minister. She was able to arrange a meeting between the Prime Minister and the young couple. Asha and Kumar dressed up in their best clothes that day, and did I tell you already that they looked like figures cut out of a fairy tale? They made an impressive pair as they stood anxious and eager with a bag full of artifacts on the long marble floor of the Bangabhaban.

When they had waited two hours, the heavy wood panels swung open at last, and indeed, in walked the Prime Minister in flesh and blood. She wore a Rajshahi Silk saree with iridescent peacocks. She smiled on them and bestowed her hand upon their bowed heads. Kumar was a very smart man. He quickly showed the Prime Minister all his art. The last object he took out of his sack was a miniature study of the Father of the Nation. It was the bust of a young Father, robust and bespectacled, smiling with that touching generosity and confidence. An invincible Father who would protect the nation and all its people. The Prime Minister looked at the bust and cried for the Father of the Nation. She held the bust in her hands and fondly ran her fingers over the lines of his kind face, the face that promised a great nation and sanctuary for all.

"Oh," said the Prime Minister. "How you must respect my father to have made this work of love."

"This bust is also a symbol of hope," said Kumar. "The Father of the Nation kindles hope in each and every soul."

The Prime Minister cried some more, on account of the fact that her father had been assassinated, and that

280

many people had forgotten the hope that he represented. Nobody spoke of that anymore.

"Apa," said Asha. "If you wish, we can make a life-size bust of the Father."

"A life-size bust!" cried the Prime Minister. "What a wonderful idea. Make one and show it to me. I shall commission you to make one right now, and I will decide where to have it placed. We must bring hope back to this country."

And so Asha and Kumar had gotten themselves a project beyond their imagination. A project that great artists and architects would kill for. Naturally the NGOs expected great returns from the project and lent this wonderful and talented couple all the money they needed. We formed a committee among ourselves and raised about One Lakh Taka. A lot of money. This Kumar, he was a genuine artist. In a different story, he could have been a Jainul Abedin, or a Picasso. But this is a true story.

Finally, at the end of a year, Kumar finished his life size project. He had worked with black clay, dabbing and coaxing with his fingers until there emerged a bust of sparkling and confident eyes, a wide and strong chest, a nose large enough to shelter the entire nation, and a smile of great softness and hope. By this time the couple had a flower-like baby girl. Asha often brought the baby to the NGO offices and we played with her. We were all very fond of the couple, you see.

The Father was magnificent, a figure in action. The lines of his throat were taut with the effort to speak, finger lifted into the air, his face beaming with love and courage. It was impossible, even for a nation that had forgotten their Father, not to be moved by such an image. The NGOs arranged a second meeting between the Prime Minister and the couple. The Prime Minister was on a tour of local NGOs. It was planned that she would view the bust in one of the credit NGO offices. We spent days locating the bust in exactly the right place, heightening its effect, its message of hope and prosperity. Asha wore a golden saree and put red ribbons in her long hair. Kumar himself wore a long-sleeved navy blue shirt tucked in khaki pants, and slick, polished shoes.

The Prime Minister swept in wearing a pale blue Dhakai saree, with one end carefully flung over her head as it was close to elections. She laughed in her easy manner and chatted with many of the lowly staff. Her smile dazzled the room. When she saw the bust, she stopped. She was very happy to see the bust. She gathered Asha to her bosom and cried. She made a joke to Kumar about his ability to make dreams come to life, and Kumar laughed with great hope lodged in his throat. A TV camera focused on the intimate group. Many pictures were taken.

But the Prime Minister must have forgotten that she had made a promise, or that she had commissioned the project, given her word that her office would buy the bust. She made no mention of taking it or displaying it anywhere. After the photos were taken, she walked away with her long train of security men, the echoes of her easy laughter trailing behind. The Father looked on uncertainly, a wasted mound of clay.

Confused and dumbfounded, Kumar and Asha tried to sell the statue elsewhere. But indeed the nation had lost hope, either in its Father or in art itself. Nobody was buying into the faith symbolized by the Father of the Nation. Time passed and the NGO workers grew anxious. We called meetings. How would we account for the One Lakh taka we had lent? How would we get it back from this failed couple? One by one, the NGOs started to press Kumar to pay back the principle. He was an able rickshaw-puller, after all. Surely, some of that money at least could be recovered. Slowly, the polite requests turned more insistent and desperate. The workers of some of these NGOs visited their home and waited for Kumar. Kumar began to stay away from home till they were safely gone. Some of the NGOs even put local hoodlums to the task of collections. Kumar spent his time hiding, running away. Asha She was known to rush into our offices with her baby, throw herself at our feet, and crying, wild-eyed and her hair flying at all angles.

One day, someone, perhaps someone hired by a money-lender, perhaps even one of the NGOs present here today, poured kerosene over their house and set it on fire. We moved the family to another place. Asha and Kumar tried to borrow money from other NGOs and even local loan sharks, to pay back the committee. Several of us tried to find them jobs. Asha's hair flew more wildly, and her baby wailed loudly in her arms. They lived on the run, sometimes appearing on a doorstep begging for mercy. I was worried myself about getting Naripakkha's money back. I was also applying polite pressure. My colleagues assured me that these people would be able to come up with the money if only they wished to: "Long-term dependence on credit has spoiled them," they said.

Then, one day, Kumar disappeared. We must not be too harsh on him. He couldn't handle it anymore. His shoulders were thin and his eyes were dark and big. He fled the land of hope (some of my colleagues think he escaped to Kolkata), hoping perhaps simply for survival. This left Asha and her baby girl. The flying Asha with flying hair. Flying from hoodlums who sifted through her belongings of oil-stained pillows and darkened aluminum pots looking for something to give, anything to make up the loan. But Asha had nothing she could sell to pay back or stand on her feet again.

Asha began to come to me in the middle of the night, at my house. She stayed away from offices now. Her hair, she did not even brush it. Her sari was just a bundle of cloth now, loose and wrinkled, sagging, discolored. She had no angles anymore, all of her seemed to be melting daily, all the edges softening till it was hard to define her at all.

"Apa, these men keep calling," she said to me one night. "They want to sell me to this place in Pakistan."

I trembled as I gathered her to my chest. With my wide arms, I encircled both mother and baby, as if I could bar them from all that lay in wait just outside my doors. Then I didn't see Asha again for a long time. Perhaps she had lost faith in my love, ineffectual as it was.

But one night Asha appeared at my door again. It was a rainy night in June. The kind of night when the rain doesn't let up. The trees danced demoniacally and the water itself reminded me of Natyaraj, a dancing god in his chariot galloping down the alleyway. We were at dinner, eating wet khichuri with fried omelet. Someone knocked wildly at my door. The servants opened the gates and called me.

When I came out to see, there she was, Asha. When I invited her in, she walked up the driveway to the verandah. With one hand, he held on to her baby girl, who now walked. But she would not come inside the house. A rickshaw waited in the shadows beyond the gate, the rickshaw-puller bunched up inside his hood.

She didn't tell me then, but she had already made up her mind. The brothel in Karachi had suddenly become a living option. That night, she said nothing. But I knew. And the way she walked, it was different. There was suddenly something different about Asha that made me look sharply at her, again and again.
When she had reached me on the verandah, I noticed that in her other hand she held a large jute bag.

She knelt at my feet on the wet verandah and untied the knot on the bag. She brought out the formidable bust of the father, a blackened and stained father, whose head lolled about helplessly in the sack.

"You keep this," she said.

She touched my lashes and kissed the tips of each of my fingers, as if kissing herself good-bye. She was as dramatic as she was beautiful. I noticed that Asha's eyes were steady, sad and large. No longer wild. She stood towering over me. She had always been taller, but now she stood straight, and, I suddenly realized, she was wearing high wooden clogs. Her shoulders were flung out on either side, thrusting a greeting to the world, carving a piece for her body out of the air.

"Didi, I shall go now."

Asha took her daughter by her arm and walked back to the gate. She slipped through the small door, stooping to get through. Then she turned and laughed at me.

I could not think of a way to intervene. I stood with my two bare feet planted solidly on my humble mosaic floor, and I accepted the inevitable. I was simply a witness. Asha had solved her own problem.

But tell me, my respected colleagues, how do you feel about trafficking now? And how do you propose to eliminate this great evil?

Those assembled waited silently for Sona's words to fade into the air. Dr. Rashed asked a clerk to open the windows for good measure so that the uselessly sentimental words could fly away. Then the powerful people of the nation resumed their policy discussions. A little cold air must have blown in from one of the windows because several had to clear their throats first.

Exit

Sooner or later they had to face the world. After six months in Houston, they were invited to their first dinner party. They bought a new dress for their year-old baby, whose name was Shabnam. A very new dress of red slanting stripes that made her look striking. Shabnam was beautiful because of her hair; dark curls fell dangerously over her eyes. She had inherited her hair from mother Haya, who, before leaving for the party, wrapped a large dupatta around her head, covering everything.

They arrived at the party in the suburbs of Katy in a rental car from Enterprise and rang the doorbell. They crossed the large expanse of sparkling white marble floor to the pristine white carpet of the living room, and they made it without incident. They settled down on the edge of the cream-colored leather sofa, backs arched at forty-five degree angles to the seat, and they tried to disappear into oblivion. The room was so immense that they could do that, in spite of all the other guests. The hostess was a friend of friends in Dhaka, an elegant woman who had short hair and was very nice. "May I get you anything to drink?" she asked Haya.

"No, no, thank you," Haya said, craning backward, away from the offer.

The hostess had a daughter. A four-year-old, who, her mother professed, had been waiting eagerly to meet the baby. The child, slender like her mother, had long hair which fell straight to her waist. She sat on the floor watching a cartoon on a flat screen TV. She paid no attention to Shabnam.

"Don't you want to play with the baby?" the hostess asked her.

The child shrugged.

It had been clever of Haya to cover her head with a dupatta. As the doorbell rang, there were many others, the suitably religious-minded, who wore a scarf, a dupatta, or the end of a sari gathered over their heads. To anyone else, Haya might have been one of them. These women asked her name and approved of it.

"Haya means shame, propriety," they explained to her.
Haya nodded.

Then the hostess said to all the children sitting on the carpet in front of the mothers, "Okay, you can go upstairs with all the kids." Instantly, the children vanished, were banished, from the living room. The hostess picked up Shabnam and gave her a push too. Shabnam had barely learned to walk.

"She was okay here," Haya said, but it was really a whisper, and the sleek hostess with the short hair had moved on.

The men walked out onto the balcony. The women lounged on the leather sofas, their shalwar kameezes iridescent under the bright chandeliers as their bejeweled hands circled the air in wide arcs. Not many people spoke to Haya. Haya was happy. There was nothing to say.

If someone had asked, "What do you do?" she would have answered, "Nothing."

If someone had asked, what does your husband do, she would have answered, "Nothing."

"And how long have you been in Houston?"

"No time."

She leaned back slowly and found the back of the sofa.

Shabnam's cries reached downstairs and ricocheted in the white living room. Haya ran upstairs. When she reached the stairs and peered up the banister, she found Shabnam standing precariously at the top of the stairs, surrounded by four older girls about to push her.

"Baba!" Shabnam cried, calling for her father. Then seeing Haya, she cried, "Amma!"

Haya ran up the stairs. The four girls looked very angry with Shabnam. They stood with hands at their waists, arms angled like the handles of urns. Their beautiful hairs glistened under their hair bands and shook with their anger. "Tell her to give back my Barbie," the hostess's daughter commanded.

Haya looked in Shabnam's arms. Shabnam was clutching a Barbie wearing a blazing pink dress with beautiful brown curls that fell over her eyes.

"*No!*" Shabnam said.

Haya tried to coax Shabnam, then she wrestled the doll out of Shabnam's arms. The girls made her uncomfortable. She picked up Shabnam and fled to the stairs. But Shabnam would not be carried and screamed till Haya was forced to let her down.

For the next half hour, Shabnam laboriously made her own way down the carpeted steps, holding onto the railing with her fat fingers and sometimes slipping. Then she walked up the stairs again one at a time. The girls were disgusted when Shabnam reached the landing. They tried to push her down.

"Go away!" They said. The hostess's daughter was especially annoyed. She wagged her finger at Shabnam, her hair dancing down her back.

"You're just a baby. Go away."
Shabnam looked small and feeble, smiling at the girls stupidly, trying to make friends. When Haya had to be in the hospital, Shabnam went the Barnes & Noble in the medical center, near their hotel with her father, every day. It was their new ritual, without Haya. Day after day, Shabnam threw herself fearlessly into the world of mothers and children, confidently joining the circle of other children around the toy train set in the center of the children's section.

After going up and down the stairs several times, Haya positioned herself at the top of the stairs to keep an eye on Shabnam. The older girls turned on the TV to watch *Cinderella*. They sat primly pressed together on a white sofa, a row of vibrant colors, healthy skin and healthy hair. As Haya watched the movie along with the girls, Shabnam tried to sit on the sofa, putting a knee up on the sofa and pushing her body forward with her head. She landed on one of the girls and knocked heads with her. The girl screamed in pain, clutching her head. Haya reached out to console the girl, but then withdrew her hand with its gnawed fingers. The hostess's daughter grabbed her friend and gave her a fierce loyal hug.

The she turned bitterly to Shabnam, "You have hurt my friend, you stupid girl! Now leave!" She was upset and near tears.

Something in her powerful voice got through to Shabnam at last, and Shabnam started to cry. Haya picked her up, rubbed her head, and carried her downstairs.

The third time Shabnam made it up the stairs, her father took her. The girls were in the closet of the playroom, jumping and screaming, and their carefree laughter could be heard from the living room. Shabnam was trying to jump and scream with the others.

The hostess's girl cried, "She! She! She has hurt my friend and now she is messing up my house." Haya heard them from the living room, which gave her a strange feeling, the quality of not being somewhere and yet knowing what was happening in your child's life. Shabnam's father carried her downstairs.

One of the women in the living room pointed to Shabnam and her father as they came down the stairs and said to Haya, "Your husband takes care of the child? You're so lucky!"

Haya did not say anything.

The slender hostess plopped down next to Haya, running her hands through her apple-scented hair, asking Haya, "How is your health?" In her other hand she held a glass of Fanta that clinked with ice.

"Fine," Haya said.

The hostess raised the glass to her face and sucked on the straw. There was only ice left at the bottom of the glass, and the hostess sucked noisily on the ice. The ice made Haya close her eyes and stiffen her nostrils. The nurse in the infusions room at the hospital always gave Haya a Styrofoam cup of iced apple juice before she put the needle in. After four sessions, it was a ritual. The nurse parted Haya's blouse and pricked gently with a needle, connecting her to the saline drip. Then Haya lay back with a magazine and her husband collected chocolate from the white counter to settle down for the long session.

The hostess stood up, patted Haya on the shoulder and left, commanding, "Mingle! Don't hide."

Haya turned her chin away from the leather fabric of the sofa and faced the expatriate Bangladeshis in Houston. They spoke of daycare centers, the sales at Garden Ridge, and the projects at the office. Then they talked about raising kids.

"I can't believe you are following your child around," the women said to her.

"My daughter runs about the house," said a woman in a *katan* sari. "She trips and falls. I don't bat an eyelid." Her hair was up in a bun: a single Chinese hairclip pinned it in place.

"Yes," said her companion on the sofa. "How else would they learn to take care of themselves?" Her hair was down, a luxurious reddish-brown mane about her shoulders. "She's going up and down the stairs," Haya explained, pulling the scar more tightly about her bald head. "She only just learned to walk. She might fall."

"*No,*" a third woman said energetically. "No, that is completely the wrong approach. Have you just come from Bangladesh?"
Haya nodded.

"Listen," continued the woman, "the latest theory in child development is that you must raise a responsible child, able to take care of herself. Let her defend herself. You won't always be around."

"Yes," Haya said, listening intently.

The drama upstairs continued. Shabnam climbed down and then made her way up the stairs again, and the older girls invented a chorus.

"Go. Go!" they cried, gathered on the landing.

They jumped and screamed and made faces to scare her. Then they tried to push her down the stairs, their little fists on Shabnam's shoulders and forehead. Haya was at the dining table getting her food, lathering her rice with yoghurt to slide it past her ash tongue. She left her plate on the table and ran upstairs. When the girls saw Haya, they stopped mid-track, and commanded her to take away the baby. Shabnam was whimpering.

Haya stood watching them all. It was coming true, her worst fear, that if she turned her back, her child would be in danger. The world was full of people who could harm Shabnam.

She spoke sharply to Shabnam. "Don't touch this. This is *theirs*." She snatched away Shabnam's slippery hand from the tails of her *kameez* and carried her writhing body angrily to her husband.

"Isn't it time to go?" she said, as Shabnam screamed and snot streamed down her mouth.

The men in the living room turned their heads when they turned to leave. The women ignored them. Only the host and hostess came away with them to the door.

"Why is she crying?" the host asked.

"She wants to climb the stairs," the hostess said. "All babies like the stairs."

The hostess's daughter stood on the steps, waiting anxiously for Shabnam to leave. "She is *just a baby*," she cried as they left. "She can't speak or climb stairs or anything. She can't do anything without her mommy!" Shabnam screamed and kicked her feet as she was carried out the door.

They drove back in silence. Shabnam screamed in her car seat until she fell asleep. An hour later, they reached their tiny hotel room tucked at the edges of the medical center and put Shabnam in her bed.

"I've never seen a child like that girl in that house!" Haya cried indignantly.

"Kids can be mean!" Her husband said, "Maybe it's the age."

Later, they lay in bed, clutching each other. There was a deep anxiety about their embrace nowadays, an effort to keep time still and yet move it beyond the horror of the present. He ran his fingers over her bare head.

"You know what I really mind," she said, "is that she left so humiliated in everybody's eyes. She's better than that. She can play with other kids and get along."

"We won't let it happen again," he said. "Next time we'll prepare her."

The next day, they made sandwiches and dissected the people at the party.

"What I don't like about them is how settled they are," Haya gossiped. "So *showy*."
Her husband cut the sandwiches neatly with a plastic knife, passing a piece of bread to Shabnam who lay on the carpet surrounded by playing cards.

"Yes," he said, "all the men talked about cars and green cards."

"And all the women," she said, "talked about sofa designs."

But two days later, when they had judged everybody at the party, they knew they still hadn't hit upon the source of their anxiety. They had all three shared in their moment of defeat, but how to right it? When Haya let herself think, she sensed that their defeat was the taste of absence already, the feeling of nonexistence when she still existed, of powerlessness when she still had the power to protect her child, the feeling of being paralyzed by a future that had not yet raised its ugly head.

Then they were invited again. The phone clamored in the forgotten corner of their room, shocking them, two days after Haya had finished her treatment.
"A farewell party in your honor," said this hostess over the phone. "To celebrate the end of your treatment and to say good-bye since you're leaving us so soon." This time, they were determined that Shabnam should make the right exit. They bought her a black velvet dress with a bow at the waist and black leather party shoes, because the last time she had worn plastic. They took her to libraries and parks all week, negotiating her relationship with the world. On the night of the dinner, just as they were about to leave, Haya went back to the mirror in the bathroom and let the scarf drop from her head. She unraveled the silky material in her hands till the layers fell apart, soft and transparent. She left it on the wet countertop behind her.

They arrived at the door of a three-story mansion and rang the doorbell. Like last time, they bent down to take off shoes. They walked across a crowded room full of people, settled people who weren't dying and who had hair. Haya had hair growing at the periphery, like a circus ring. She let Shabnam drop to the floor and gave her a deep embrace, an embrace of supreme confidence, before Shabnam melted into the sea of jostling kids.

Then Haya faced the room herself. The hostess came smiling toward her, pointing with a scintillating hand somewhere above.

"I thought it would be better for the children to play upstairs. I hope that's all right. Your sweet daughter's so tiny."

"Yes," said Haya. "That will be fine."

Two Women

The two newlyweds sat giggling at Hasan and Khalida's dining table. The long table took up the entire space in the rectangular room, and was always full of food and guests, at all hours, on all days of the week, throughout the year. Sunlight poured in through the window on the narrow wall. The newly married Mamun sat next to his wife, his plump fingers dipped in soupy lentils, looking on adoringly as his wife blushed and showed off the henna on her hands.

Mamun had just married Shumi in Bangladesh last year. Two months ago, he had flown back to bring her to Atlanta and married her again in court in America, so that they could apply for her green card here. It was much faster this way, than processing from Bangladesh, which could take up to a couple of years sometimes, he said. Shumi was young, pretty in a pink three-piece shalwar kameez suit, her face pale and pink like all Sylheti girls, the lipstick a glossy ice cream pink, her eyes large and set a little too wide apart, the eyebrows unfashionably thick but striking, the nose a little too big, but the nostrils flaring with beauty.

"I had it done by the same artist who did my henna on my wedding night," she said, lilting the words in a childish singsong voice, as she admired the handiwork on her hands. "Look!" she commanded, holding up her hands.

Mamun, sitting next to Shumi, took up her palms in his own to examine them, rubbing them with fat fingers. "Beautiful."

They all kept looking at Shumi's hands. There were deep long veins in blood red, with blackish red patterns hanging from them, little leaves and curved moons, swirling in and out of each other, traditional *kolka* shapes, dark, like dried blood; mesmerizing.

Both men, the newly wed Mamun and Khalida's husband Hasan, were gloating over the young woman. But Khaleda reasoned generously that Shumi was barely older than a child; such a young person could be forgiven her vanity and self-absorption, as could the two men fawning over her. Khalida felt pity for the young woman. Shumi had just graduated from university. She was alone for the first time, away from her parents and her homeland. She was so much younger than Mamun and Hasan, and even Khalida. She's not really flirting, Khalida told herself. She can't help it.

Khalida herself wore henna on her fingertips, dipped blood red, two gold bangles, one on each wrist, for her husband's well-being, and bell-shaped gold earrings passed down to her from her mother. She put these on daily, all the entrapments of a happy marriage, ensconcing her in safety. She was skinny as a reed, drawing snorted comments from her mother-in-law who was established upstairs permanently. Her cheeks were hollow, her eyes sunk in their sockets, with dark lines underneath, and her hair, too, was falling out, tied back in a mouse-thin ponytail. Her doctor had advised her to eat more to gain weight.

Khalida's life was not without joy. A long, married life didn't lose its preciousness, it only deepened with time, she thought. Hasan was a good-looking man, with his tucked-in shirts, always ironed fresh, clean, pearly nails, a head full of black hair, clean shaven, a nice sweater on top, his teeth white and even. There were her little boys, five and seven, and the house and the garden. Within the walls of this house, she felt protected, a precious safety earned through years of effort. There was a remarkable peace in her domesticity.

In the course of a few months, Shumi and Mamun were back at their dining table, quarreling. They had been constant guests at Hasan and Khaleda's house since Shumi had arrived in Atlanta, having dinner with them almost every weekend and sometimes on weeknights. Khaleda didn't mind. She cooked enough for an extended family anyway. Her mother-in-law lived with her, and Hasan's five elder sisters, who all lived in Atlanta, dropped in at the house on Peachtree Street at any time of the day or night. Hasan had trained Khalida to cook for a large family from the beginning of their marriage.

The day he had brought Khalida to America from England, to this very house, Hasan had said to her, "My sisters and their families are all coming over. They want to eat from your hands tonight."

Khalida's mother had trained her and her younger sister for this role their entire lives. Together, the two sisters had learned to cook with their mother in their tiny London flat, pouring in oil, bending over sputtering pans, stirring in turmeric, red chili pepper, garlic, and onion. Khalida had been especially trained in Sylheti cooking, in the intricacies of processing the dried, salted fishes and the various sour fruits that gave Sylheti dishes their distinctive taste.

Shumi confessed that she could not cook at all. Over dinner, with her fingers dipped in the tender beef curry Khaleda had simmered for hours, Shumi said, "My mom always said to stay away from the kitchen..."

"Why? She was afraid you would get burnt?" her husband Mamun quipped.

"No!" Shumi snapped. "She wanted me to study. She said, most girls know how to cook, but how does it help them to learn how to serve others? You're going to learn something that serves you, she said."

"Yeah, you're right. Your education didn't serve me in anyway. I go to bed hungry every night," Mamun muttered.

Khaleda was worried to see them fighting like this. Hasan had been saying that he was concerned about his friend: Mamun looked thinner, whereas most men gained weight after marriage. If anything, Shumi looked plumper, her clothes fit more tightly around her chest. Her arms looked more rounded, the gold bracelets snug on her wrists.

"You insult me all the time!" Shumi screamed.

Khaleda's two sons were working on their homework at the dining table. They looked up startled. Khaleda made them pick up their books and bags to go to their room upstairs.

"I'll come up and help you brush your teeth later," she whispered to them.

They kissed her on both cheeks, their plump faces next to her own furry skin, their soft white down brushing against her nose, and disappeared up the carpeted stairs.

Shumi began to cry loudly. "He's going to Haj with his family, without me, leaving me behind."

"Why don't you take her?" Khaleda asked Mamun.

Hasan and Mamun were childhood classmates from their school days in Sylhet. Mamun looked up to Khaleda as his friend's wife, since she had been married first.

"She doesn't want to go!" Mamun protested, throwing up his hands in exasperation.

Shumi sprang up from the table, her fingers still dry with food. She was still pretty, wearing a red kameez that she had just unpacked from her suitcase (she had still not worn all the outfits she had brought back with her from Bangladesh).

"He does everything for his family! And nothing for me," she sobbed.

"It's my family's tradition to go to Haj every year," Mamun protested, still sitting, food in his mouth.

The louder Shumi sobbed, the angrier her husband became with her. Khaleda stood up, embracing Shumi, stroking her chin, and took her away to the kitchen with her arm around the younger woman's shoulders.

"His family lied to us!" Shumi cried, washing her hands at the sink. "They said he was working for a big company. That he was an engineer. They lied about his age too! They told lies about everything–his education, job, age."

They stood in the narrow, dark kitchen with its grease-sputtered stove and grimy walls, overlooking the garden where Hasan toiled every day, planting vegetables from Bangladesh. He had smuggled in seeds and saplings through relatives who had traveled to Bangladesh. There were giant red tomatoes, Bengali squash, Bengali beans, okra, bitter cilantro, eggplants, cilantro—a whole jungle of cilantro like weed —, and a special kind of Sylheti lemon tree planted in a pot that he wheeled into the garage in the winter: a vibrant sight out of the narrow window of the dark kitchen.

Out of sight of the men, Khaleda tried to explain Mamun's situation to Shumi. He was very close to his mother, she said. His father had died early, and his mother had raised her two sons on her own in Atlanta, working in people's houses, as a nanny, tailor, or cook, or catering, doing anything she could to earn money, to send her son to college. Then Mamun had a stroke while he was at college. That was why his words were slurred.

He became a taxi driver, because his mental condition made most jobs too difficult for him to handle. Shumi should understand these things, have pity on him, Khalida reasoned.

Hearing Khaleda's words, Shumi sobbed louder. "That's just the trouble," she pleaded. "His family lied to my family. They didn't tell us about his stroke or his health condition. They didn't tell us that he hasn't got a degree. They told us he was barely thirty, when he is forty. And they sent us a false picture. When my mother saw him at the wedding, he was so ugly she fainted."

"Hush, don't say such things," Khaleda said. But her heart melted with pity for the girl.
Shumi's shoulders heaved as she sobbed. "I feel trapped. I don't know what to do."

"Time will heal everything," Khaleda said. "Don't act rashly. Focus on yourself. Finish your studies, then get a job. He is a US citizen, so that makes everything easy for you. Focus on getting your degree and your citizenship. Has Mamun applied for your green card yet?"

"Not yet," Shumi sniffed. "He has been busy."

"Get your green card. Be practical. Focus on that."

Khaleda was not ashamed to be giving such advice. It was the same advice that her mother had given to desperate young women in England, Sylheti girls much younger than Shumi who had been married in their first bloom and shipped abroad. They would come to Khaleda's parents' home and cry on her mother's shoulders, their hearts breaking. Stonewalled by scolding mothers-in-law, oblivious husbands, and a large family of in-laws demanding obedience, many of these women became insane. As a young girl, Khaleda had witnessed beautiful girls begin to hallucinate, mutter to themselves, have nervous breakdowns, and get shipped back home to their parents. Once, a young bride had hanged herself from the ceiling fan, although nothing was said in the community afterward.

"Please, focus on yourself. Act rationally. The rest will take care of itself," Khaleda pleaded with Shumi, remembering all the other young women.

At first, Shumi seemed to take Khaleda's advice to heart. The next time Khaleda saw Mamun and Shumi, it was Eid, which fell in the summer that year. Khaleda's house was packed with family. College-age nieces adorned in satin outfits and costume jewelry and nephews in ties and pressed shirts crawled in all the rooms. Her sisters-in-law sat back on her well-worn sofas demanding tea. They had brought their mother downstairs, with much screaming and shouting from all sides. Khaleda's mother-in-law was fat and she had gout in her legs.

Khaleda was glad that she stayed upstairs most of the time, although she also complained that the old lady kept her on her toes. Khaleda had to run upstairs ten times a day, because the old lady kept asking for things.

Her drawing room was dirty. With the two boys, who liked to carry on their chemistry experiments with household items and play football inside the house, and the endless turnabout of guests, Khaleda had given up long ago on keeping a nice home. There were dust balls in the corners and the old sofas kicked up fluff when anyone sank into them. The carpet had uneven dark patches. Thick curtains all around made the interior dark. Khaleda rolled with her everyday reality. She let the boys do their homework on the carpet of the drawing room, while her husband watched American football on TV, and she sewed, like her mother had taught her, or knitted when the weather permitted, as she used to in England, while watching the game with her husband. When her sisters-in-law were over, they all sat together with pots of tea and a big bowl of spicy trail mix, watching Hindi movies together.

"Khaleda, why don't you gain weight? You would look nice." Her sisters-in-law sat in front of her and complained among themselves that she was like a stick. She didn't look pretty even when they adorned her in Sylheti finery, in oodles of gold necklaces that came down to her chest, gave her gifts of hanging earrings and heavy brocade outfits.

"How can I gain weight?" Khaleda retorted, sitting back on the sofa and pointing at her stout mother-in-law, who sat scowling in an oversized chair that Hasan had bought especially for her. "The old lady calls me all day. The doctor told me to eat a plate of rice at every meal, but before I can digest the rice I'm running up and down the stairs again."

The sisters-in-law roared with laughter at this. The mother-in-law snorted in anger. Her two-hundred-pound body spilled from the oversized chair. "I talked to Helal," she said, referring to her eldest son, who lived in Long Island. "I said to him, Helal, your wife didn't produce any sons, so you should marry again." This apparent non sequitur was a jab at Khaleda, to tell her that she could marry her son Hasan off again if she chose to.

Her daughters laughed uproariously at her dumb cruelty, for she was old and had no power, and Khaleda laughed with them. Everyone helped themselves to the food Khaleda had cooked: biriyani, spicy goat, buttery tender beef, and sweet yoghurt chicken curry called chicken korma for the little ones. The sisters-in-law had brought sweets that they and their daughters had made, staying up all night kneading milk, dough, and sugar with their hands.

Hasan entered the drawing room with Mamun and Shumi. Shumi was wearing yet another outfit that Khaleda had never seen before. It had been a year and she had still not run out of new dresses. She looked paler than before, her face wan and not quite so pink, the lips dull. Khaleda stood up to greet her, embracing her.

"Bob called to wish us Eid Mubarak," Hassan said to Khaleda.

"How is Bob?" the sisters teased Hasan.

Hasan owned a Bengali grocery shop. He was a good businessman and his customers liked him. One customer in particular, Bob, a swarthy man in his fifties, bought ten bags of basmati rice at a time, only from Hasan's shop. Over the years, he had learned to use all the Indian spices—cumin, turmeric, coriander, even whole spices.

"Bob is getting old and worried about whom to leave all his property," Hasan said seriously. "He is very depressed."

"Tell him to leave it to you," the sisters joked crudely.

Hasan was the only one of his seven siblings who had not graduated from college. The rest of them were engineers, accountants, or doctors. Now his nephews and nieces were headed off to college. He had come to America on a student visa, lost interest in hi studies, and dropped out casually. Because he had not finished college, Hasan couldn't get an H-1 visa through a professional level job. But his siblings in Atlanta had begged him to stay on in America, for their sakes, so they could all be together. He had been young and careless, and he had agreed, not thinking it a big deal to stay beyond his student visa. His siblings had set him up with his first store. He made good money. There was nothing wrong with their lives, Khaleda thought. They had a house, two beautiful children, a good income. But Hasan still didn't have documents. They had hired a lawyer. Every few months, they turned up to court to fight their case. How shocking it was for Khaleda, a British citizen, to arrive in America and find out that she was illegal here! But she tried not to think about it. Khaleda turned to Shumi, seated beside her. "How are you?" she asked solicitously.

"Good! I enrolled in a master's program for next year. In Business. I'm going back to school. I'm changing my visa to a student visa."

"How about the green card?"

"It was faster to do this first. Mamun is still getting the documents ready for the green card."

"Oh, good." Khaleda said.

"And my mother is coming to help me with cooking and cleaning so I can study."

"Oh, that will be good. You must bring Auntie here to visit," Khaleda said, thinking that with Shumi's mother helping with the housework there would be less conflict between the husband and wife.

Mamun, overhearing, said, "Did you hear Shumi is getting into a master's program? She will be very educated." He seemed proud of her, fussing around her, bringing her a plate of food, tea, sweets.

After dinner, when they were gathered in the living room with tea and sweets, Mamun turned to his friend.

"Hasan, can you draw Shumi's henna on her hands?"

Hasan nodded. He was not only good at gardening, but also good at any kind of arts and crafts. Shumi brought out a tube of chemical henna from her handbag. But Hasan said he had fresh henna in the fridge, plucked from his own tree, and went to get it. He had made the paste himself.

When the three disappeared to the kitchen, the two lovebirds and Hasan, Hasan's sisters said, "They seemed to have made up? Are things okay between them?"

Another cried, "I thought they were about to separate! Khaleda, do you know anything?"

"She's so cheap, she never has people over. She eats at your place every day. Has she ever cooked for you?"

Out of decency, or loyalty to Shumi, Khaleda didn't say anything.

"I don't approve of her," Hasan's eldest sister said, looking seriously at Khaleda. "Be careful, she might steal your husband. I don't understand women like her. She doesn't cook for her husband. Her mother-in-law called and told me she never even asks for advice on how to cook."

"She's too fast," his second sister said. "She doesn't wear saris."

"She's very young," Khaleda said lightly, blowing on her tea to cool it.

"I don't know, I feel sorry for Mamun," Hasan's eldest sister said. They had known him since he had been a child. "He looks sloppier since his marriage, don't you think? His shirt is wrinkled. His pants sag."

"I heard the mother-in-law tortures her," Khaleda defended Shumi. "She doesn't let her take care of Mamun, she is so possessive."

"That's what the naughty girl told you," said the sisters in law. "Auntie is very nice."

"Apparently, Mamun's mother lied about Mamun, didn't tell the girl's family about his stroke or his age or not having a degree?"

"Come on, that's trivial. She should put it behind her and be a good wife," they said. Khaleda's mother-in-law, who had dozed off, woke up momentarily and agreed with them. "Mother-in-law comes first." They all laughed at the old woman. When the three returned, Shumi made Hasan draw the whole pattern out in ink in a notebook before she would let him paint on her hands. At last, satisfied, she stuck out her hands with the palms up. Hasan sat on the carpet and knelt over her hands, holding a homemade tube. The fresh henna with its strong earthy odor spilled out onto Shumi's palm like green dragon's blood. It was a rare moment of joy for Shumi, with her husband looking on lovingly and all the women of Atlanta sitting around admiring her, for once.

After the party was over and all the cups and plates had been cleared, the notebook page with the henna pattern still lay on the carpet of the dusty drawing room, in a corner among some abandoned toys.

Khaleda rarely left the house. When she did, she felt afraid; her heart fluttered. She didn't drive if she could help it. In England, she had driven from one city to another. She used to take the train by herself to the bank where she worked. But in America, she stayed put at home.

Fortunately, Hasan had a great relationship with all the people around them. He was the one who made friends with all the parents at their sons' school, making sweets for Jack's mom, fixing David's dad's car for him when he had a flat tire, making a gift of fresh vegetables from his garden or a free bag of loose leaf tea from his shop to his sons' teachers. He was a neat-looking short man, with a full head of black hair, smiling, ever gregarious. People took to him easily.

The only time Khaleda left home for a long time was when she had to go to the hospital to deliver her third baby. It was a complicated pregnancy from the start. At first, the doctors couldn't get a heartbeat for the fetus; they said the pregnancy wasn't viable. Then they said it was fine. But it was always like that, one thing after another. When she was seven months pregnant, the doctors told them that the baby's heartbeat was weak. There was something wrong. They had to admit her in the hospital to watch over her. Khaleda felt she would die, trapped alone in the sterile hospital room, away from her two young sons. They were allowed to visit her once. They put their plump little hands around her neck and cried and misbehaved, till Hasan pulled them away from her. Khaleda and the boys cried. Then Hasan and her sons left and Khaleda was sobbing in the empty white room.

The baby was born with a hole in her heart. They had prayed for a girl, but now they had a daughter who was fighting for life. An emergency surgery by the doctors saved her life. Hasan was ecstatic in his gratitude to the doctors. He kept thanking them, bringing them gifts of sweets cooked by his sisters and fresh vegetables from his garden, carefully tied with colored rope. The baby stayed in NICU. Hasan went to visit, chatting with the nurses, answering their questions about gardening. The elderly Southern nurses took to him like a son. But the whole hospital stay was an ordeal for Khaleda. Only when she and the baby both came back home, she felt she could breathe at last.

The summer turned to fall. The baby had trouble breathing. Khaleda sat in the drawing room throwing out one bib after another filled with vomit from the baby, staring out at the vibrant fall colors of the trees in her backyard. She felt happiest looking out this window, over the backyard, fenced in securely. The windows on the front end of the house facing the street made her nervous; someone from immigration could walk in from the street at any moment and knock on the door, demanding answers. She closed her eyes as these worries invaded her weak mind. Sometimes, she would have to get up with the baby and walk, shaking out her shoulders and legs and arms, to get rid of the thoughts.

Her mother-in-law called from upstairs. "Khaleda, I need water! The jug is empty. Please. I'm dying. Have some pity on the old woman…"

Khaleda sat back down and let the old woman's voice fade to a querulous moan and then silence. Her little girl mewled like a small animal, barely human. The child's eyes were too big in the shrunken face, like that of the children Khaleda had seen in paintings of the Bengal famine. Her ribs jutted out from her thin chest. From the beginning, she had been on medications. There were doctors' visits. Hasan always took time off from the store to accompany Khaleda and the baby to the doctor's office. He wept, holding on to the doctor's hands; tears streaked his cheeks. They responded to him gently. Khaleda could barely look at them. She was not used to interacting with Americans. She looked away anxiously.

Finally, one day in the fall, the doctors said the baby was mostly out of danger. Life felt a little normal. They were all five sitting in the drawing room. The boys were watching TV lying on the carpet. Hasan had given them their dinners, which he had cooked himself. Khaleda was feeding the girl, who had some color in her cheeks at last. She sat in a highchair with a dirty rag on the tray while Khaleda spooned goo into her thin mouth. The doorbell rang and Mamun and Shumi arrived, after many months. Since Shumi had enrolled in the graduate business program, she rarely came to the house. Mamun still visited sometimes, when they were having dinner, to grumble about his rude mother-in-law and about the lack of food at his home.

"Well, hello strangers!" Hasan called out affectionately. "Where were you? Visiting Mars?"

The boys thought their father's joke was hilarious

and laughed uncontrollably. "There is no life on Mars," they kept repeating.

"Why don't you go out for a smoke with Hasan bhai?" Shumi suggested to Mamun tightly. Her eyes were rimmed red. As always, she wore a pretty printed cotton kameez, but it was wrinkled. Her face was faded and her hair red and unoiled.

Hasan and Mamun walked out to the backyard. The two women could see them framed in the window, walking, looking at the vegetable garden.

"Khaleda Apa, I'm pregnant!" Shumi wailed. Khaleda left the baby in her highchair and came to sit beside Shumi, comforting her by putting her arm around the girl's shoulders awkwardly. "That is good news. Congratulations," she said.

The boys looked at Shumi with concern.

"Go upstairs," Khaleda said to them, wanting to protect them from this knowledge of women's misery. Her sons ran out of the room with wide eyes. She could hear them running up the stairs noisily. Her mother-in-law shouted that they were making too much noise.

"I don't want a baby!" Shumi wailed. "I—I want to leave him!"

"Leave him?" Khaleda was shocked. She put down the baby's food on the carpet. The girl, who was not interested in food anyway, did not seem to mind, watching TV with frozen eyes.

"I was thinking of leaving him, and now this happened." Shumi sobbed.

"Why do you want to leave?"

Shumi wiped her eyes and sniffed, her cheeks stained with tears.

"This is joyful news, Shumi!" Khaleda cried. "You're just depressed because of hormones," she said, recalling her own irrational depression during each of her pregnancies. "Believe me, having a baby is the most joyful experience of being a woman. You'll have someone that you're willing die for."

"Mamun and I are always fighting."

"Lovers' quarrels. All couples fight."

Outside, the sky grew grey, and a shadow fell over the bright red and orange trees. The two men walked about, oblivious to their tears and recriminations inside the house.

"No, they're serious arguments!" Shumi sobbed and hiccupped. She started to pull off the tight gold bracelets from her plump hands, then she yanked off the gold wedding band. "It's unbearable!"
Khaleda stood up and switched on the lights in the room, shocked by the violence of the younger woman. She could hear the men opening the back door, coming back inside.

"I'll make some tea," she said. "You have to be practical," she went on, a little coldly. "You're young. You can't let emotions rule your heart. You have to be calm and raise the kid. Did you apply for your green card yet? You have to get your green card. Perhaps you'll grow to love your husband. Don't be foolish. You're acting silly. What do his age or his looks matter? He's a good man."

"He drives a taxi!" Shumi spat out disdainfully. "He's old. He slurs his words." She picked at a tissue in her hands, tearing it to shreds.

The men walked into the room. Mamun noticed Shumi's face and started to argue with her, his cheeks flaming and his voice cruel. Husband and wife fought, Shumi wailing, standing in Khaleda's drawing room. Khaleda's mother-in-law shouted to stop all the shouting. Khaleda interrupted their argument, to ask Mamun, "Why haven't you applied for her green card yet?"

He said he hadn't gotten around to yet it because of some missing documents.

It was fall again. Khaleda was once again sitting in the drawing room. The orange and yellow and red leaves and wet earth framed her windows again, as the baby watched TV. She was fourteen months old and still not walking. Khaleda and Hasan were worried about her. The boys had just left for school, and Hasan was working at the store, so it was the two of them again. They had developed a routine. The girl watched crtoons on TV while Khaleda watched Hindi serials on her phone. Sometimes they switched, and the child played on the phone, while Khaleda watched on the big screen. A few times a day, she shrugged herself out of the warm sofa and got up to go to the kitchen, to find some oatmeal or banana or rice to feed her daughter, trapping the child in the highchair to mechanically spoon the mush into her mouth. Sometimes, her mother-in-law shouted for something and Khaleda ran upstairs. Then she ate her vitamins because the doctors had told her to put on weight.

The doorbell rang. Normally, Khaleda didn't like answering the door. But she knew it was Shumi, dropping off her baby at Khaleda's home. Shumi had come on other days, begging her to keep the baby in an emergency, when the nanny had not come. Shumi's mother had flown back home to her ailing husband, after successfully helping her daughter to get a divorce. The marriage had ended, but Shumi had not forgiven

Mamun. Every time they met, Shumi broke down in remonstrations against her ex-husband.

"Hello, my darling," Khaleda greeted the younger woman.

Shumi set the heavy car seat with her baby on the floor in the foyer, at the bottom of the staircase. She no longer wore Bengali clothes. She was dressed in a synthetic blouse, black dress pants, and cheap fashion jewelry.

"Thank you for doing this."

"No problem," Khaleda said mechanically.

She didn't try to advise Shumi anymore, but she thought it absurd that Shumi had ended her marriage without applying for a green card. It was beyond her reasoning. Khaleda had been trained by her mother to be a good wife, as all good Sylheti girls her age had been, but she had no other kind of knowledge. She had no advice for the girls nowadays going off to college, trying to get job interviews. She had no wisdom to give them, but she envied them. She felt a hole in her heart sometimes for all the things she could have been, given another chance.

"My school is so demanding, I have classes and projects all the time," Shumi said. "Thank you so much for doing this."

"Are you almost finished with your degree?" Khaleda asked mechanically, bending down to coo at the baby girl, pink and beautiful like her mother. The baby gurgled happily and stuck out her wriggling fingers.

"Yes, I have just this semester's exams. Then I go home."

"Right." Khaleda didn't say anything more, although she wondered if Mamun would let her take the child, or if she planned to leave without her child.

"Thank you," Shumi said again. "Bye!"

"Bye!" Khaleda waved, before closing the door behind her.

Then she watched from the glass window, as Shumi walked down the driveway in her slacks and heels and climbed into her car to drive away, leaving Khaleda standing in the middle of her domesticity, with the two babies and the old lady upstairs.

One morning, Mamun came to Khaleda's door instead of Shumi, telling her to keep the baby. The baby was pink and beautiful in a pink dress, her face plump and alert, the white down soft on the fat pink flesh, healthy whereas her own little girl was frail and thin, watching TV in the drawing room. Mamun swung the car seat and handed it over carelessly to Khaleda, who tipped from its weight. The baby giggled in delight. Her name was Mona.

"Keep her," Mamun commanded. "I have to work. I'll be back."

"Okay," Khaleda said. "Are you alright?"

She looked at him with concern, like a mother, wanting to feed him and take care of him, but he hurried out, slamming the front door behind him. She stood near the stairs holding the heavy car seat with the wriggling baby. Her own baby, whom they still did not call by a name because they were not sure she would live, cried from the drawing room.

"Oh, Khaleda, I need to go to the bathroom," the old lady called from upstairs.

By midday, Khaleda had things under control. Mamun and Shumi's baby was napping in her car seat, on the carpet floor. Her own baby had fallen asleep in her highchair, her mouth open pathetically as she snored with her head against the plastic back. Khaleda slumped back in her sofa and turned on the TV on low volume. She watched the same kind of TV she would watch as a girl in their London flat, some corny American sitcom on TV or a Hindi movie on the VCR. Hasan brought her Bollywood movie videos from his store.

The doorbell rang again.

Shumi had come to take the baby. It was fall, and it had been raining steadily for days. The leaves lay wet and soggy on the damp grass. There were beads of sweat on Shumi's upper lip. She looked disheveled, her hair untidy, as if she didn't care about her appearance anymore. Khaleda studied her in shock, to understand why she looked so changed. The girl had cut her hair short. Her nails were short and unpolished.

"I didn't know you were picking up the baby. It's no problem for me to keep her. What's wrong?" Khaleda asked solicitously. She was normally too polite to probe, part of her British reserve.

"Nothing," Shumi said quickly. She marched inside in her noisy heels. She never asked about anybody, Khaleda thought. Not about the boys or her daughter or about her mother-in-law.

Khaleda followed Shumi to her drawing room, where the two babies snored. The TV was off. The room was dark and peaceful.

"Thanks. I'll take the baby," Shumi said, picking up the car seat.

"Take care of yourself," Khaleda said. "You need a man's love. Will you marry again?" She hoped someone would love this girl again and return her to her prettiness.

Shumi walked to the front door without speaking. Khaleda followed her.

"Thank you, but you don't have to worry about me." Shumi said sternly, her mouth set in a flat line, closing the door behind her.

An hour later, Mamun appeared at the house with Hasan.

"Where is Mona? What did you do with the baby?" They both accused Khaleda.

Both men were sweating as heavily as Shumi, in sharp contrast to the cool air inside. Khaleda's baby daughter woke up in her highchair and started to cry. The school bus dropped off their two boys in front of the house.

"Oh, my God!" Mamun was shouting, clutching his hair as he paced about the drawing room.

"What have you done?" Hasan accused Khaleda savagely. He was a gentle man who barely spoke above a murmur with Khaleda.

"What did I do?" Khaleda asked, still not understanding.

She picked up her crying daughter and walked around the room with her, rocking her mechanically. The girl vomited. The boys opened the fridge and rummaged inside loudly, complaining that there was no food. The house stank of stale food and vomit. Khaleda was afraid that her mother-in-law would start hollering too, if she woke up from all the noise.

"I have to call the police!" Mamun shouted.

He ran to the landline phone at the foot of the stairs and wrapped his plump fingers around the receiver. Khaleda ran after him with the baby in her arms.

"No! Don't call any police to this house," Khaleda cried. "Call the police from your own home."

She still didn't understand what was going on. Mamum pushed her hand away, shouting, "Well, my daughter went missing from your house, because of your negligence, so I'll damn well call the police from this house."

"No!" Khaleda shouted back savagely. "For the sake of my family, no!"

Mamun bared his teeth at her, hissing at her, nose to nose with her, but he put the receiver down.

After Mamun and Hasan left the house together, and Khaleda had fed the boys and comforted them, and pulled out their homework, and the girl had dozed off to sleep on the sofa, Khaleda finally figured out what had happened: She was mortified that she had been so naïve. Shumi had stopped going to school in her depression and dropped out of school, so she had fallen of status and couldn't live in America anymore. She intended to leave the country with the baby. She was kidnapping the baby, according to Hasan and Mamun.

Over the next few days, the three—Hasan, Mamun, and Khaleda—, sat huddled together over the dining table, eating food together, their hands dried in cold *daal* and rice, arguing and worrying together. Shumi and Mona were still missing. The police were looking for them.

"Legally, the baby belongs in America," Mamun said.

"Come on, let it be. She's angry. She will be in touch soon," Khaleda pleaded.

She felt her old sympathy for Shumi rise up again. She remembered the pretty, young girl sitting at her dinner table only a few years ago blushing in her pink outfit. It had been such a normal marriage. What had gone wrong?

"It's all her mother's fault," Khaleda said.

"Legally, she cannot take the baby without my permission!" Mamun shouted angrily.

"The police will find her eventually," Hasan said.

"Unless she left the country already."

Mamun's relatives were already on the lookout for Shumi in Dhaka and in Sylhet. But there was no trace of her leaving the borders with her passport.

Eventually, the police found her. She had crossed Atlanta and had been driving toward New York. They found her in Jackson Heights at her uncle's house, her mother's brother. Mamun agreed not to press charges against her, but he took her to court and the judge ordered that she couldn't leave Atlanta with the baby without the judge's knowledge. The court took possession of the baby's passport.

"Well, that's over," Mamun said happily. He had returned to ask Khaleda to look after his daughter again. "All's well that ends well. This time, don't let her in. Whoever rings the bell, don't answer the door!" He laughed.

"What will happen to Shumi?" Khaleda asked anxiously.

"She'll have to leave the country, won't she? She hasn't got papers. Unless she stays on, like an illegal." Khaleda bit her lips and rubbed her taut forehead with bony fingers. "The poor girl. The baby needs her mother."

"Now, don't feel sorry for her. This divorce was their idea. Shumi's idea and her mother's."

320

"I know. I know." Khaleda put her hand on Mamun's shoulder to calm him. She still felt bad for Shumi. She worried about her, this young woman, alone. What decision would she make?

Shumi called Khaleda on her cell phone one day while Khaleda was feeding Mona and her own little girl at the same time.

"Your husband took my baby from me!" Shumi cried hysterically. "I'll call immigration on him."

"You're speaking nonsense!" Khaleda cried. "We have nothing to do with this. This fight is between you and Mamun."

"No, I'm not. I mean it!"

Khaleda dropped the phone and screamed. Both the babies started to cry.

Within hours, the police were at the house and at the store, looking for Hasan. They didn't find him at either place. First, he went to his elder sister's house and then to New York, in Long Island, where his brother Helal lived. He stayed there for six months before eventually returning home. His sister's son managed the store till the police eventually stopped looking for him.
But Khaleda would never forget the day the immigration officers came to her door. For years, for her entire married life, she had apprehended this moment. When it happened, her heart dropped. She opened the door. Her body was cold. She spoke to them mechanically in her British accent. No one was interested in *her* immigration status. The two infant girls were crying in the drawing room, a constant background noise in her life. Her mother-in-law was upstairs, thankfully silent, probably dozing. There was a light drizzle, and the officers'

clothes were wet. They spoke to Khaleda politely but sternly, asking her for permission to enter. Several men walked through the house, going through the rooms methodically. One man climbed the stairs but managed to come down again without waking up her mother-in-law. Then they left. They never came back. But their boots stomping through the house echoed in Khaleda's ears for years afterward.

When the officers left, Khaleda walked to the drawing room and picked up Mamun and Shumi's baby (her own had cried herself to sleep), thinking, she would never forgive Shumi. Her heart rang with bitterness against the young woman who had walked into her life and tried to destroy it so carelessly.

When the boys came home, she kissed them repeatedly and held them too tightly, till they complained and wriggled out of her grasp. That night, she checked on the old lady officiously, giving her water again and again, oiling her hair, and massaging her legs. She even looked at her little girl who had been born with a hole in her heart, with courage and finally decided on a name for her. "Beena." Khaleda whispered it breathlessly.
The little girl stared back with her enormous eyes out of her thin face. Khaleda placed her bony hands on the two sides of Beena's thin face, smiling as she looked into the child's eyes.

A year passed before Khaleda saw Shumi again. Khaleda was still at home. Still wearing a nightdress. When she opened the door in the same tight foyer, she was shocked to see Shumi standing outside her door, after such a long time. She tried to form a smile, genuinely surprised at the visit, but she also remembered what the girl had done.

"May I come in?" Shumi asked timidly.

Khaleda stepped away from the door. Shumi followed her to the dining room, where a small window faced the front street. A transparent curtain screened it, protecting it from the outside, while offering up sunlight. "Sit." Khaleda dragged out a chair from the table and sat down herself.

The plastic tablecloth was still covered with breads crumbs and jam. She was not a good housewife still. Shumi kept standing.

"How is...how is your little girl?" Shumi asked.

"Good. She's in daycare now."

"How is Hasan Bhai?" Shumi asked innocently, as if she had not tried to end their lives.

"Fine," Khaleda answered tersely. She felt bitterness and pain spreading across her face.

But Shumi didn't say sorry. "I am going back to Bangladesh. Without my baby."

"So you have been living here illegally?"

"Yes. You don't know how I survived. Doing odd jobs. Staying with friends. I was broken. I am leaving for home." She cried noisily, but Khaleda didn't respond. "You were right about having a baby. That baby meant everything to me. I am nothing without it. So when I am whole again, if I can, I will try to come back for her."

Khaleda nodded. They never saw Mamun anymore, so she had no news of their situation. He had remarried, and therefore no longer needed her services to take care of his daughter.

"Good," she said flatly.

"I wanted to see you before leaving," Shumi said. "You were so kind to me. You were my only friend."

Khaleda forced herself to look at the girl, who was looking pretty again. She wore little earrings in her earlobes and her hair was combed neatly. She wore a pretty white top and grey slacks. There was color in her cheeks again. And on her hands, Khaleda noticed, she was wearing blood red henna again. Although she said she was poor and broken, something of her old youth and independence had returned to Shumi.

"You look the same to me," Khaleda said in a gentler voice.

"And you. This house too," Shumi gestured around her. "This a favorite spot for me."

Khaleda laughed harshly. This was no compliment, since the house was always dirty, always out of her control. There was an endless train of guests. Papers and rubbish floated from one room to another. Lost, forgotten scraps of things turned up suddenly in drawers or on the floor. She had no control over who came and who went, who ate the food she cooked.

"And are you sure about your decision to leave your baby behind?" Khaleda asked.

Shumi nodded. Her cheeks colored with bitterness and her eyes narrowed. "What happened to me was awful! I was a beautiful, young girl. I was married to this older ugly guy. I deserved better!"

Light floated through the window, throwing patterns on the plastic cover. If Shumi had asked, Khaleda would have told her that her mother-in-law had died a month back, so Khaleda had the house all to herself undisturbed for a few hours a day now.

"You must remember me as I was. So young and so pretty." Tears of self-pity pooled up at the corners of Shumi's eyes. "Please, show me some pity."

"Why should I feel sorry for you? *I* was married when I turned eighteen. I was my mother's firstborn child. We were close," Khaleda answered harshly.

"Yes, but please, tell me, wasn't it unfair, what happened to *me?*" Shumi continued. Her mouth was contorted in a horrible grimace like a little girl crying.

"And *I* was married to a man ten years my senior in another country," Khaleda said. "So I got married and I came here to be with my husband in another country and start a new life. And when I got here, I discovered that my husband had no papers. No one had told me. My parents didn't know. I found out after I was married that I was illegal. So this became my life. I live here as an illegal and daily I fear that my husband or both of us will be taken away. That is my life. And I was a British citizen."

"Well, why don't you live in England?" Shumi asked. She had pulled herself out of her thoughts. "Because this is where his family is. His life is here. His business."

Shumi nodded. She turned to go, as if she understood she would get no sympathy here.

Out of the corner of her red eyes, Khaleda saw a piece of paper with an intricate pattern drawn in black ballpoint pen of a henna design, that Hasan had drawn for Shumi years ago.

"Okay, then," Shumi said.

"Keep well," Khaleda said, walking her to door. She closed the door eagerly behind the fragile young girl, closing it to all that she did not understand.

Made in the USA
Middletown, DE
15 March 2022